Supporting the Spirit of Learning

This trilogy is dedicated to all children whose natural giftedness is not recognized under our current educational structure. Within each one of them lie the beauty and wisdom of the whole world, and so we are choosing to honor their unique and diverse strengths—their spiritual essence. They have touched our hearts and filled us with love. They are the individual stars that together form the galaxies. We invite them to fill our lives with their special light and help us learn from and appreciate the kaleidoscopic world in which we live.

Supporting the Spirit of Learning

When Process Is Content

Editors
Arthur L. Costa
Rosemarie M. Liebmann

CORWIN PRESS, INC.
A Sage Publications Company
Thousand Oaks, California

For information address:

Corwin Press, Inc.
A Sage Publications Company
2455 Teller Road
Thousand Oaks, California 91320
E-mail: order@corwin.sagepub.com

SAGE Publications Ltd.
6 Bonhill Street
London EC2A 4PU
United Kingdom

SAGE Publications India Pvt. Ltd.
M-32 Market
Greater Kailash I
New Delhi 110 048 India

Printed in the United States of America

Library of Congress Cataloging-in-Publication Data

Main entry under title:

Celebrating process as content : toward renaissance learning /
editors, Arthur L. Costa, Rosemarie M. Liebmann.
p. cm.
Includes bibliographical references (p.) and index.
ISBN 0-8039-6311-4 (cloth: acid-free paper).—ISBN
0-8039-6312-2 (pbk.: acid-free paper)
1. Education—United States—Curricula. 2. Curriculum change—
United States. 3. Curriculum development—United States.
I. Costa, Arthur L. II. Liebmann, Rosemarie M.
LB1570.C395 1996
375'.00973—dc20 96-10144

This book is printed on acid-free paper.

97 98 99 00 01 02 10 9 8 7 6 5 4 3 2 1

Editorial Assistant: Kristen L. Green
Production Editor: Michèle Lingre
Production Assistant: Sherrise Purdum
Typesetter & Designer: Andrea D. Swanson
Indexer: Mary Kidd
Cover Designer: Marcia R. Finlayson

Contents

Foreword

Peter M. Senge

The Tragedy of Our Times

Gordon Brown, former dean of the MIT School of Engineering, used to say, "To be a great teacher is to be a prophet—for you need to prepare young people not for today, but for 30 years into the future."

At few times in history has this admonition been more true than today. Yet if we look at the process, content, and achievements of public education, can any of us be confident that we are preparing young people well for the future in which they will live? Are we contributing to the capabilities of a 21st-century society to govern itself wisely, to prosper economically and culturally, and to generate insight into pressing problems and build consensus for change?

We stand poised at a turning point in history, with unprecedented challenges, some of which are literally unique in our history as a species. For the first time in our evolution, human beings have the power to fundamentally alter the natural environment within which we all live. No generation has ever had to face problems such as global warming (or cooling) and deterioration of the ozone layer. We are now the first species in the history of life on this planet that systematically destroys other species. No generation has ever had to confront the prospect of human activities that literally alter the gene pool and the evolutionary process. The nuclear arms race, now 50 years old, has entered a new, potentially more dangerous stage, with many nations involved. No generation before has ever had to live with the prospect of nuclear terrorism.

Within the United States, we are faced with uncontrollable government deficits and an unprecedented breakdown of the traditional family structure.

No generation in America has ever had to confront such wholesale mortgaging of the future—simultaneously borrowing from the next generations to support our current standard of living and leaving "no one at home" to raise that generation.

The common denominator of all the problems above is that they are *systemic* problems. The destruction of the environment, the arms race, and the erosion of community and family structures are not isolated problems with singular causes. They arise from the interactions, often over long periods, of diverse forces of change worldwide—forces such as technological progress, shifting societal values, global economics, and continuing population growth. Such problems cannot be understood by breaking them apart into components, and they will only be exacerbated by the "business as usual" politics of polarization and special interest groups. There are no villains to blame, no simple problems to fix. As the cartoon character "Pogo"—the first systems thinker in popular U.S. culture—said, "We have met the enemy and he is us."

A system of public education inevitably rests on public consensus regarding the skills, knowledge, and attitudes that will be needed by future citizens. Today, I believe our traditional consensus regarding the goals and process of public education leaves us dangerously vulnerable in a world of expanding interdependence. We have all been taught to analyze complex problems and to fix the pieces. Our traditional education process—indeed our theory of knowledge in the West—is based on reductionism, fragmenting complex phenomena into components and building up specialized knowledge of the parts. Moreover, our traditional educational process is based on competition and individual learning. This educational process, founded on fragmentation and rivalry, starts in elementary school and continues right through university, getting worse and worse the further one "progresses" in higher education. Literally, to be an "expert" in our society is to know a lot about a little. Such an educational process can never lay a solid foundation for understanding interdependency and for fostering genuine dialogue that integrates diverse points of view.

Concerns today with public education focus on achievement relative to traditional standards. But the real problem lies with the relevance of the traditional standards themselves. Preparing citizens for the future with the skills of the past has always been the bane of public education. Today, it could be the tragedy of our times.

A Leading Edge of Change

Given the profound changes that are unfolding all about us, it is not surprising that we are witnessing a massive deterioration of traditional institutions worldwide. In a world of rapid change and growing interdependence, large, centrally controlled organizations have become virtually ungovernable. The former Soviet Union, General Motors, and IBM, one-time paragons of power and control, all suffered massive breakdowns of their central nervous systems in the 1980s. The fundamental problem became the management system itself—the inability to effectively coordinate and adapt in an increasingly dynamic world, the inability to push decision making to "front lines," and the inability to neutralize traditional political power blocks committed to self-interest over common interest.

The failure in our traditional system of management is driving extraordinary change in the institution in which I spend most of my time—large business enterprises. Perhaps no sector has been forced to confront the startling changes of an interdependent world more rapidly than business. Because businesses literally compete against one another around the world, if one company or one part of the world makes significant headway in developing new skills and capabilities for a dynamic, interdependent world, it quickly gains advantage. Others have to play catch-up or go out of business.

This is precisely what began to happen in the 1960s and 1970s, first with the Japanese, followed in rapid succession by the Koreans, Taiwanese, Singaporeans, and the other "Asian tigers"—what eventually became known as the total quality management (TQM) revolution. TQM represented, in the words of the Japanese TQM pioneer Ishikawa, "a thought revolution in management," based on such "radical" notions as "continuous improvement" (i.e, continuous learning) and focusing on "processes," not just products—how we are doing things, not just measuring the results of what we have done. TQM included a principle that everyone is part of a larger system, and the question should be not "What is my job description?" but "Whom do I serve?" Extended to the enterprise as a whole, this principle implied that everyone in the enterprise needs to understand who the enterprise intends to serve—its "customers."

But TQM was merely the first wave of far more sweeping changes in traditional, centrally controlled bureaucratic organizations. Today, process-oriented management is being extended beyond basic manufacturing processes, the traditional focus of TQM, to thinking of everything an organization does as processes and to considering major reengineering of processes as well as continuous improvement. This is leading to new ideas about organization design—decentralization and network organizations, and even "virtual corporations," in which large numbers of highly autonomous operators interact, in effect, to create the scale of a large enterprise. Clearly, effective knowledge workers, whether they operate in networks of smaller enterprises or "networked," process-oriented larger enterprises, will need new skills and capabilities to understand complexity, communicate in ways that integrate diverse points of view, and build shared aspirations and mental models. In fact, without such new skills and capabilities, these new organizational forms may never come into being because they rely as much on the "soft technologies" of reflective conversation and systems thinking as they do on the "hard technologies" of information systems and telecommunications. In addition, in my view, running below the surface of these diverse changes may be a return to some guiding ideas from traditional management wisdom, ideas lost in the drive to reduce the art of management to a purely rational, quantifiable, mechanical model. These include ideas such as that an enterprise should exist to serve society, to contribute in some important way, and that this alone is their basis for sustaining a profit; that there is no substitute for passion, personal vision, excitement, and belief in what one is doing; and that profits when they are earned are more like oxygen than an end in and of themselves—they enable the enterprise to stay in the game and continue to generate and contribute.[1]

This whole cluster of changes in guiding ideas, core capabilities, management focus, and organization design represents a fundamental shift in our entire system of management and the overarching ethos of organizations, from "controlling organizations" to "learning organizations." This is the only ethos that seems compatible with organizational health in a world of growing interdependence and change.

The basic problem with all of this is that it is not easy. It takes years to develop the skills and knowledge to understand complex human systems, to learn how to think and learn together across cultural boundaries, to reverse years of conditioning in authoritarian organizations in which everyone "looks upward" for direction, and to build genuinely shared visions and promote "looking sideways" to see the larger systems of which each is a part. Equally challenging are the patience, perseverance, and extraordinary commitment required to develop these skills and understandings in the context of corporate environments still dominated by authoritarian, control-oriented cultures.

A Lagging Edge of Change

The more we understand the skills, knowledge, and beliefs needed to succeed in an interdependent world, the more we see the folly of thinking that we can focus exclusively on our system of management and ignore our system of education. Probably no one became more identified with the early stages of the quality management revolution than the American Dr. W. Edwards Deming. Shortly before Dr. Deming passed away in December 1993, I had an opportunity to ask him, "Dr. Deming, could the system of management you propound ever be widely implemented in the United States in our business enterprises if it is not implemented in our schools?" His simple answer was "no."

Having worked now for 20 years at developing the particular capabilities that seem vital to "learning organizations" in business organizations, it becomes clear that Deming was right. Isn't it silly to begin developing systems thinking capabilities in 35-year-olds who have spent the preceding 30 years becoming master reductionists? Isn't it grossly inefficient to begin developing reflectiveness, the ability to recognize and challenge one's own mental models, with successful adults—who to be successful in school and work had to become masters at solving problems rather than thinking about the thinking that generated the problems? Isn't it naive to think that we as adults can suddenly master collaborative learning, when so much of our lives has been devoted to win-lose competition and proving that we are better than each other? Shouldn't *personal mastery,* the discipline of fostering personal vision and working with "creative tension," be a cornerstone of schooling? Educators often speak of the ideal of lifelong learners—people with a keen sense of purposefulness, who are self-directed and good at objective self-assessment. Isn't it hypocritical to espouse personal vision and mature self-assessment when so much of traditional schooling is devoted to learning what *someone else* says we should learn and then convincing *them* we've learned it?

Increasingly, business people are recognizing the tragic neglect of fundamental innovation in public education. And they are moving from corporate contributions and public relations to action. For example, Electronic Data Systems (EDS) has a corporate policy that allows any employee to take time off each week with pay to volunteer in public schools. Intel employees have worked to start new public schools in Arizona and in statewide educational reform movements in Oregon and New Mexico. Ford employees are teaching systems thinking and mental models in community colleges in Detroit. Motorola has started its own "summer camp," teaching basic science and technology for children of Motorola employees.

But little is likely to take hold, spread, and grow from such isolated experiments until there is a widespread revolution in professional *and* public thinking about the nature and goals of public education for the 21st century. How will the traditional skill set of the industrial era have to be expanded for successful workers and citizens in the knowledge era? How must the traditional education process be transformed? How must traditional ideas of what constitutes "school" give way as more and more of the content of traditional education becomes available over the Internet? What will educational institutions commensurate with the knowledge era actually look like?

There will be no easy answers to such questions. My guess is that two cornerstones to the new system of education will be elevating the learning process to comparable standing with the content of what is learned and making high-level thinking and learning skills, such as systems thinking and collaborative learning, as important as traditional skills of reductionistic thinking and individual problem solving. These could indeed be two elements of a thought revolution in education.

Who Will Lead the Transformation?

Recently, my wife and I attended an awards assembly at our teenage son's school. Our 5-year old son, Ian, was with us. When the winner of the first award was announced, Ian turned to Diane and asked, "Mommy, is only one child getting an award? So, the other kids don't get an award?"

What does a 5-year-old see that the sophisticated educators do not see? Why can he see the system as a whole—all the kids—and the educators see only the pieces, the "exceptional" kids? Maybe it's simply because the professional educators have spent their whole lives in schools. Maybe, despite their knowledge about learning theory and research, they also have the hardest time seeing beyond "the way it's always been done." Maybe the leadership that will be needed must come from all of us.

In 1994-1995, I participated in a series of satellite broadcasts on learning organizations.[2] One of these shows involved three kids from the Orange Grove Middle School in Tucson, Arizona, a school that has been integrating systems thinking and learner-directed learning throughout its curriculum *and* management practices for more than 5 years. The clarity, articulateness, and composure of these young people (ages 13 and 14) deeply impressed the other participants, mostly corporate managers doing the same types of work within their businesses. As the program went on, many of the most penetrating insights were offered by the young people. When the moderator asked who would like to offer any closing remarks, Kristi Jipson, an eighth-grade student at Orange Grove, said,

> I'd really like to say to those parents who say that "a book and a ruler is what it's all about," that you really need to talk to kids. If you talk to us, you'll see that we are really excited about what we are learning now. Before, you only needed to learn the "book and ruler" stuff. But now, as this program shows, businesses are changing, and by the time we get there this is what will be going on, and we'll need to know it.

One of the most forceful voices for innovation in the Catalina Foothills District, in which Orange Grove is located, has been a group of senior "citizen champions," many in their 70s and older, who in the words of Luise Hayden, became "enrolled in a revolution." They formed the Ideals Foundation with a vision of "entire curricula" organized around

> demonstrating how the parts relate to the whole. The foundation should benefit all children who are capable of learning, quickening their academic growth and enlarging their future aspirations and opportunities for school and career success, regardless of their present level of achievement. It should be a search for methods whereby students can use their own learning advances to help another, in a sustained and mutually supportive relationship.

The profound rethinking of public education required today cannot be led by any one constituency or professional group. The future is the responsibility of us all. And *all* includes those who have seen most of the past and those who will see the most of the future. All must participate, and all must lead.

Notes

1. Such ideas may seem naively idealistic, but that is only because of widely shared mental models about business, not because of any careful study of successful enterprises historically. For example, Royal-Dutch Shell's study of long-lived companies—business enterprises that have survived for more than 100 years—found virtually exactly these characteristics (see deGeus, 1995).

2. The broadcasts were a series of three programs on *Applying the Principles of the Learning Organization* (1994-1995), sponsored by a learning partnership of the Associated Equipment Distributors (AED) Foundation, the Association for Supervision and Curriculum Development (ASCD), The Learning Circle (TLC), and the PBS Adult Learning Services. The programs were coproduced by The Learning Circle and N.A.K. Production Associates.

References

deGeus, A. P. (1995, January). *Companies: What are they?* [Speech delivered to the Royal Society of the Arts]. Available from the MIT Center for Organizational Learning, Cambridge.

The Learning Circle and N.A.K. Production Associates (Coproducers). (1994-1995). *Applying the principles of the learning organization* [Satellite broadcasts]. Sudbury, MA: The Learning Circle.

Preface to the Trilogy

Arthur L. Costa
Rosemarie M. Liebmann

> When we no longer know what to do we have come to our real work and when we no longer know which way to go we have begun our real journey. The mind that is not baffled is not employed. The impeded stream is the one that sings.
>
> *Wendell Berry*

Each new journey begins with a quest, a yearning to move beyond present limits. As we tried to envision the future needs of our learners, we were taken aback by how little we actually know about the world in which they will live. Numerous studies guided our way, but in reality, these are only predictions of a time we cannot fathom. Change is with us, and it seems to be invading our lives at an ever more rapid rate. Not only are we feeling the personal transitions, but organizational change, which has been traditionally slow, is responding to a faster and more demanding society.

This trilogy provides educators with a bold but responsive perspective on curriculum intended to serve learners well into the 21st century. In today's complex and intelligence-intensive world economy, organizations can no longer rely exclusively on the intelligence of those few at the top of the pyramid. The amount of clear thinking required to meet the demands for speed, flexibility, quality, service, and innovation means that everyone in the organization must be involved. The organization must engage the acumen, business judgment, and systemwide responsibility of all its members.

Processes for the Workplace

Students entering the marketplace must come fully equipped with the skills that enable them to be lifelong learners. They must bring into the workplace their ability to think for themselves—to be self-initiating, self-modifying, and self-directing. They must acquire the capacity to learn and change consciously, continuously, and quickly.

The members of future organizations will require skills beyond that of content knowledge. The new employees must possess process skills. As Peter Senge addresses in the foreword, community members will be and are expected to go beyond just fixing problems to anticipating what might happen and to searching continuously for more creative solutions.

Societal Processes

The development of such a learning society depends on people's willingness to define the relationships between the individual and the community. The collective nurturing and understanding of our interdependence is essential if we wish to ensure our survival on this earth. More and more facets of society are beginning to challenge the traditionally held views of reductionist thinking. We are recognizing the need to see the world not only through the eyes of the individual but also as a part of a greater system in which connections are as important as differences.

Our society further recognizes a growing need for informed, skilled, and compassionate citizens who value truth, openness, creativity, and love, as well as the search for personal and spiritual freedom. We hear statements about community, interdependence, a balance in all areas of one's life, and making work an arena for self-discovery. This implies that the school's curriculum must be open enough to accept an androgynous perspective.

In an age in which self outweighs all other considerations, popular society is responding to the media because they appeal to the senses, not thoughts. The advertising industry is geared to selling the sizzle to the senses and not the steak to the cerebrum. An Anheuser-Busch commercial delivers the following message: "Why ask why? Drink Bud Dry." Or simply put, don't think, just drink! The media deliver the message that image is everything and substance is nothing. A recent Mazda commercial advocates, "Buy the car because it feels right." And Nike T-shirts are emblazoned with the statement, "Just Do It," which sends a message that impulsivity, rather than deliberation, is valued in this popular society.

Many persons are currently concerned with the increasing violence in schools, communities, and the world. Yet the media send a message that rules are unacceptable—"On Planet Reebok there are no rules!" The effect of the media as forces in learning cannot be underestimated. Education, therefore, must begin to help learners understand that not every opinion is worthwhile and that experts should be consulted. Educators must assist the young in moving away from the episodic grasp of reality created by the media.

These are not new thoughts but rather part of the continual quest for meaning as humans increase their knowledge base. Our desire to improve the current educational system has been founded on the erroneous belief that more of the same techniques and strategies will make all the difference. Yet if we consider the following quotes and their accompanying dates (from *Newsletter of the Curriculum and Supervisors Association,* 1994), one is left thinking that more of the same may in fact not hold the answers:

> More than eleven-twelfths of all the children in the reading classes in our schools do not understand the meaning of the words they read. —Horace Mann, 1838
>
> It is the opinion of high school teachers that from one fourth to one half the pupils are not greatly benefited by their course of study. These students lack interest, industry, effort, purpose, and are feebly endowed. —A Boston School Official, 1874
>
> A "despairing teacher" sent the *New York Times* samples of students' atrocious writing. —1911
>
> The president of the Carnegie Foundation complained, "In a large number of institutions the teaching has become enormously diluted." —1923
>
> The *Elementary School Journal* reported a "chronic problem facing American schools: a significant proportion of children were practically unable to learn to read under the prevailing methods of instruction." —1929
>
> The New York Committee on Delinquency in the Secondary Schools reported a "wide array of reckless, irresponsible, and anti-social behavior, with instances of violence, extortion, gang fights, and threats of bodily harm. There was vandalism against school property, private property, and pupils' personal possessions; there was theft, forgery, obscenity and vulgarity." —Early 1950s (p. 1)

The current education problems are the result of business as usual.

The re-visioning of education now required is so profound that it reaches far beyond the questions of budget, class size, teacher pay, and the traditional conflicts over the curriculum. In truth, the current industrial model of education is largely obsolete.

Processes of Meaning Making

Educators, in conjunction with other stakeholders, must begin to address the purpose behind the content. They must ask themselves the question, "Why do we do what we do at all?"

The exploding array of information makes it more impractical than ever to cover content at the expense of in-depth treatment. We are on the verge of a paradigm shift—content will become the mechanism by which we teach process. This shift will embrace the child's natural love of learning. As Senge (1990) has stated,

> Children come fully equipped with an insatiable drive to explore and experiment. Unfortunately the primary institutions of our society are

> oriented predominantly toward controlling rather than learning, rewarding individuals for performing for others rather than cultivating their natural curiosity and impulse to learn. (p. 7)

Content can no longer be the end in and of itself but the tool by which people learn to make meaning for themselves or to solve the problems for which they do not have answers.

In the past, educators have considered knowledge as static. This concept has influenced how we view a student's ability to learn. Valued is the possession of information, thus excluding the dynamic processes by which information is acquired and applied to authentic challenges. In the words of Deepak Chopra (1994), we "have become obsessed with the child's weaknesses, hiring tutors to make up for his [her] deficiencies, instead of looking at his [her] strengths and nurturing the natural talents." Not all children can be mathematicians, scientists, artists, authors, poets, musicians, historians, and so forth. Children come for a purpose unique to who they are, a purpose appropriate to the overall mosaic of life. It is time educators value individuals for their natural skills and talents, instead of trying to create clones, all possessing the same abilities.

Each human being has an inestimable potential for higher-order thought. As a result, we believe processes should be at the center of education. According to Chopra (1994),

> We think of the human body basically as a physical machine that has learned to think. Consciousness becomes the by-product of matter. The reality is that your physical body is not a frozen anatomical structure, but literally a river of intelligence and energy that's constantly renewing itself every second of your existence.
>
> I'd like to propose that we are not physical machines that have learned how to think. Perhaps it's the other way around: We are thoughts (and impulses, consciousness, feelings, emotions, desires and dreams) that have learned how to create physical bodies; that what we call our physical body is just a place that our memories call home for the time being.
>
> Understanding that consciousness is the creator of the mind and body, I think, is really necessary for us to survive and create a new reality. Not only is the body a field of ideas, but so is the physical universe we inhabit.

Curriculum: A Shared Purpose

All institutions are changing as the relationships between employee and employer, woman and man, offspring and parent, and student and teacher alter in deep and permanent ways in response to the need for all to contribute their intelligence, creativity, and responsibility to society.

The dilemma of what to teach and how best to teach dates from early colonial times. In the present controversy, educators and those outside education wrestle with basic skills, which can be seen as quantifiable measures of the success of education, versus intellectual skills, which are essentially qualitative and require authentic forms of assessment.

The importance of establishing a shared purpose for education in a culturally diverse country needs to be understood. As one corporate executive stated,

> Schools have no alignment on purpose. It is as if someone blows the whistle and starts the football game but forgets the goalposts and the markings on the ground. The players are simply running around and the game keeps going on, but we have no idea if we are winning.

To be effective, an organization must have a clear vision or shared purpose, clear insights into current reality, and a willingness to work at closing the gap between the two. Until schools begin to recognize the changes in society, focus on new visions for students that are congruent with these changes, and come to grips with the current state of reality, the industrial model of education will be perpetuated in an intellectual, community-modeled learning society. As the old smokestacks of the industrial era vanish from the horizon, so must the industrial model of education. We need to reawaken in our students the joy of learning to use and develop their intellects.

Toward a Process Curriculum

Tomorrow's workplaces will require the following characteristics: flexible and customized production that meets the needs of the consumer, decentralized control, flexible automation, on-line quality control, work teams of multiskilled workers, delegation of authority to workers, labor-management cooperation, a screening procedure for basic skills abilities, a realization that the workforce is an investment, a limited internal labor market, advancement by certified skills rather than by seniority, a recognition that everyone requires continuing training, and employees with broader skills as opposed to specialists. Therefore, education needs to focus on

- The development of thinking skills
- Self-assessment integral to learning
- Opportunities for students to actively construct knowledge for themselves
- Learning environments that develop cooperative problem solving
- Skills that are learned in the context of real problems
- Learner-centered, teacher-directed management
- Outcomes that ensure all students have learned to think

Anthony Gregorc (1985) expresses this focus well:

> The intent of education is to aid the student in realizing that he/she is a thinking person equipped with a personal knowledge bank and a decision-making instrument called a mind. Each student is expected to realize that he/she has a personal set of truths, opinions, biases, and

> blind spots which guide attitudes and actions. The educational process is intended to demonstrate how the student uses his/her thinking mind, how he/she learns from others and how he/she is affected by the environment. (pp. 98-99)

Ernest Boyer (1993) of the Carnegie Foundation saw the need for the following outcomes for students: being well-informed, acting wisely, continuing to learn, going beyond isolated facts to larger context and thereby discovering the connection of things, and seeing patterns and relationships that bring intellectual or aesthetic satisfaction.

We believe that the purpose of education is to enhance and develop the natural tendency of human beings as meaning makers. Humans' curiosity is aroused as we search for the meaning behind ambiguous principles and concepts. It is this continual search that promotes technological as well as personal advancements. When engaged in this search, we experience moments of illumination and moments of total change of heart. Educators need to return to learners their willingness to be playful, courageous, trusting, and risk taking. We need to invite them to reach for their outermost limits at all times. We need to create environments that allow students to practice freely without fear. We need to build not only strength of body but strength of character and strength of mind.

Where are we now? Csikszentmihalyi (1990) states,

> In the past few thousand years—a mere split second in evolutionary time—humanity has achieved incredible advances in the differentiation of consciousness. We have developed a realization that mankind is separate from other forms of life. We have conceived of individual human beings as separate from one another. We have invented abstraction and analysis—the ability to separate dimensions of objects and processes from each other, such as the velocity of a falling object from its weight and its mass. It is this differentiation that has produced science, technology, and the unprecedented power of mankind to build up and to destroy its environment.
>
> But complexity consists of integration as well as differentiation. The task of the next decades and centuries is to realize this under-developed component of the mind. Just as we have learned to separate ourselves from each other and from the environment, we now need to learn how to reunite ourselves with other entities around us without losing our hard-won individuality. The most promising faith for the future might be based on the realization that the entire universe is a system related by common laws and that it makes no sense to impose our dreams and desires on nature without taking them into account. Recognizing the limitations of human will, accepting a cooperative rather than a ruling role in the universe, we should feel the relief of the exile who is finally returning home. The problem of meaning will then be resolved as the individual's purpose merges with the universal flow. (p. 41)

For what should educators strive? Many of the answers lie in the chapters of these books. We need to develop holonomous thinkers—people who understand their individuality as well as their interdependence. We need to equip every member of society with the skills to survive in and contribute to a chaotic universe that is in constant change. All members need the strength and courage to live their lives to the fullest by giving their unique gifts back to the universe. Perhaps it is time that we as educators found the courage to open Pandora's box and release the butterfly inside.

> The solution which I am urging is to eradicate the fatal disconnection of subjects which kills the vitality of our modern curriculum. There is only one subject-matter for education, and that is Life in all its manifestations.
>
> *Alfred North Whitehead*

References

Boyer, E. (1993, March). *Keynote address.* Address presented at the national conference of the Association for Supervision and Curriculum Development, Washington, DC.

Chopra, D. (1994, September). *Ageless body, timeless mind.* Presentation given at the Boundless Energy Retreat, Somerset, NJ.

Csikszentmihalyi, M. (1990). *Flow: The psychology of optimal experience.* New York: Harper & Row.

Gregorc, A. (1985, Fall/Winter). Toward a redefinition of teaching, instructing, educating, and training. *Curriculum in Context,* 97-100.

Newsletter of the Curriculum and Supervisors Association. (1994, June). p. 1.

Senge, P. (1990). The leader's new work: Building learning organizations. *Sloan Management Review, 32*(1), 7-22.

Preface to *Supporting the Spirit of Learning*

Arthur L. Costa
Rosemarie M. Liebmann

> New frameworks are like climbing a mountain—the larger view encompasses, rather than rejects the earlier more restricted view.
>
> *Albert Einstein*

This trilogy, *Process as Content,* invites a new vision of education and literacy. As we enter a world in which knowledge doubles in less than 5 years (and is projected to double every 73 days by the year 2020), it is no longer feasible to anticipate the future information requirements of an individual. We must look differently and with greater depth at what learning is of most worth. We need, in the words of Michael Fullan (1993), to take a "quantum leap" (p. 5) in how we think about and develop curriculum.

This second volume in the trilogy, *Supporting the Spirit of Learning: When Process Is Content,* examines some issues and changes necessary in curriculum, instruction, staff development, assessment, parent communication, and technology. Contributions from practitioners, researchers, and theoreticians respond to the questions of what curriculum, instruction, assessment, and staff development would be like if process were content.

Because of increased knowledge on how the brain learns, because of paradigm shifts from the new sciences, and because of societal needs to engage in systems thinking, the time has come to shift our focus from the *what* of knowledge (content) to the *how* of learning (processes)—from, as Seymour Papert

(1991) states, "instructionism to constructionism" (p. 24). We need to nurture the skills, operations, and dispositions that will enable individuals to solve problems when answers are not readily known. Educators need to embark on radical reforms that shift away from content to process and need to value the collective intelligence of the group, as well as the intelligence of each learner.

As we began to collect the authors for this trilogy, repeated concern over our vision surfaced, namely, were we reversing the dichotomy from content being highly valued and prized—so much so that process has almost been excluded—to process being the primary emphasis and content forgotten? The answer to this question is a firm, resounding "No!" We, as editors and authors, believe strongly in the duality that both are required and must be intertwined. We are not suggesting that content be devalued. We are suggesting that content be viewed from the perspective of how it enhances and accomplishes the development of processes. It is not a dichotomy of inclusion versus exclusion (either/or) but rather an interaction (both/and).

> Process—the cluster of diverse procedures which surround the acquisition of knowledge—is, in fact, the highest form of content and the most appropriate base for curriculum change. It is in the teaching of process that we can best portray learning as a perpetual endeavor and not something which terminates with the end of school. Through process, we can employ knowledge, not merely as a composite of information but, as a system for learning. (Parker & Rubin, 1966, p. 1)

We propose that when humans operate at their peaks of efficacy, there is a congruence between what they are thinking, feeling, and doing. This concept is supported by Thomas Moore (1992), who notes,

> An eternal question about children is, how should we educate them? Politicians and educators consider more school days in a year, more science and math, the use of computers and other technology in the classroom, more exams and tests, more certifications for teachers, and less money for art. All of these responses come from the place where we want to make the child into the best adult possible, not from the ancient Greek sense of virtuous and wise, but in the sense of one is an efficient part of the machinery of society. (p. 53)

If we accept that there is currently a shift away from the industrial model of society to a learning society, then the focus of education needs to shift also. The change will require a movement away from a content-driven curriculum to a curriculum that provides individuals with the skills necessary to engage in lifelong learning.

Simultaneously, the role of the educator needs to shift from the information provider to one of a catalyst, coach, innovator, researcher, and collaborator with the learner throughout the learning process. The development of the learner's unique abilities becomes the central focus of the learning environment.

The intent of the book is to influence curriculum decision makers at all levels—teachers, administrators, school board members, test constructors, textbook authors, legislators, and parents—and to support them in thinking anew about the role of restructuring the curriculum in the school.

We believe that the most critical, but least understood, component of restructuring in the school reform movement is the restructuring of curriculum. Curriculum, in the broadest sense, is everything that influences the learning of the students, both overtly and covertly, inside and outside the school. Curriculum is the heart—the pulse of the school; it is what drives everything else. Curriculum is the currency through which teachers exchange thoughts and ideas with students and the school community. It is the passion that binds the organization together.

Current reform movements are driven by national, state, and local mandates, reorganization of time concerning the school day and the school year, redistributing the power of decision-making processes, investing in technology, and recombining interdisciplinary teams and subjects. These and other such reforms constitute the *how* of delivery, not the sum and substance of what we are all about. When we begin to address the very heart of the organization, the driving component—curriculum—then all other reform efforts will fall into place. We have been building new reform structures around old-fashioned curriculum. Therefore, this book offers a bold proposal: Redesign the curriculum as the main component of re-visioning the school.

Such radical shifts in our current thinking require a clear articulation of process education. The first book in this trilogy, *Envisioning Process As Content: Toward a Renaissance Curriculum,* addresses what is meant by process and what some of these processes are. We presented supportive literature from the new sciences and the expectations of performance from America's corporations to underscore why the time is right for such a shift in thinking about education.

This second book in the trilogy, *Supporting the Spirit of Learning: When Process Is Content*, explores questions about curriculum and instruction, for example: What would instruction, assessment, and staff development be like if process were the content? The last book, *The Process-Centered School: Sustaining a Renaissance Community,* presents suggestions and strategies for those embarking on the journey of transforming education into a process-oriented paradigm.

We invite you, the readers, to play with these visions, thoughts, and ideas—to elaborate, change, or modify them in ways that best meet the needs of your learning organizations. They are offered to you as a way to stimulate your own growth and learning. Process, by its very nature, enables a dynamic response to the environment that surrounds us.

As people continue to recognize that knowledge speaks to us not in a single voice but with many, we will simultaneously accept that there are multiple ways of thinking and understanding. As Marvin Minsky (1987) has stated,

> Everyone can benefit from multiple ways of thinking about things. Understanding something in just one way is a rather fragile kind of understanding. You need to understand something at least two different ways in order to really understand it. Each way of thinking about something strengthens and deepens each of the other ways of thinking about it. Understanding something in several different ways produces an overall understanding that is richer and of a different nature than any one way of understanding. (p. 103)

We invite you to consider curriculum in a different way—to enter a world of learning that permits greater freedom, greater control, and, in the end, more thoughtful learners. From this increased freedom, we will generate eager, autonomous, interdependent, lifelong learners.

References

Fullan, M. (1993). *Change forces: Probing the depths of educational reform.* Bristol, PA: Falmer.

Minsky, M. (1987). *The society of mind.* New York: Simon & Schuster.

Moore, T. (1992). *Care of the soul.* New York: HarperCollins.

Papert, S. (1991). Situating constructionism. In I. Harel & S. Papert (Eds.), *Constructionism.* Norwood, NJ: Ablex.

Parker, J. C., & Rubin, L. J. (1966). *Process as content: Curriculum design and the application of knowledge.* Chicago: Rand McNally.

Acknowledgments

We wish to acknowledge the valuable contributions of each of the contributors to this volume and this trilogy. Their contributions represent a vast range of diverse views and, at the same time, reflect a common focus, dedication, and commitment to promoting process-oriented education. They have been patient with our prodding, agreeable to our edits, and supportive of our mission. For their time, energies, and talents, we are forever grateful.

We also wish to acknowledge Alice Foster of Corwin Press, whose encouragement and support sustained us during the 3-year duration of this project. We also wish to express our thanks to the editors at Corwin Press who assisted us greatly with refining the manuscript.

Arthur L. Costa
Rosemarie M. Liebmann

About the Authors

Anthony Colella is a graduate professor at Seton Hall University, specializing in leadership/management training and industrial psychology. He holds a Ph.D. degree from Fordham University and a postdoctoral certificate from Harvard University. An educator and lecturer for 25 years, he conducts seminars and workshops for public and private school administrators, law enforcement and government personnel, health care professionals, and corporate leaders. His lectures focus on research in change theory, the thinking-learning process, and the mind-body connection. As a certified reading and learning disabilities consultant, he has also worked with children and adults in diagnosing and prescribing effective learning practices for exceptional individuals. As a specialist in the field of child growth and development, he has been a teacher and administrator in the public and private arenas as well as the owner and director of a private school in New Jersey.

Arthur L. Costa is Emeritus Professor of Education at California State University at Sacramento and Co-Director of the Institute for Intelligent Behavior in Berkeley, California. He has served as a classroom teacher, a curriculum consultant, and an assistant superintendent for instruction and as the Director of Educational Programs for the National Aeronautics and Space Administration. He has made presentations and conducted workshops in all 50 states and in Mexico, Central and South America, Canada, Australia, New Zealand, Africa, Europe, Asia, and the islands of the South Pacific. Author of numerous journal articles, he edited *Developing Minds: A Resource Book for Teaching Thinking* and authored *The Enabling Behaviors*, *Teaching for Intelligent Behaviors*, and *The School as a Home for the Mind*. He is coauthor of *Cognitive Coaching: A Foundation for Renaissance Schools* and coeditor of *The Role of Assessment in the Learning Organization: Shifting the Paradigm* and *If Minds Matter*. Active in many professional organizations, he served as President of the California Association for Supervision and Curriculum Development and was the National President of ASCD from 1988 to 1989.

John Edwards is Associate Professor of Education at James Cook University in Townsville, Australia. His major research interests are professional performance, the creative management of change, the rediscovery of the joy of teaching, how people think, and the direct teaching of thinking, particularly lateral thinking. Improving performance and thinking in Australian business and industry is the focus for a major government-funded study that he and his coresearchers will complete in 1997. His career includes experience as a research metallurgist, a writer, a science teacher and department head, and a science education specialist at an international center in Southeast Asia. He lectures and consults widely throughout Australia, the Pacific, Southeast Asia, Europe, and the United States in both educational and business settings.

Rafi Feuerstein is Assistant Director of the International Center for the Enhancement of Learning Potential and Director of the BENEHEV Bloomfield Institute for Dynamic Assessment, focusing on the Learning Potential Assessment Device within the International Center. He received rabbinical certification from the Yeshiva of the Rav Kook Center in Jerusalem in 1988 and is currently the Rabbi of his kibbutz, Ein Tzurim. He received his B.A. from the Hebrew University in Jerusalem in psychology and philosophy and is continuing there on his advanced degree in cognitive psychology.

Reuven Feuerstein is Professor of Psychology at Bar Ilan University School of Education, Adjunct Professor at Peabody College-Vanderbilt University, and Founder and Director of the International Center for Enhancement of Learning Potential/Hadassah-WIZO-Canada Research Institute in Jerusalem. He is internationally recognized in the fields of cognitive psychology, special education, and human growth and development. At the University of Geneva under Jean Piaget and André Rey, he earned diplomas in general and clinical psychology. He received his Ph.D. in developmental psychology from the Sorbonne. His theory of Structural Cognitive Modifiability and Mediated Learning Experience led to the Learning Potential Assessment Device, the cognitive intervention program of Instrumental Enrichment, and the Shaping of Modifying Environments. He has received the Variety Club International Humanitarian Award, the French Government's Chevalier dans l'Ordre des palmes Académique, and the Israel Prize for education. He has led intensive work to improve the lives of individuals with Down syndrome, blindness, and other disabilities.

Robin Fogarty is a leading proponent of thoughtful classrooms and trains teachers throughout the world in cognitive strategies and cooperative interaction. She taught all levels from kindergarten to college, served as an administrator, and consulted with state departments and ministries of education. She has trained teachers and administrators in the United States, Canada, Puerto Rico, Australia, New Zealand, Russia, and the Netherlands in thinking, transfer of learning, and integrating the curricula. She consults for several provincial and state departments of education in their current reform efforts. She has authored, coauthored, and edited numerous publications. Her recent works include *The Mindful School: How to Integrate the Curricula; The Mindful School: The Portfolio Connection; Integrating the Curricula with Multiple Intelligences: Teams,*

Themes, and Threads; Think About . . . Multiage Classrooms; Multiple Intelligences: A Collection; Student Portfolios: A Collection of Articles; and *Block Scheduling: A Collection of Articles.*

Robert J. Garmston is Professor Emeritus of Educational Administration at California State University, Sacramento, and is Executive Director of Facilitation Associates, an educational consulting firm specializing in leadership, learning, and personal and organizational development. He is Codeveloper of Cognitive Coaching and Co-Director of the Institute for Intelligent Behavior (with Arthur Costa). He has authored numerous publications on leadership, supervision, and staff development. He has made presentations and conducted workshops for educators, managers, and professional trainers throughout the United States and in Canada, Europe, Asia, and the Middle East. Formerly an administrator in several school districts, he was Principal in the Sunnyvale School District, Director of Instruction at the Live Oak School District, and Superintendent of the Bellevue Union School District. Active in many professional organizations, he served as President of the California Association for Supervision and Curriculum Development from 1989 to 1991 and as a member of the Executive Council for the Association for Supervision and Curriculum Development at the international level from 1991 to 1994. He has served as consultant to diverse groups at the local, state, national, and international level.

Gwen Gawith is a teacher educator, author, and illustrator from Auckland, New Zealand. After training and experience in management, graphic arts, librarianship, and education, she specialized in information literacy and learning design. She has written numerous articles and nine books and has run workshops for teachers throughout Australia. She currently coordinates learning programs in information studies for New Zealand teachers. The Centre for Information Studies offers specialist postgraduate courses in information studies, teacher-librarianship, and information technology to teachers throughout New Zealand and has also pioneered unique school-based information literacy courses used by principals for whole-school staff development.

Bena Kallick is an educational consultant providing services to school districts, state departments of education, professional organizations, and public sector agencies throughout the United States. She received her doctorate in educational evaluation with Union Graduate School. Her areas of focus include group dynamics, creative and critical thinking, and alternative assessment strategies in the classroom. Formerly a Teachers' Center Director, she also created a Children's Museum based on problem solving and invention. She was the coordinator of a high school alternative designed for at-risk students. Her written work includes "Literature to Think About" (a whole language curriculum), *Changing Schools Into Communities for Thinking,* and *Assessing the Learning Organization,* coauthored with Arthur Costa. She has also coauthored audiotapes including "Creative and Critical Thinking: Teaching Alternatives" and "Collaborative Learning: Strategies to Encourage Thinking" (with Marian Leibowitz). She is Cofounder of EXEMPLARS, a company designed to facilitate teachers' networks and communications about performance assessment. She has taught at Yale University School of Organization and Management, University of Massachusetts Center for Creative and Critical Thinking, and Union Graduate School. She is on the boards for JOBS for the Future and the Apple Foundation.

Michael Keany is Principal of Manhasset High School. He has also been a middle school principal, curriculum developer, director of an alternative program, and secondary science teacher. An author of science texts and developer of instructional equipment, he has been a teacher trainer at the university level. He has also served as a school board member for 12 years.

Marian Leibowitz is an educational consultant for school districts, state departments of education, professional organizations, and agencies throughout the United States and abroad, including giving seminars for groups such as ASCD and I/D/E/A. Her major focus is restructuring of schools—leadership, change, instructional design, curriculum, and assessment. She has taught children who are gifted and has consulted for numerous school districts in the establishment and evaluation of programs serving students with special needs. She has been a Learning Disabilities Teacher/Consultant, Chapter I Coordinator, Director of a Title III Mainstreaming Project, Special Education Coordinator at EIC/Central, and Assistant Superintendent for Curriculum and Instruction in Teaneck, New Jersey. She was a site visitor for the U.S. Office of Education Secondary School Recognition Program and works extensively in staff development and program evaluation at the secondary level. She is currently working with school districts in restructuring schools, with major projects in Albuquerque, New Mexico; Stamford, Connecticut; New Rochelle, New York; Lorain, Ohio; and Adrian, Michigan. She is past president for the New Jersey Association of Leading Consultants and chapter president for the Council of Exceptional Children, as well as past president of the New Jersey Association of Supervision and Curriculum Development. She was named to the ASCD panel studying Restructuring the Teaching Profession and was cofacilitator for the ASCD consortium of school districts involved in efforts at restructuring. Rider College, the Northeast Coalition of Educational Leaders, and the New Jersey Association of Supervision and Curriculum Development have recently honored her for her outstanding contributions to the field of educational leadership.

Rosemarie M. Liebmann is Director of the Institute for Continuous Learning Systems, a private consulting firm; Director of Curriculum and Instruction, Livingston School District, Livingston, New Jersey; and Adjunct Professor at Seton Hall University, South Orange, New Jersey. She attained her Ed.D. from Seton Hall University and has done extensive work in the field of human resource development. Her doctoral thesis probed the holonomous skills required of a literate society. This research has led her to a recognition of the need for society to return to valuing personal and interpersonal spirituality. She has extensively researched the ancient art of shamanism as well as feminist spirituality. Having served in the educational field for 25 years as a teacher and administrator, she seeks to help others through the use of Cognitive Coaching. In her work as lecturer, workshop leader, educator, and author, she aspires to model for others that our minds will blossom only when we permit the buds to open. The richness of learning and experiencing the world around us is the nutrients for the soil of our spirits.

Timothy Melchior was appointed Principal of Memorial Junior High School in Valley Stream, New York, in 1978. He and his school have received numerous awards and recognition for the school's programs, especially in teaching thinking. He is the developer of Counterpoint Thinking and the author of articles about teaching thinking, Edward de Bono's CoRT Thinking Program, supervision, staff development, and change and leadership. As a researcher and consultant, he has worked with educators and school districts throughout the United States, has spoken at national and international conferences, and has worked for major corporations. He retired from his principalship in June 1996 and is now Vice President for Corporate Development for Cardone, Gordon and Associates, a company that specializes in investment instruments for employees of nonprofit organizations.

Sandra Parks serves as a curriculum and staff development consultant on teaching thinking for schools and conducts annual seminars for the Association for Supervision and Curriculum Development. She was Founding President of the Indiana Association for the Gifted and taught gifted education courses at the University of North Florida and the University of Miami. Since 1981, she has been Director of Thinking Works, an instructional materials resource center in St. Augustine, Florida. With Howard Black, she coauthored *Building Thinking Skills* and *Organizing Thinking*. With Robert Swartz, she coauthored *Infusing the Teaching of Critical and Creative Thinking Into Content Instruction* and codirected the National Center for Teaching Thinking, host for the Sixth International Conference on Thinking. She presently serves as chairman of the board of directors of the Network to Improve Thinking and Learning.

Vito Perrone is Director of the Teacher Education Programs and member of the Learning and Teaching Faculty at the Harvard Graduate School of Education. He has been a secondary school teacher of history and social studies and continues to be deeply involved in the life of elementary and secondary schools. He was Professor of History and Dean of Common Learning and Graduate Studies at Northern Michigan University (1962-1968); Professor of History, Education, and Peace Studies and Dean of the New School and Center for Teaching and Learning at the University of North Dakota (1968-1986); and Vice President of the Carnegie Foundation for the Advancement of Teaching (1986-1988). Since 1972, he has served as Coordinator of the North Dakota Study Group on Evaluation, a national organization of teachers, school administrators, community organizers, and university scholars. He has written extensively on educational equity, curriculum, progressivism in education, and testing and evaluation.

Stanley Pogrow is Associate Professor of Educational Administration at the University of Arizona, where he specializes in instructional and administrative uses of computers. He is the developer of the HOTS program, a thinking skills program for educationally disadvantaged students, and SUPERMATH, a new approach to pre-algebra for all students.

Louis Rubin is Professor of Curriculum and Instruction at the University of Illinois, Champaign-Urbana. He has taught at Stanford University, the University of California at Berkeley, the University of Nebraska, and Emery University, as well as Simon Fraser University and the University of British Columbia in Canada. He has published an extensive array of articles dating from 1960 and is the author-editor of 11 books, including a two-volume *Handbook of Curriculum, Facts and Feelings in the Classroom* and *The Future of Education: Frontiers in Leadership and Artistry in Teaching.* He was formerly the Director of the Communications Coalition for Educational Change in Washington, D.C., and Director of the Center for Coordinated Education in Santa Barbara, California. He has served as a consultant to UNESCO, the U.S. Department of Education, the Ford and Kettering Foundations, and numerous state departments of education and several foreign nations. A frequent speaker, he has lectured in Europe, Asia, Africa, and South America.

Yaron Schur is Director of the Institute for Instrumental Enrichment within the International Center for the Enhancement of Learning Potential. He is a specialist in the System Oriented Approach of the Feuerstein Instrumental Enrichment cognitive intervention program, which is used in school classrooms and industrial environments. He is also concerned with the bridging of Instrumental Enrichment to the teaching process in curriculum subjects. He has developed a curriculum for the teaching of astronomy in middle-level schools within Israel that emphasizes the development of thinkings and uses up-to-date teaching aids. Before joining the ICELP, he was an inspector in the Israel Ministry of Education in charge of the implementation of national reform in technological education. He received a Presidential award as volunteer of the year in 1980 for his work with street gangs. He was the first recipient of the Weizman Institute of Science's national award for best physics teacher in 1985.

Peter M. Senge is a faculty member of the Massachusetts Institute of Technology and Director of the Center for Organizational Learning at MIT's Sloan School of Management, a consortium of corporations that work together to advance methods and knowledge for building learning organizations. He is author of *The Fifth Discipline: The Art and Practice of the Learning Organization* and is coauthor (with colleagues Charlotte Roberts, Rick Ross, Bryan Smith, and Art Kleiner) of *The Fifth Discipline Fieldbook: Strategies and Tools for Building a Learning Organization.* He is also a founding partner of the management, consulting, and training firm Innovative Associates. He has lectured extensively throughout the world, translating the abstract ideas of systems theory into tools for better understanding economic and organizational change. His special interests and expertise focus on decentralizing the role of leadership in an organization to enhance the capacity of all people to work productively toward common goals. His work articulates a cornerstone position of human values in the workplace, namely, that vision, purpose, alignment, and systems thinking are essential if organizations are to truly realize their potentials. He has worked with leaders in business, education, health care, and government. He works collaboratively with organizations such as Ford, Federal Express, Motorola, AT&T, Intel, Electronic Data Systems (EDS), Harley-Davidson, Hewlett Packard, and Royal/Dutch Shell. He received a B.S. in engineering from Stanford University, an M.S. in social systems modeling, and a Ph.D. in management from MIT.

Robert J. Swartz is Co-Director of The National Center for Teaching Thinking and was the sponsor of the Sixth International Conference on Thinking. He is also Professor of Philosophy at the University of Massachusetts at Boston, where he developed the Critical and Creative Thinking Program. He is a consultant for several school districts and professional agencies. He is coauthor of *Teaching Thinking: Issues and Approaches* and a series of handbooks for elementary grades and secondary grades, *Infusing the Teaching of Critical and Creative Thinking Into Content Instruction* (with Sandra Parks).

Marilyn Tabor is Senior Associate of the Institute for Intelligent Behavior. As a national consultant, she specializes in personal and organizational development, learning, and leadership. Her particular interests include the facilitation of group process, multidimensional applications of Cognitive Coaching, and development of the adaptive organization wherein leading and facilitating occur in collaborative work cultures. As a Coordinator of Curriculum and Instruction, she worked directly with administrators and teachers in a district of 31 schools. She models Cognitive Coaching in the ASCD video training program *Another Set of Eyes: Conferencing Skills,* and Reflective Conversation in the video accompanying the California State Department of Education training program *Preparing Support Providers to Work With Beginning Teachers.*

Barbara D. Wright is in private practice as a psychotherapist. A native of Winnetka, Illinois, she attended schools that modeled theories of education espoused by scholars as distant as the 16th-century educator John Comenius and as recent as John Dewey and Carlton Washburne. Her progressive education brought an early awareness of the need for implementation of child-centered concepts in public education. She attended the University of Rochester, New York; Rutgers University; and Drew University, where she earned her Ph.D. Although her field of expertise is in psychology, she has long been interested in questions of learning in a school setting as well as in the exploration of feminist theory pertaining to education.

1

Process as Content in Education of Exceptional Children

Reuven Feuerstein
Rafi Feuerstein
Yaron Schur

Thoughts without content are empty. Intuitions without concepts are blind.

Kant, 1958, p. 61

Introduction

If we consider the great changes that are happening, as if by rapid mutations, in many dimensions of human conditions, concern with the nature of education and the curriculum to prepare children for confronting the future era is legitimate. The new culture requires continual adaptation for survival. The need to produce changes in the curriculum, by creating new educational approaches, requires an analysis of the changes that must be addressed to plan the modern educational and instructional endeavor. Understanding the special

AUTHORS' NOTE: We would like to acknowledge that this chapter was written with the generous sponsorship of the Hadassah-WIZO Organization of Canada during the presidency of Judy Mandleman, as well as that of the rest of the Founding Members of the International Center for the Enhancement of Learning Potential, chaired by Sidney Corob, C.B.E. We thank them for their support. In addition, we would like to thank Hadassah Susson for her editorial assistance.

nature of changes with which humans may be faced may better enable us to look for ways of preparing the young generation for their encounter with the new era. In this chapter, we conceptualize the types of expected changes that will require a typology of adaptational responses.

When we look at the past developments and the evolution of the interaction between human organisms and their environment, we are constantly confronted with the process of mutual impact between the partners of this interaction. Human beings change the environment, creating new components, structures, and modalities of action. Thereafter, to benefit or sometimes survive these changes, humans subsequently have to change themselves in whatever dimensions are required.

The transformation from a culture of gatherers and hunters to one of laborers and producers was accompanied by many changes in the dependence-independence dimension between individual and group. While gatherers depended on limitations of the existent food available, laborers produced the food. The greatest marker in this shift, however, was the new greater distance at which this interaction took place. For gatherers, the distance between the individuals and the food was almost zero. Food production created a new distance between the need expressed by hunger and its gratification in satiation. This new distance was accompanied by processes that affect the mental functioning of the human organism: from direct, immediate recognition of the food to be gathered in response to hunger, to the representation of the food as a future, often delayed answer to the need expressed by hunger. Between the need (hunger) and the goal (food), a chain of means to reach the goal has to be inserted in an established given order. This order may even be accompanied with delays in gratification, such as not eating the grains that will be used as seeds, despite the immediacy of the sense of hunger. Thus, human beings had to learn to increase the distance at which they interact with their world.

In his monumental presentation *Urdistanz und Beziehung* (Primary Distance and Relationship), Martin Buber (1960) defines the difference between animals and humans by their different interactions with their environment. While animals' interactions are with a realm (*ummwelt Berreich* in Buber's terminology) that includes only those parts of the outer world that are relevant to their immediate needs, human beings have a world whose existence is recognized, experienced, elaborated, organized, grouped, and categorized, irrespective of the immediacy or the remoteness (or distance) from their needs.

This distance between human beings and the world, in contrast to the lack of distance between animals and their realm, is, notably, the dualistic nature of the human-world interaction compared with the adualistic nature of animal-realm interaction, which creates a relationship. Relationship is the direct product of distance. Only when distance is created by the distinctiveness and the mental, logical differentiation of individuals from the environment will the relationship become more complex, richer, and multidirectional.

The concept of distance encompasses the dimensions of time, space, internality, externality, and the distances produced by the mental processes. These processes are manifest in the production of substitutes of reality through the process of encoding this reality into signs, symbols, and traces, which then need to be decoded. Classification of dimensions of reality that differ in many aspects but have in common one conventionally chosen dimension entails a distant perspective, one from which differences are not perceived or volitionally ignored in favor of the common trait used for establishing inclusion in the conceptual group. The processes of classification, of categorization, and of establishing relationships are all modes of action performed at distances that only the dualistic mode of interaction between human beings and the world permits. Piaget (1966) described the passage from an adualistic to a dualistic mode of interaction with the world as a developmental, stage-related process.

The establishment of such a dualistic relationship, however, is made possible by a process-oriented activity of the human mind. The content-oriented approach confines activity to the immediacy of the concretely perceived object or event on which humans operate. Limiting learners to the acquisition of content knowledge is acting like gatherers and hunters, who gratified their needs by the adualistic immediacy of their realm and the immediate presence of the gratifying object. In contrast, orienting learners to the process involved in the production and generation of knowledge is acting like the laborers who have to plan ahead to reach goals that are remote from the immediately accessible reality. Thus, human beings have to form internal mental images of future reality and insert the chain of actions necessary to reach the goals that they have constructed mentally.

The distance at which humans operate on the world, both externally and internally, will determine the nature of the process that they will have to employ in this operational interaction. If the spatial distance is such that the visually emitted message is not received, then a process of encoding the message in a way that the distance will not obstruct its transmission will have to be instituted. Reading written messages became the way by which temporal distances were overcome and information became transmissible. The operations that create interaction over distances are based on mental, cognitive processes that become more complex as the remoteness of the target increases.

We contend that characterizing the changes in the various dimensions of the world is a constant increase in the temporal and spatial distances at which humans have to operate. This makes content learning of little value unless it is accompanied with the processes that are necessary to transform the specific content into a source of generalization and to transform the generalization to the newly generated contents. Both transformations depend on process. Yet what is presently offered in educational and instructional systems is all too often reduced to an inventory of facts. This is true even when this inventory includes mathematical rules and quasi operations. Devoid of their underlying processes, these rules remain purely technical and limited to the immediate realm, rather than transferable also to the distant world.

Content Education

When we apply the question of content versus process to the instruction and education of exceptional children, we are confronted with a system of instructional methods, didactics, and teaching goals whose major aim is to keep individuals at zero distance from the object, events, and experiences on which they operate. Lack of belief in the propensity of these individuals to modify their cognitive structures, irrespective of the type and quantity of intervention offered, makes their teachers extremely reluctant to establish distance from what is concrete, sensorially perceived, and directly experienced.

The sources of information are used as models of imitation, and reality is reproduced by the organisms perceiving it. The generation of new, previously untransmitted information is impossible because of the lack of the processes necessary for such production. Everything to be learned is kept in proximity, to the point that little is left over on which the mental processes might operate. When exceptional children are asked for the years in which they were born, the standard answer resembles, "I don't know. My father, mother, or somebody else knows. I never was told. I didn't study it. I am not suppose to know what was not told or taught to me." Often, however, the children know their ages and the current date and are even able to subtract. Missing is the process orientation that will make them use all the existent information as parts of the equation leading to the generation of new information.

The absence of process leaves the individuals in a passive state, acting as reproducers of gathered information with little, if any, readiness to act as generators of the needed information. Many of those who are introduced to knowledge and skills are not offered the necessary insights to operate on the reality with which they are confronted. An admittedly extreme example will give the paradigm of this strategy of teaching with a zero-distance approach.

During a description of the methodology applied to train adults with mental retardation to function in society, a lecturer pointed out that it was important for such individuals to learn how to use the supermarket. The first step for achieving this goal was to teach them how to enter the supermarket. From this came the need to teach the various ways of opening different styles of doors to supermarkets. We quote the lecturer's description of the proposed teaching solution: "We took a minibus and went from supermarket to supermarket and showed them the doors that are pulled, dragged, pushed, et cetera." The concept of "opening," which provides the guide to discovering and adapting to new forms of the same function, was not offered. Therefore, the students would have to remain at zero distance between them and the variations of opening—at a time when humans can open a valve in a satellite that is millions of miles away by pushing a button!

Much of the content-oriented approach has a similar modality of teaching. In general, the didactics applied in special education represent zero distance between the learner and the facts to be learned. Process becomes vital when the learned facts become distant enough to require a relationship to be established between them. Education, both in general and in particular of exceptional individuals, encourages the extensive use of all the senses in learning all aspects of the facts, stimuli, or events imparted. The integration of the various senses is considered to be the high peak of the teaching process. The uniqueness of the object is stressed, rather than its common traits that can be found in many other things. These commonalities, when educed through comparative behavior, become the source of the analogical, syllogistic thinking so vital in all daily and academic thinking activity. Their introduction becomes the way to establish the process of inference, important in anticipatory planning behavior.

But the behaviors related to higher mental functions cannot be achieved by simply exposing individuals to knowledge-based content or even to skill information. The underlying processes with their accompanying awareness must be the animating factor of all content learning. The task of process learning is not only to make the facts "visible" but also to make these facts "seeing" ones. Process learning turns the image into its component concepts and translates the essence of the image.

To consider such process not only as essential in the guiding of adaptive behavior but also as accessible to people who are usually limited to concrete, sensorial, fact-seeking experiences—in other words, to persons with mental retardation—we have to believe that the limitations ascribed to them are not fixed by the "G" factor that is weakly represented in their mental structure. Rather, we have to believe that new, previously nonexistent cognitive structures can become implanted and activated despite their low manifest level of functioning. The underlying belief of their teachers will powerfully determine whether the necessary means will be created, shaped, and applied to produce the necessary structures.

These means will not be simply additional bits of information or skills but processes of learning that permit the use of bits of information to produce new ones. Wherever underlying belief fails to recognize the developmental options of individuals, educational efforts will be reduced to implanting the content that is considered to be necessary, pragmatic, and accessible. Content will be chosen that is relevant to the individuals at the given point in their lives. Thus, the "world" presented to them will shrink to zero distance into the realm of mere biological needs.

The predominant interest in curriculum content limits unnecessarily the educational and experiential horizons of many children and turns them into dull, uninterested adults. The father of Simon, a young man with Down syndrome, pleaded not to "teach his son things he doesn't know because it will make him feel bad." Indeed, Simon, a high-functioning person with a strong memory and a great wealth of knowledge that he gathered from extensive reading (working as a librarian), was not able to solve tasks requiring spatial orientation, did not recognize the right hand of the person standing in front of him, and drew the waterlines in inclined bottles totally against the rules of gravity (Figure 1.1).

It took us literally only minutes to help him improve his spatial orientation by emphasizing the process of representation of the movement that enabled him to place himself in the position of his partner and to change the water from its familiar position in an upright bottle to an awareness of the constancy of the water's level, irrespective of the bottle's position. When confronted with the achievements of his son, the father admitted to having protected him from exposure to these and many other tasks, choosing to teach him only those contents that he considered necessary for Simon's immediate survival or already familiar enough so as not to require any mental processes to master them.

Many parents and educators withhold vital functions from their children and students because these functions are considered inaccessible to them and irrelevant to their future or their current functioning. Thus, it is rare to find individuals with Down syndrome even at such advanced ages as 20 or 30 years

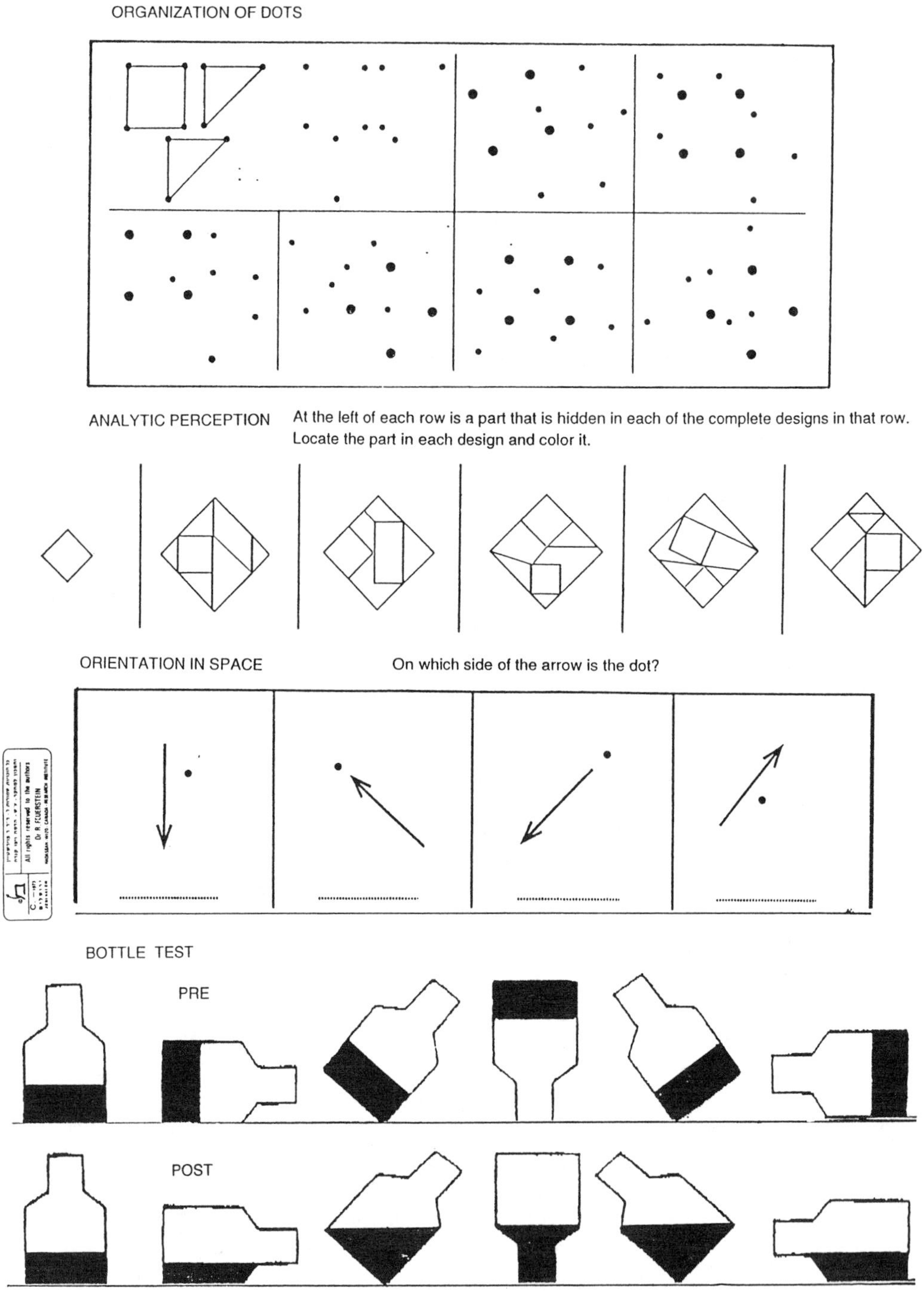

ORGANIZATION OF DOTS
ANALYTIC PERCEPTION
At the left of each row is a part that is hidden in each of the complete designs in that row. Locate the part in each design and color it.
ORIENTATION IN SPACE
On which side of the arrow is the dot?
BOTTLE TEST
PRE
POST

Figure 1.1. Examples From Feuerstein Instrumental Enrichment, Including the Pre- and Post-Piagetian Bottle Test

SOURCE: Compiled from Instrumental Enrichment instruments. Copyright © by Reuven Feuerstein and the Hadassah-WIZO-Canada Research Institute, Jerusalem, Israel. All rights reserved. Reproduced by permission.

who know how to light a match. Such knowledge is viewed as dangerous because the hypotonia of their peribuccal areas prevents them from blowing out matches with their lips. In any case, it is projected that they will never have to do it because they are not involved in cooking and so forth. Thus, they are not taught the skill that would be safe if it were also mediated to them that flames always rise. Therefore, after having been lit, a burning match could be held safely in a vertical position without burning their fingers and could be extinguished by rapidly waving the hand that is holding it.

By the same token, math is taught mechanically as a content, not only in almost all special education classes but also in many regular schools. Thus, the students, even gifted ones, are not made aware of the *process* underlying their technical skills. The Piagetian concept of "groups" requires the formulation of processes that Piaget refers to as *operations* once they have been crystallized into perceivable activities. Few children, however, understand how such groups of activities form relationships of affinity and of differences, grouping and classifying, encoding and creating substitutes of reality, with the operational formal thinking necessary to approach the world at increasing distances. This awareness cannot be instilled without using process as the content of the instructional mediation interaction.

Attempts to Introduce Process

The need to introduce process into educational activities has certainly given rise to many attempts, both theoretical and practical. Unfortunately, the practical, technical approaches have had by far the upper hand so that many programs have been generated without guidance from a sound theory.

The behavioral schools have adopted an "atheoretical" approach that denies the need or possibility of manipulating anything but individuals' overt behavior. The "engineering" nature of behavioral intervention has little to do with processes that may affect the very structures that determine overt and mental behavior.

On the other hand, the cognitivistic genetic Piagetian school considered process as the major determinant of development and looked for the predecessors of formal operational thinking in the early processes of interaction between child and object world, interaction regulated by assimilation-accommodation processes. Yet these processes, according to the Genevan school, still could not be affected by a specific or even general intervention of a human mediator who tried to accelerate the processes ahead of the time they were seen to be scheduled by the maturational process, which was said to follow a universally fixed sequence of developmental stages.

These processes, according to Piaget, were the combined product of their central nervous system maturation and the organisms' activity during direct exposure and interaction with the world of stimuli. Piaget did not see development as the product of an interaction with an initiated, intentioned adult who acts as mediator between the learner and the world. Piaget (1966) questioned the need to attribute to the human partner of an interaction a specific role in the evolvement of intelligence or the processes of thinking. He proposed that to the extent to which the interaction with an adult affects the individual, it does not differ from the effects produced by the individual's encounter with an object whose new characteristic will create accommodation by the very process of assimilation that it has generated. The organism exposed to new dimensions will be affected by them only to the extent that these stimuli respond to the phase-specific needs of the organism. Only the relevant stimuli will be selected for this process. (In this way, Piaget paradoxically comes close to the concept of "realm" discussed earlier.)

Aebli (1950), one of Piaget's first students who attempted to turn the Piagetian developmental theory into the point of departure for a didactic, ended up by proposing that if Piaget's theory is taken seriously, then either (a) the individuals have reached the stage that makes an operation accessible and understood, in which case it does not have to be taught or mediated to them, or (b) the individuals have not yet reached this stage, in which case teaching or mediating will not help. Nonetheless, the Piagetian epistemological school has provided the great benefit of a deep analysis and understanding of the cognitive processes that underlie the development of higher mental functions. Vygotsky's (1934/1986) theory described the development of cognitive functions by pointing to sociocultural origins, including the role of the mediator as representative of the sociocultural environment that enhances and accelerates their development.

Mediated Learning Experience

Mediated Learning Experience (MLE), plays a pivotal role in Feuerstein's theory of Structural Cognitive Modifiability (SCM) because it explains the universal phenomenon of SCM and offers guidelines for a systematic intervention, serves as the basis for turning content into process. In this theory, MLE, as the modality of interaction unique to human existence, is considered as the proximal factor that determines the flexibility and plasticity of the human mind that then leads to SCM.

MLE is a quality of interaction that is marked by three universal parameters, notably,

1. *intentionality* and *reciprocity*, which animate mediators who interpose themselves between the organisms and the impinging world of stimuli;
2. *transcendence*, having the major characteristic of increasing the "distance" at which human beings can interact with their "world"; and
3. *meaning*, which provides the *why* and *what for*, that is, the emotional, motivational energetic factor that makes the mediatee accept the mediational process and the content at hand (see Figure 1.2).

The role of MLE is not limited to the transmission of knowledge and the presentation of facts. Rather, it is the source of transformations and the orientation of the learner to formulate relationships between the perceived facts. MLE generates the processes that underlie elaboration of the perceived data. (See Feuerstein, Klein, & Tannenbaum, 1991, for further details.)

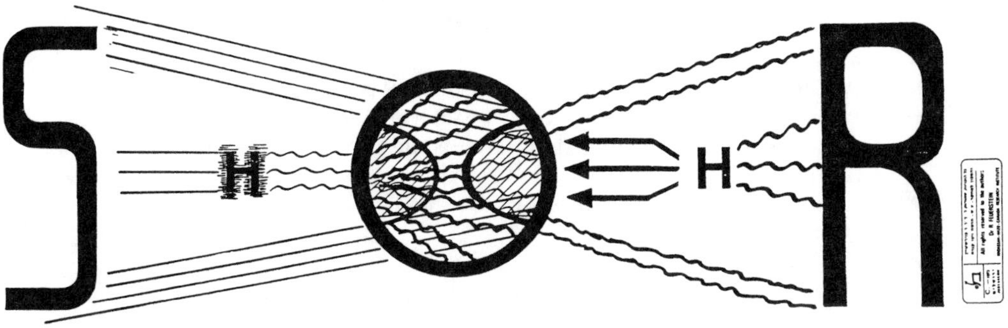

Figure 1.2. Mediated Learning Experience Model

NOTE: S = stimulus, H = human mediator, O = organism, and R = response.

SOURCE: Didactic materials of the International Center for the Enhancement of Learning Potential and the Hadassah-WIZO-Canada Research Institute. Copyright © by Reuven Feuerstein and the Hadassah-WIZO-Canada Research Institute, Jerusalem, Israel. All rights reserved. Reproduced by permission.

The Mental Act and Its Phases

The three phases of the mental act—input, elaboration, and output—are closely interrelated. Elaboration is the central processing site, where relationships are produced via comparative behavior, problems are defined, and solutions are generated from the data gathered on the input level. This is done through systematic search and volitional, intentioned choice of multiple sources of information. The input processes are guided by the tasks that are set forth during elaboration and the need for logical evidence that monitors it. The products of the elaboration process are shaped in the output phase of the mental act using language that is both at the disposal of the thinker and accessible to the receiver of the product (Table 1.1).

The three phases of the mental act must be conceived of as the components of processes that are involved, to a greater or lesser degree, in perception, registration, elaboration (storage and retrieval), and formulation and shaping of the thinking product. Data storage and retrieval can find their corollary processes in the three phases of the mental act. Stored data are the source input. The mnema (memory), comparative behavior, logical evidence, and inferential thinking are elaborated and follow the rules of the elaborative process (except for dreams). The output that represents an encoded form of the stored information becomes the source of further mental activities. (See Table 1.2.)

Any acquisition of content is strongly affected by processes, of which the complexity or level of abstraction of operations will strongly depend on the distance at which the organism-environment interaction takes place. Therefore, can or should teachers teach and transmit content, offering learners stimulus events that they will experience directly, without first or at the same time making available the processes that are necessary for the significant acquisition, elaboration, and integration of this content?

Table 1.1 The Cognitive Map: Components of the Mental Act

- The universe of content around which the mental act is centered
- The modality or language in which the mental act is expressed
- The phase of the cognitive functions required by the mental act (input, elaboration, and output)
- The cognitive operations required by the mental act
- The level of complexity
- The level of abstraction
- The level of efficiency with which the mental act is performed

SOURCE: Didactic materials of the International Center for the Enhancement of Learning Potential and the Hadassah-WIZO-Canada Research Institute.

Individual Learning Differences as Related to Extent of Mediation Interaction

Unfortunately, current instruction usually does precisely this, as is well documented. Students who are overwhelmed by data gain little insight into the processes that generated the data. Yet this type of content-oriented learning does not cause in all learners the same degree of harm. Some achieve an adequate way of functioning despite the sterile way in which they were taught. Some shake off all the learned "facts" as soon as they are no longer valuable—after grades, for example. Some never register the taught facts, failing to grasp their essence. Finally, large masses of children and adults are literally completely deprived of the contents and facts because they are considered unable to grasp them because they have been labeled retarded, mentally handicapped, or learning disabled. In these cases, absent was not only the process but also the contents, and in particular the skills to gather them, the orientation to look out for them, and all the mental processes related to these activities.

We contend that differences between individuals in their readiness and their propensity to benefit from direct exposure to stimuli and from formal and informal opportunities to learn are strongly contingent on the amount, nature, and duration of mediational interaction that they were given during the formative periods of their life. The MLE endows learners with the psychological tools on the input, elaboration, and output levels that turn direct exposure to stimuli into a source of new and powerful processes. Classroom content-learning that is devoid of process orientation is less harmful to students who come to school already armed with the processes required to make from the facts, events, skills, and formulas offered the tools for further learning and for adaptation to new areas of functioning. MLE creates the mental plasticity that turns human beings into an open system. Referring to the Piagetian genetic conception of the assimilation and accommodation process that affect the schema, we contend that the process that is generated by MLE renders the schema flexible enough to accommodate itself following its assimilation of new stimuli.

Table 1.2 Deficient Cognitive Functions

The locus of the deficiencies resulting from the lack of mediated learning experience is peripheral rather than central. It reflects attitudinal and motivational deficiencies and lack of working habits and learning sets *rather than* structural and elaborational incapacities. Evidence of the reversibility of the phenomenon has been provided by clinical and experimental work—especially through dynamic assessment (Learning Potential Assessment Device). The LPAD has also enabled the establishment of an *inventory of cognitive functions* that are undeveloped, poorly developed, arrested, and/or impaired. These cognitive functions are categorized into the input, elaborational, and output levels.

Impaired cognitive functions affecting the *input level* include those impairments concerning the quantity and quality of data gathered by the individual when confronted by a given problem, object, or experience. They include

1. Blurred and sweeping perception
2. Unplanned, impulsive, and unsystematic exploratory behavior
3. Lack of, or impaired, *receptive verbal tools* that affect discrimination (e.g., objects, events, relations, etc., do not have appropriate labels)
4. Lack of, or impaired, spatial orientation; the lack of stable systems of reference impairs the establishment of topological and Euclidian organization of space
5. Lack of, or impaired, temporal concepts
6. Lack of, or impaired, conservation of constancies (size, shape, quantity, and orientation) across variation in these factors
7. Lack of, or deficient, need for precision and accuracy in data gathering
8. Lack of capacity for considering two or more sources of information at once. This is reflected in dealing with data in a piecemeal fashion, rather than as a unit of organized facts.

The severity of impairment at the input level may also affect ability to function at levels of elaboration and output, but not necessarily so.

Impaired cognitive functions affecting the *elaborational level* include those factors that impede the efficient use of available data and existing cues:

1. Inadequacy in the perception of the existence and definition of an actual problem
2. Inability to select relevant versus nonrelevant cues in defining a problem
3. Lack of spontaneous comparative behavior or limitation of its application by a restricted need system
4. Narrowness of the psychic field
5. Episodic grasp of reality
6. Lack of, or impaired, need for pursuing logical evidence
7. Lack of, or impaired, interiorization
8. Lack of, or impaired, inferential-hypothetical "iffy" thinking
9. Lack of, or impaired, strategies for hypothesis testing
10. Lack of, or impaired, ability to define the framework necessary for problem-solving behavior
11. Lack of, or impaired, planning behavior
12. Nonelaboration of certain cognitive categories because the verbal concepts are not a part of the individual's verbal inventory at a receptive level, or they are not mobilized at the expressive level

(continued)

Table 1.2 Continued

"Thinking" usually refers to the elaboration of cues. There may well be highly original, creative, and correct elaboration that yields wrong responses because it is based on inappropriate or inadequate data on the input level.

Impaired cognitive functions at the *output level* include those factors that lead to an inadequate communication of final solutions. Even adequately perceived data and appropriate elaboration can be expressed as an incorrect or haphazard solution if difficulties exist at this level.

1. Egocentric communicational modalities
2. Difficulties in projecting virtual relationships
3. Blocking
4. Trial and error responses
5. Lack of, or impaired, tools for communicating adequately elaborated responses
6. Lack of, or impaired, need for precision in communicating one's responses
7. Deficiency of visual transport
8. Impulsive, acting-out behavior

The three disparate levels were conceived to bring some order into the array of impaired cognitive functions seen in individuals who are culturally deprived. Yet interaction is occurring between and among the levels that is of vital significance in understanding the extent and pervasiveness of cognitive impairment.

SOURCE: Didactic materials of the International Center for the Enhancement of Learning Potential and the Hadassah-WIZO-Canada Research Institute.

Increased Need for Process Learning

In summary, process learning as the content of choice is today more than ever necessary in the instruction of activities in all educational sectors: regular functioning students, including those who are gifted, whose confrontation with the increasing interactional distance also increases considerably the adaptational requirements; students who are "culturally deprived," who have not been given, and therefore a priori not received, the mediational experience necessary for generating the cognitive processes; and those exceptional individuals whose development requires a specialized form of mediation to become modifiable, irrespective of the distal etiology of their conditions such as organicity, chromosomal disorder, emotional deprivation, or environmental determinants of mental behavior such as MLE and process learning (see Figure 1.3). Increasing sectors of the greater population will depend on the process—because of the simultaneous diminishment of MLE offered and the increased need for it.

Once the need for process learning has been established, we are confronted with the question whether it is possible. Are people, in particular, exceptional learners, accessible to process learning? It is obvious that the lecturer who took his trainees to the seven styles of doors to teach how each should be opened did not believe that the concept of "opening" can be taught at a "distance" from the

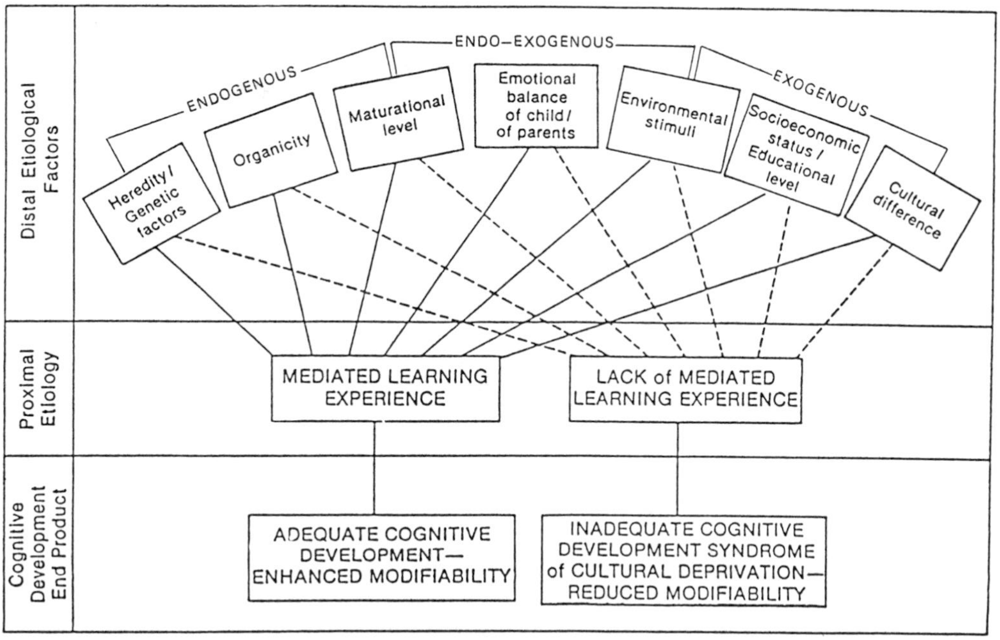

Figure 1.3. Distal and Proximal Etiology of Differential Cognitive Development
SOURCE: Adapted from "Mediated Learning Experiences: An Outline of the Proximal Etiology for Differential Development of Cognitive Functions," by R. Feuerstein and Y. Rand, 1994, *Journal of International Council of Psychology, 9/10*, p. 14. Copyright © by Reuven Feuerstein and Hadassah-WIZO-Canada Research Institute, Jerusalem, Israel. All rights reserved. Used by permission.

opening object. All too often, the superordinate concepts necessary to adapt the operation to a variety of conditions are thought to be inaccessible to individuals with mental retardation. In this chapter, we will not be able to discuss at length the propensity of individuals with mental retardation to benefit from process learning that is based on the mediation of higher mental processes, abstract representational thinking, and inferential operational activities.

Ample experimental and empirical data, however, support our belief in the accessibility of individuals with mental retardation to higher mental processes. Our data have proved that the deficiencies in the elaborational phase, the central and operational site of the mental act, are much more readily and easily modified in these individuals than the input and output phases that are peripheral. These peripheral phases are resistant to modification because they are more crystallized and mechanically elicited. Representational abstract thinking is often more efficiently elicited when teaching exceptional individuals with the help of the concrete sensorimotor modality, as is usually done in special schools and sometimes also in regular education.

Process Learning in Dynamic Assessment

We have chosen Grace Arthur's Stencil Design test as one of our dynamic tests for evaluating the learning potential of individuals who are low functioning. (See Feuerstein, Rand, & Hoffman, 1979, for more details on the Learning Potential Assessment Device [LPAD]). This test consists of a series of colored and perforated stencils that when superimposed on each other, produce a given design. Children were given 4 minutes for trial-and-error behavior to successfully construct the respective design. A thorough analysis of the reasons that these children did not construct the design pointed to the impulsivity that was encouraged by the nature of the task, which allowed them to freely manipulate the stencils (at zero distance). This obstructed the way to internalized mental processes. The children manipulated the stencils in a random way, disregarding the color and shape of the design, superimposing different colors on solid designs with the belief that the color from beneath would become visible. Even if the children constructed the right design, they often did not see that it was the right one because they did not compare their production and the required design. Zero distance of the sensorially concrete modality turned out to be a source of impulsivity and of many other cognitive deficiencies at the input, the elaboration, and particularly the output level.

On the basis of these findings, we decided to present the task in a representational modality. For this end, we printed the stencils with the perforated parts in gray color. The children could not manipulate the stencils but instead had to represent for themselves the outcome of their decisions to choose a particular stencil and place it in a given order in the production of the design. The "distance" was increased, and the total reliance on the sensorimotor modality was replaced by representational, anticipatory planning and inferentially derived information.

This resulted in a significant decrease in the deficient function that had led to inappropriate, inadequate behaviors. The number of successful tasks increased substantially. Many of the children were even able to verbally formulate rules and strategies that they discovered once it became impossible to act in an immediate, manipulatory way. The change in the nature of the task imposed an interactional distance that could be transversed only by internal mental representational abstract means. The activities, initially sensorimotor and concrete, were turned into a process-based activity, accompanied by awareness and insight that led, in many cases, to the discovery and even formulation of strategies, rules, and generalizable modes of functioning.

Modifiability of Exceptional Children

We refer to this process as Structural Cognitive Modifiability because the change that is produced within the individual goes far beyond a change in the specific unit of content information. This double orientation—the interaction at distance in space and time (operating on historical events) and the activation of internalized, perceptive processes—is what best defines human beings and their double-routed "traveling," conquering increasingly distant outer and inner spaces.

Exceptional children in special education are often denied this double route. The "royal way" to their education is considered to be the sensorimotor and concrete path at a zero distance. Other ways are—if not totally obstructed—at least not encouraged and not mediated. Often, it is thought that multiplying the channels of sensorial input—visual, haptic, and aural—will ultimately bring about the desired generation of new information through their integration and coordination. The empirical and experimental data do not confirm this outcome.

On the contrary, hypotrophy is often observed through time in certain propensities of developmental children to become more able to act operationally. This can be explained only by the "addiction" that is often produced by the educational process to the "facts" that have to be acquired through rote learning, by the strong emphasis on the knowledge base, irrespective of its limited relevance, and by the little demand that is laid on operational activity of the individuals to produce their responses. For example, observe a trivia quiz in which rapidity is the decisive factor in the acceptability of the response. This process develops not reconstruction—much less construction—of information but rather only direct, immediate retrieval of stored data, preferably in an automatic manner.

We do not want to mislead readers; we are not against overlearning through repetition and crystallization of certain activities when it is necessary to make cognitive functions more easily accessible and therefore more efficient. For these purposes, learning content is necessary. We consider the lack of three dimensions inadequate, however. The first is that even acquisition and crystallization of knowledge strongly depend on the cognitive mental process that underlies and accompanies learning activity (for example, the role of cognition in the acquisition of reading and the role of organizational processes in the construction of memory). The second is that once acquired, through learning and overlearning, the content should not become an inanimate body of knowledge, wherein little or no changes are possible or required. Finally, the underlying process, as a sequence of operations, should also become the target of crystallization to be efficiently used and applied.

Educators are often confronted with the tendency to transmit, teach, and mediate a rule, a principle, or an operation but with a hit-and-run strategy that leaves little space for crystallization and automatization of the acquired operation, which would render it more retrievable and applicable to other situations. Indeed, many programs that are designed to produce critical thinking and other process-oriented techniques do not do enough to turn the acquired principles, rules, and strategies into habits that will ensure their use whenever necessary.

One of the subgoals of the intervention system developed from MLE, notably Feuerstein Instrumental Enrichment (FIE), is precisely habit formation through repetition—but process oriented rather than mechanical. Here we have used the principles described by Piaget as the circulatory reactions—primary, secondary, and tertiary—that are various types of repetitions from simple to highly valued reproductions. The principle that rules the repeated *activity,* rather than the task, is emphasized. Instrumental Enrichment, which consists of various cognitive tasks, directs the learners to diverse cognitive functions. It presents the learners with numerous repetitions of the task to be learned, but the task is never the same. The variations in the task first require rediscovery of the situation and adaptation of the strategies to the changed condition of the task that the repetitions create. Although the habit of formation is addressed to the process, the variation of the tasks requires the constant adaptation of the process.

Process-Oriented Enrichment Programs

In consideration of the increased adaptational requirements that face individuals in this era, the greatly reduced mediational interaction offered nowadays, and the evidence that MLE may modify significantly the learning propensity of exceptional children and adults, regardless of the etiology, age, or severity of their condition, the need to offer systematic intervention programs is becoming evident. This trilogy itself is, indeed, a testimony to the search for ways to increase the cognitive processes underlying instructional activities. People differ, however, as to how to reach this goal. Under certain circumstances, these variations may correspond to differences between individuals to whom the program is applied.

A number of broad categories are apparent. The first is to enrich directly the repertoires of individuals with strategies that may become helpful in specific situations. Such programs are known as problem solving, lateral thinking, creative thinking, and so on. These will come close to relating process as content. This type of intervention may have its limits with people who have deficient cognitive functions that have to be corrected for them to become able to benefit from this approach.

Another category includes programs of *infused intervention* that consist of content-centered curricula. These programs use knowledge and specific skills such as languages, math, history, chemistry, and physics as opportunities to enrich the process repertoire of learners by infusing operational thinking into the content. This thinking is accompanied by reflective awareness-generating activities. This approach has the advantage that it responds in an immediate way to the difficulties experienced by learners, which are the concern of the teacher.

Children who have difficulties in reading, math, or other school skills may be given reinforced regimens in the area of their weaknesses, to which is added the process-infused operational thinking. The results obtained from this approach vary in their significance. Later in this chapter, we will discuss some of the problems related to the infused modality. But at this point, we want to point out that there are large masses of students whose cognitive functions do not allow them to benefit from content teaching and who first need to acquire the prerequisites of thinking that are necessary for learning to take place.

Here we present a third category: a dual modality of content instruction and process enrichment. The two-course approach is like parallel roads on the opposite shores of a river that are connected by many bridges. Ideas and principles cross from one side, and content crosses from the other. The exercises are structured to act as a means to construct representation, imaged abstract, and constructive, creative modes of interaction with stimuli, events, and processes (Figures 1.4 and 1.5; see Feuerstein, Rand, Hoffman, & Miller, 1980, for more details).

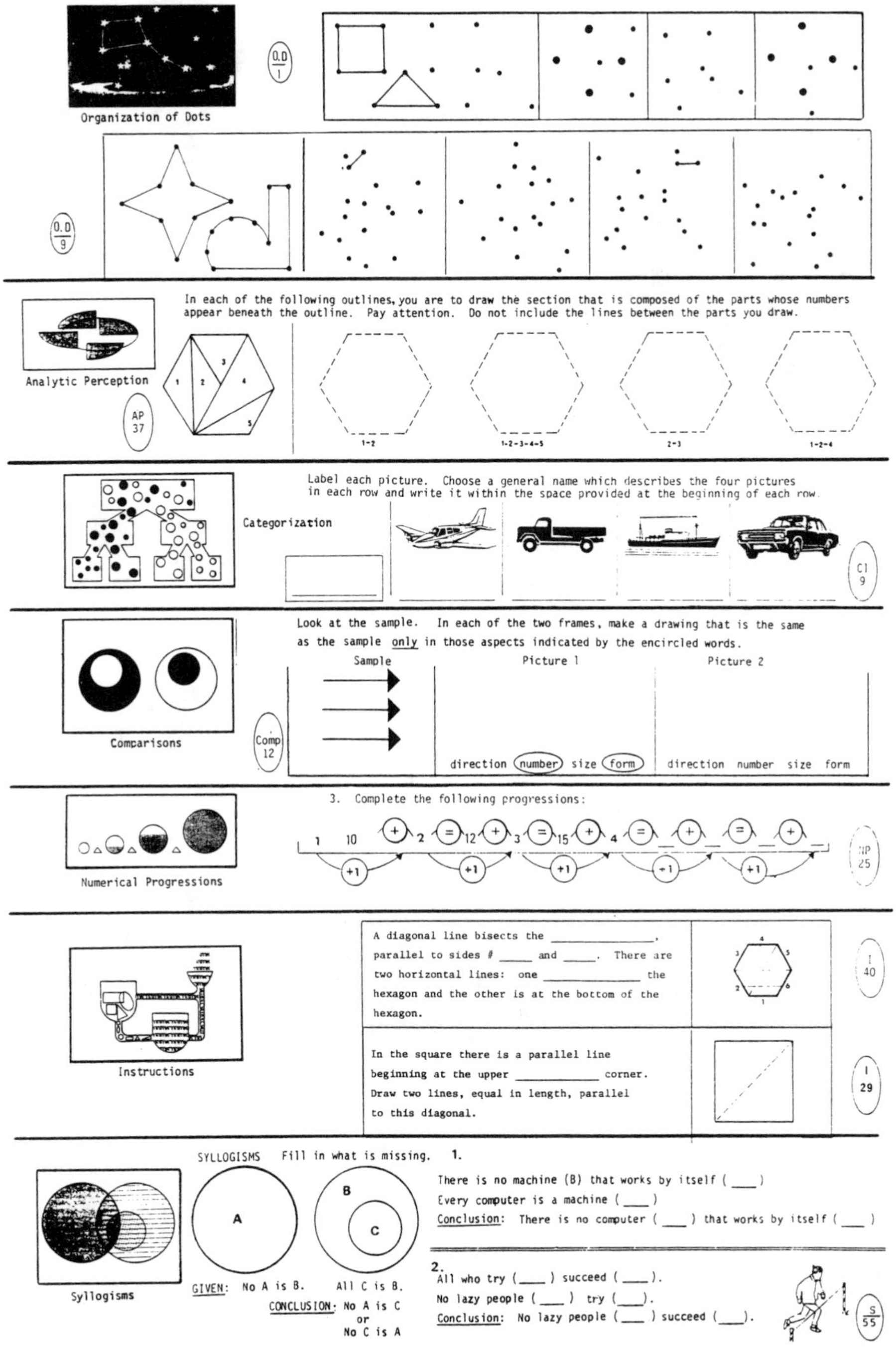

Figure 1.4. Examples of Sample Tasks From Feuerstein Instrumental Enrichment

SOURCE: Compiled from Instrument Enrichment instruments.

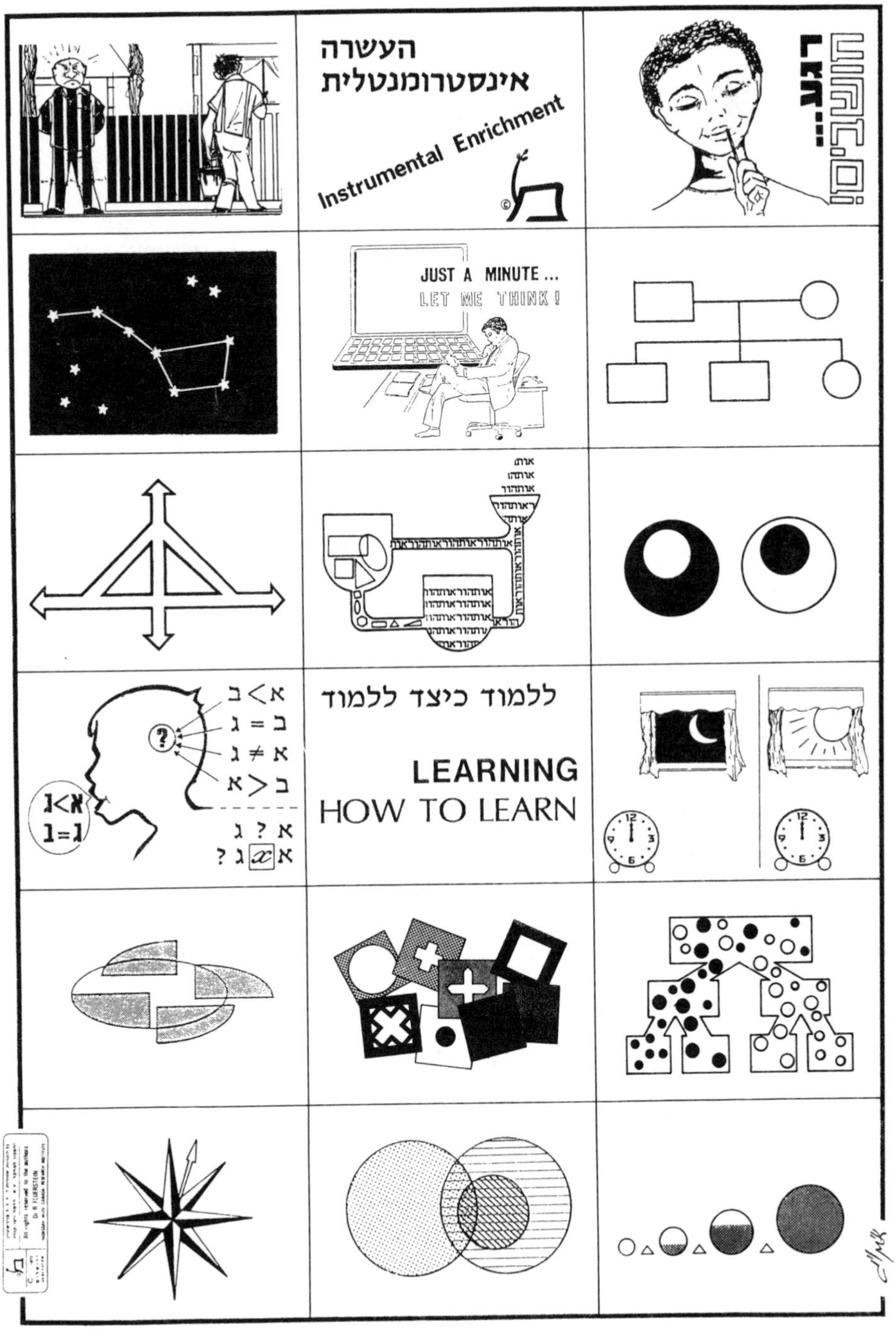

Figure 1.5. Compilation of the 14 Symbols of Each Instrument of Feuerstein Instrumental Enrichment

The process activities, by virtue of their being "content free," represent "distance" with which individuals interact for the sake of the processes they engender. The individuals are enticed to engage in their mastery, not from immediate need—as is all too often stressed by education—but in an autotelic way. To reach the goal, we have even avoided the incentive of grades for the learners' achievements and discouraged individual competition. Individuals compete only with themselves. They are encouraged to learn about the changes that are produced within themselves following their interaction with distance.

This choice of a content-free modality for mediating the process of learning has triple rationales: to overcome resistance by the students, the learning materials, and the teacher. Students are all too often material oriented, interested only in mastering the knowledge. Students often consider learning the process an imposition if it is done in competition with the content to be mastered and may then act impatiently. The constant mediational intervention of the teacher serves as the bridge that makes the FIE program relevant to the subject matter. The resistance of the knowledge-based curriculum is another reason that restrains the use of the infused model. Despite its frequent obsolescence, content is still necessary and cannot and should not be abandoned. Process learning cannot be done in a vacuum. Subject matter to be animated by process has a structure, a rhythm, a succession, and an order that has to be respected by the teaching act. Infusion may disturb the structure of the specific subject matter. Finally, the process-oriented program too has its own rhythm to be respected. Subordinating it to rules of content learning renders it inefficient. That is why FIE is presented as a separate course of study with bridging to the subject content.

The major goal of FIE is to increase the learning propensity of learners by equipping them with the prerequisites and processes of learning. It uses a "noninfused" modality. The prerequisites of learning are instilled through tasks in which the content is irrelevant to the curricular program. Rather than directly teaching reading or reading components, FIE produces the focusing, scanning, segregating, and cognitive elaboration of activities that will prove vital for reading processes on different levels.

We create the prerequisite activities underlying mathematical operations, such as comparative, summative, and logical manipulational behaviors, rather than math itself. We produce representational processes and enhance conceptualization of space and how to mark various orientations in space rather than teach geography. We teach concepts of time, sequences, and relationships—such as causal or teleological—that will help organize historical events through processes rather than teach chronological lists of names, dates, and events to be memorized. We teach family relationships, not to teach who an uncle or an aunt is but rather to make familiar terms known as the point of departure for relational thinking.

The FIE program is applied by teachers who are specially trained to act as mediators. FIE is best performed in the classroom with a strong cooperative component that makes the mediational interaction more efficient through its amplification by group processes. Bridging organizational, analytic, comparative, and other process-oriented behaviors to the subject-content is best done by the learners themselves first proposing possible applications from their own ideas and experiences. Teacher-mediators then offer the overall orientation for the processes of generalization and transfer. They create relationships of affinity between the mental function that underlies the problem-solving behavior in the FIE exercises and the characteristics of the curriculum content. Understanding mental processes and their role in adaptive behavior becomes the center of an activity that leads to the generation of cognitive, motivational structures. Awareness and consciousness generated by the conflicts and the cognitive dissonance inherent in many tasks become the source of perceptive learning.

In the last decade, FIE has undergone a number of developments based on experience gained with its application in tens of thousands of classes in 35 countries, in 17 languages, with diverse populations. FIE has been extended from child/teacher-centered goals in the classroom to the implementation of a system-oriented approach in entire schools. Psychologists, administrators, and community workers, as well as teachers, are now becoming exposed to the theory of SCM and the process-generating qualities of MLE. The approach to the students and to the learning of content is reflected in the shift in emphasis from content-product to process-thinking.

The work with the entire school system is meant to enable the teachers to use MLE and process-oriented interaction in the classroom without being compelled to fight for each change in the approach to the curriculum, which, otherwise, is often the case. From this point of view, the system-oriented approach creates a generalized atmosphere of a modifying environment. It is still up to the teachers, however, to apply the program in the process-oriented way.

Teachers, in their role as transmitters of information, producing a knowledge base, deal with two types of information. One is at a zero distance from the students, inasmuch as the content to be transmitted is familiar and the related events are mere elaboration of the known facts. The students have every right to believe that because they already know the facts to which they are now being exposed, there is no need for elaboration—similar to the example of the doors given earlier. Another example occurs when the notion of the earth as a planet is taught. The earth seems to be so familiar and trivial that attempts to make the students ponder it and see the problems that are related to understanding the earth as a celestial body are often encountered with resistance.

The prerequisites of thinking with which students need to be equipped are meant to make them question, wonder, and be curious not only about the facts but also about how the facts happen and their origin. These prerequisites create a specific need. Many children do not see the problem, because they do not create relationships between two types of data—the perceived flatness of the earth in daily life and the idea that the earth is a sphere. Perceiving this problem, "How can it be a sphere when it appears to be flat?" becomes possible only following the exposure of the individuals to data that create the contradiction and produce a state of disequilibrium that then becomes the source of questioning and a readiness to go out and look for ways to reestablish the lost equilibrium.

The cognitive processes that must be produced to turn the obvious familiar into a source of questioning, creating disequilibrium that becomes the starting point of further activities by the learners, are dependent on a set of mediational activities of teachers. Indeed, many children who receive mediational interaction start to question and see contrasting relationships between events. Therefore, they look for modalities with which to solve the problems. Even when the problems are not immediately solvable, at least the awareness of the problems and need for search are significantly installed.

The second type of content that must be given over to the students is at a considerable distance from them. Information about the Gallipolic battle in the First World War has no meaning whatsoever when the students do not have the orientation to the time and to the space in the Ottoman Empire, which is the Turkey of today. Students of history have to detach themselves from the current era and try to understand the circumstances of a different, remote, unknown place and time. They have to create the coordinates of time and space that are related to their own present, their here and now, after which they will be able to learn facts that have at first no meaning for them. They will become able to interpret the events and relate them to the conditions that existed in the particular era. Here, again, the special cognitive processes that must be produced to equip the learners with the coordinates, operational and content, are of greatest importance.

The teacher-mediators and the student-learners of FIE need to bridge the formal relational, process-oriented activities that are engendered by FIE and cross over the bridge to the content. They must bring with them the elements that have been learned and not merely stored by the student-learners. They also are accompanied by the awareness that they have acquired instruments of learning that must be applied in a way that structures the content. The content will become significant—not only "visible" but also "seeable." They will see the meaning, the relationship, and the conditions in which the content becomes understandable, important, and related to those elements that gave them meaning. This journey that is made together by the teachers and the students with the equipment that they both have—content and knowledge—turns the elements that are learned into new processes of learning. This is referred to as *modifiability.*

This modality of application of FIE has been elaborated for many years. FIE has been applied in a variety of conditions and with a variety of contents. For example, it has been used with engineers and other workers at the Motorola University in Chicago as well as in many European industries, such as SNECMA, Peugeot, and Pirelli. It has become considered as the necessary way to create in individuals who must adapt to innovative, more complex components of their work or studies the modalities of interaction that will respond to the increased distance at which these interactions take place.

Summary

We began by looking for the characteristics of the changes with which human beings have to cope and to which they must adapt. We presented the concept of increase in the distance in the organism-world interaction as characterizing the greater part of changes, irrespective of the area in which they appear. We consider this concept of distance useful because it provides hints as to what should be the nature of the adaptation that the individuals will have to make and the type of intervention required for them to become able to adapt.

In the case of special education, the situation is much more complex because exceptional individuals are considered not only to be unable to adapt themselves to the new conditions of life but also to be totally unengaged in such changes. Therefore, often they are left to interact with the world surrounding them at a zero distance. We have shown that this is absolutely illegitimate and that we must offer special, exceptional individuals a process orientation in their learning to enable them to confront the complexities of life.

References

Aebli, H. (1950). *La didactique psycholoqique* [The psychological didactic]. Neuchâtel and Paris: Delachaux and Niestle.

Buber, M. (1960). *Urdistanz und beziehung* [Primary distance and relationship]. Heidelberg, Germany: Verlag Lambert Schneider.

Feuerstein, R., Klein, P. S., & Tannenbaum, A. J. (Eds.). (1991). *Mediated learning experiences: Theoretical, psychosocial and learning implications.* London: Freund.

Feuerstein, R., & Rand, Y. (1974). Medicated learning experiences: An outline of the proximal etiology for differential development of cognitive functions. *Journal of International Council of Psychology, 9/10,* 7-37.

Feuerstein, R., Rand, Y., & Hoffman, M. B. (1979). *The dynamic assessment of retarded performers: The Learning Potential Assessment Device, theory, instruments and techniques.* Baltimore: University Park Press.

Feuerstein, R., Rand, Y., Hoffman, M. B., & Miller, R. (1980). *Instrumental enrichment: An intervention program for cognitive modifiability.* Baltimore: University Park Press.

Kant, E. (1958). *Critique of pure reason.* New York: Modern Library.

Piaget, J. (1966). Nécessité et signification des recherches comparatives en psychologie génétique [Necessity and meaning of comparative research in genetic psychology]. *International Journal of Psychology, 1,* 3-13.

Vygotsky, L. S. (1986). *Thought and language.* Cambridge: MIT Press. (Original work published 1934)

2

Generative Topics for Process Curriculum

Vito Perrone
Bena Kallick

The educational discourse has shifted in recent years from "What do we want students to know about?" to "What can students do, and what do they understand?" We begin from the premise that successful performance, which is based on understanding, is a desired end for the work that teachers and students do together in the schools. It is important, however, to bring about a rich understanding of *understanding* as a formulation. The place to begin is with teachers themselves.

When teachers are trying to formulate their own definitions of what *understanding* means, it is usually helpful for them to think about their deepest interests or intellectual passions—things they feel particularly articulate about, are in control of, and are good at. Most teachers are able to define a set of ideas, a theme, an activity, or a particular event they say they genuinely understand, not just know about. It is toward such understanding that all teaching across all subject matters should be aimed—toward something students can hold on to beyond the Friday test, the final exam, and school itself.

When students of all ages and levels of academic success describe those occasions in educational settings when they were most engaged intellectually, when their understandings were larger than usual, and when learning had a special quality, some of the following elements are common (Perrone, Gardner, & Perkins, 1996):

- Students helped define the content—selecting the *particular* subject to research, the *particular* biography to read, or the *particular* play to present.
- Students had time to wonder, to work around the edges of the subject matter, and to find a particular direction that interested them.
- Students sensed that the results of their work were not predetermined or fully predictable. Moreover, they believed teachers learned something from them.
- Topics had a "strange" quality—something common that was seen in a new way, evoking a "lingering question."
- Teachers permitted—even encouraged—different forms of expression and respected students' views.
- Students created original and public products; they gained in the process some form of "expertness."
- Students had an audience that paid attention to the details of and gave a thoughtful response to their work.
- Students *did* something—participated in a political action, wrote a letter to the editor, worked with the homeless, or developed an exhibition.
- Teachers were passionate about their work. The richest activities were those "invented" by the teachers.

So how can educators create a classroom in which these experiences are more commonplace?

Finding the Overarching Goals

Most teachers begin their planning by asking themselves questions such as these: What do I most want my students to take away? What do I want to be able to say about my students as they complete their work with me? What must I pay attention to all of the time—come back to again and again? What are some of the major stories, ideas, and formulations that need to be understood in this course of study? The answers to these types of questions help form what might be called *overarching* goals.

Some of these overarching goals may be oriented toward particular skills or habits of mind. For example, among the goals teachers might set for a secondary school history course are that students should be able to use primary sources, formulate hypotheses, and engage in systematic study; be able to handle multiple points of view; be close readers and active writers; and pose and solve problems. Teachers might want students to demonstrate their ability to listen to one another's opinions with understanding and empathy, to be flexible in their thinking, and to persist in seeking many different perspectives. At the end of the class, teachers might expect students to be able to develop a historical narrative and understand that history is created by the decisions people make and don't make.

Some goals might be related and recurrent. For example, teachers might also want students to understand the unfinished nature of American democracy; the continuing struggle for equity, liberty, and justice; the connections of past and present; and the idea that every person is a historian.

Teachers might even put all their overarching goals on the board to ensure that the students and the teachers can regularly assess what is being learned against the goals. One teacher does this by asking her students the question "What does this have to do with understanding more about . . . ?" In this way, she keeps the work of the class focused.

To help meet the larger, overarching goals, teachers need to make certain that a variety of primary and secondary sources are available for almost anything to be studied. In this regard, getting materials together would be one of the teachers' principal tasks. Teachers also should leave room for student choices, for inquiry, for interpretation, and for role playing.

Finding the Essentials

Having outlined overarching goals, teachers might then consider what content to address within the subject matter by asking, "What *one* topic would we *surely* pursue that would most likely ensure meeting the overarching goals?" and "What two additional topics or concepts would be critical in this subject area?" The teachers could continue this process until they had a fully developed set of ideas and topics for a course. In this way, they have begun to formulate *generative topics*—those ideas, themes, and issues that provide the depth and variety of perspectives that help students develop significant understandings.

Implicit in the formulation of generative topics is a belief that some ideas have more possibilities for engaging students than others. In general, such topics are central to the field of inquiry, are critical to understanding the field and its central questions, are accessible at many levels, are able to be entered from different experience levels, have a limitless quality, and are easily connected to other topics and to the world. Democracy and revolution in history, evolution in biology, patterns in math or music, and personal identity in literature are generative topics. Questions of fairness and topics that have recurring qualities (such as immigration) are also generative. Slavery has more potential as a generative topic than do the military events of the Civil War because the effects of slavery are still present. Topics related to technology are generative because they connect to so many aspects of a culture.

Given the goals in the history course discussed in the previous section, teachers would likely have units on the Constitution, the Bill of Rights, Reconstruction, Civil Rights, Women's Suffrage, and industrialization, as well as units that revolve around patterns of immigration, discrimination, violence, and peacemaking. In keeping with the interest in student understanding, teachers would also develop understanding goals for each topics—essentially considering two or three major outcomes that can be demonstrated through performances (Perkins & Blythe, 1994). The delineation of understanding goals ensures a focus on the topics under study.

Ernest Boyer (1993), in his keynote address to the Association for Supervision and Curriculum Development, suggested eight significant themes that might guide the development of overarching goals and essential topics. They are

- Respecting the miracle of life—understanding the cycles of life and knowing about birth and death as a part of the cycle
- Empowering the use of language—understanding the significance of communication through symbolic and visual language as well as print and oral forms
- Appreciating the aesthetic—understanding culture through its arts
- Understanding groups and institutions—understanding the web of social existence
- Revering the natural world—understanding the ecosystem of the universe
- Affirming the dignity of all work—understanding the significance of work of the hand as well as work of the mind and understanding producing and consuming
- Guiding values and beliefs—questions of purpose and understanding the purposefulness of others

These themes offer enormous potential for linking curriculum into meaningful overarching goals and generative topics.

Developing a Topic

As a way to think about a topic's generative potential, teachers might map the topics that emerge from their questions. We provide two maps developed by teachers. The first (Figure 2.1) relates to "respecting the miracle of life" from Boyer's list of curricular commonalities. It represents some of the possibilities developed by a group of middle school teachers. The second map (Figure 2.2) was developed by a group of secondary school teachers who were brainstorming immigration as a topic to be studied.

In general, the bigger the map, the richer the topic. After viewing their maps, teachers might choose to focus on some—but not all—of the ideas. In this regard, the old notion that it is better to pursue fewer topics more deeply has returned to education. For example, the message of the Coalition of Essential Schools that "less is more" is taking hold in more settings. Groups such as the National Research Council of the National Academy of Sciences also recommend that schools focus on fewer topics.

To choose which of the mapped topics to pursue, teachers might ask the following: Which of the topics is most likely to engage the students? Is the topic central to the field of inquiry under study? Is it accessible as well as complex? To the degree that a topic invites questions that students have about the world around them and taps the issues that students confront, it has a generative quality.

In regard to the overarching theme of empowering language, a group of teachers generated the following topics and issues:

- How can words be powerful in different contexts?

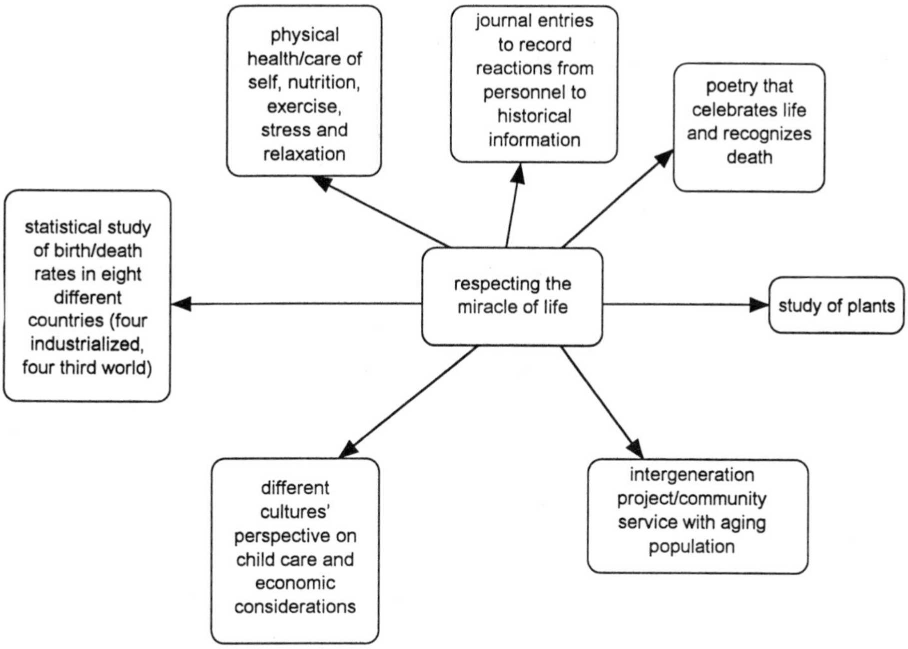

Figure 2.1. Example of Topic Map for Respecting the Miracle of Life (Middle School)

- In what ways are the power of words in music, advertising, cartoons, and literature alike? Different?
- How do words become powerful?

The teachers felt that studying the power of words in different contexts would help students understand (a) the power of their own language, (b) the use of language in different settings, and (c) imagery and metaphors as art and the craft of writing in different contexts.

Many generative topics naturally lead to inquiry, questions, anomalies, and diverse perspectives leading to research. A concern many teachers express is that when asked to do research, students often copy from reference books or other secondary sources in the library. We have found that students don't always know how to go about research. Moreover, on closer study, the following might also be the case:

- Students often cannot read or understand the various source materials.
- The questions that are being asked are easily answered by the reference material because they have not been sufficiently shaped into ways that will require the students to do original or productive thinking. Questions often are either easily answered (who, what, where, and why) or too global (e.g., how is the concept of conflict defined in world history?).

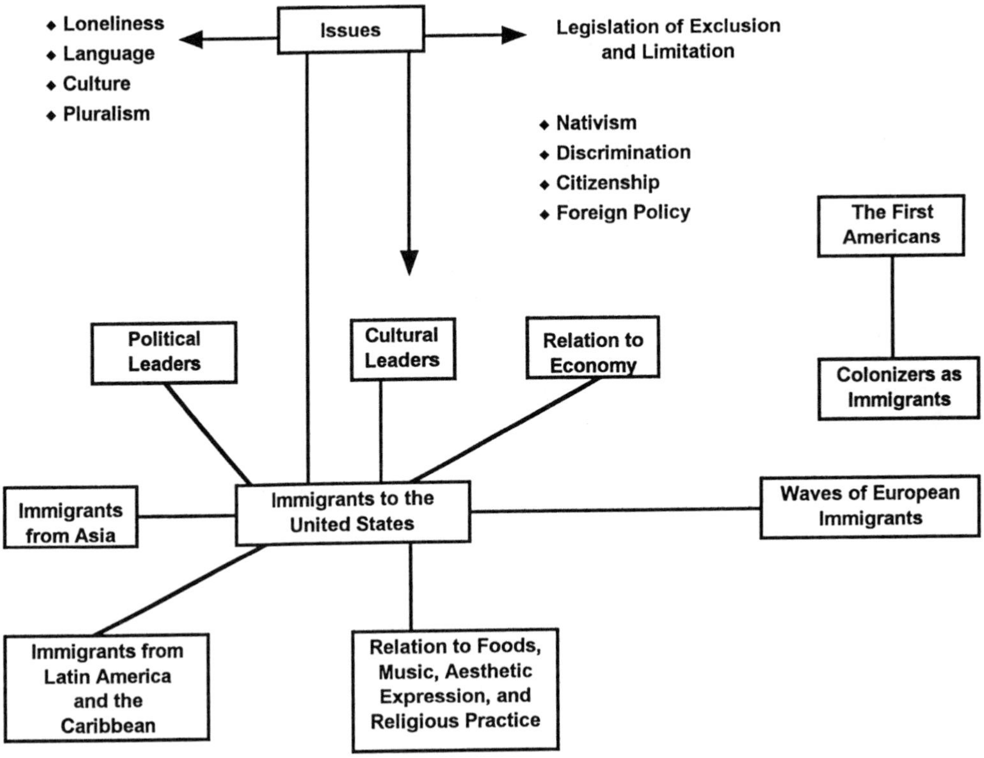

Figure 2.2. Example of Topic Map for Immigration (Secondary School)

Shaping good questions is a significant part of helping students engage in inquiry. Questions that require students to take a position around which they can offer a different interpretation or construct another path tend to be particularly productive.

In one elementary school in which we have worked, for example, students are asked in the fifth grade to study U.S. inventors as a part of their social studies unit. This study falls under the overarching theme related to the dignity of all work. Students choose inventors of particular interest. Students are then asked to learn as much as they can about their inventors. Ultimately, each student makes a presentation on behalf of his or her inventor—essentially an informed and persuasive argument to convince the class that the inventor is worthy of a statue on the town green.

For the students to present their arguments, they investigate (a) what criteria people use to decide who should have monuments representing them in a public place, and (b) who their inventors were and why they might deserve monuments. In preparation for the formal presentation of their inventors, students learn about the stories of various members of the town who are important contributors to the community—essentially learning about criteria for bestowing honor on others. They also learn to tell the stories of their inventors in ways that are engaging and that dignify the significance of the inventors' work. Finally, students answer the "So what?" question: If the inventors had not invented what they did, what difference would it have made?

For teachers, the task is to help students do the inventors unit, or other inquiry units, well. Teachers in this school have set forward in their discussions some of the following directions to guide them in helping their students with inquiry. Some of these patterns might be illuminating to those interested in inquiry teaching.

Linked Thinking

Teachers begin most inquiries with this question: What do we already know about the topic? After some general conversation, students are asked to break into small groups (even pairs is sufficient) and to think of all the possible things they know about the topic. The social skills to be focused on include these:

- Taking turns
- Relating only to the main idea
- Asking each other questions if they are not certain what someone means
- Making sure that everyone participates
- Helping the recorder get all the ideas down

Teachers then debrief the content and process with the students, giving them many examples of good responses that they heard as they walked among the students to see if they were on task and interacting in constructive ways, as well as answering and posing questions.

Categorizing

The next task is for students to categorize what they have listed so that they begin to make connections among the ideas. Once again, teachers encourage such social skills as the following:

- Being flexible in their thinking; allowing for ideas to be in more than one category if they agree that it fits
- Asking each other why the item is put in the category; what makes it fit?
- Taking turns
- Making certain that everyone is participating
- Piggybacking off one another's ideas

Teachers debrief again both content (categories) and social behaviors, making certain to have examples of both on the basis of their observations as they move around the room.

In another discussion with fifth-grade teachers in Somers, New York, we decided that the following steps would be useful for inquiry-based projects.

Step 1: Establish Important Themes and Concepts

We thought that the following themes and concepts would make a good focus, on the basis of one of Boyer's overarching themes, the web of social existence:

- When cultures meet, what is the nature of their interaction?
- What affects their relationships?
- What changes in the cultures?
- What changes in individuals?

This led in our thinking to an examination of prejudice, moving from one place to another, and why people leave to journey to other places.

Step 2: Find a Way for Students to Identify With Themes and Concepts From Their Own Life Experiences

The following are ideas that we considered to help students identify with our themes:

- What stories of immigration or migration are included in our family histories?
- How is the culture of the playground different from the culture of the classroom? What does that tell about culture?
- How are the city and the country different cultures?
- Who is in our community? How did they get here?

Step 3: Search for Meaningful National Perspectives on the Same Themes or Concepts

- What is in the news/media about this same topic?

Step 4: What Skills Do We Want to Focus on for This Unit?

In this unit, we decided that we wanted students to

- Develop an ability to analyze information
- Be able to recognize cause and effect and patterns and perspectives that would help interpret the relationships between cultures

Step 5: What Instructional Strategies Will We Use to Facilitate Inquiry-Based Learning?

Although there are many strategies, we examined the potential of the jigsaw strategy. Expert groups would be responsible for studying one of the exploring cultures: Spanish, French, English, Dutch, or other. They would be responsible for learning about

- Reasons for leaving
- What was found in the new country (America)
  All groups the explorers encountered
  Reactions and actions
- What the explorers brought back to their country

Project group options included

- Students can find a way to compare and contrast
- Students can report to the class
- Students can teach each other in their jigsaw groups

Step 6: How Does This Connect to Our Next Unit of Study?

We decided that this study would lead into the actions and reactions to the native American people when various explorers settled here. Because that seemed like a more significant study, we thought that there should be a limit to the amount of investigation and reporting that would be required from the explorers.

A recent issue of *Horace* (Cushman, 1995) outlined the following guide for what students should be able to do at the secondary level in inquiry and research. This guide represents another way to think about the scaffolds that move students along, ensuring that they will succeed with the task.

1. *Define the need for information.* For what are you going to use the information: work, play, or academics? Provide a frame of reference: Whom do you need information about, what, when, where, how, why? What do you already know? Frame and focus your question.
2. *Initiate the search strategy.* Determine for what information you will search, often by dividing your question into a number of subquestions. Brainstorm ideas and organize them visually using lists, outlines, webs, or concept maps. List key words or concepts. Identify potential sources and decide how to evaluate them.
3. *Locate the resources.* Using catalogs and other tools, search for print, audiovisual, and computerized resources in the school library. Using on-line databases, interlibrary loan, the phone, and the fax, look for information outside the school library, including community resources, government offices, and people who know the subject. Using key words, indexes, cross-references, and other search strategies, find specific information in the resources you have located.
4. *Assess and comprehend the information.* Skim and scan to identify relevant information. Differentiate between primary and secondary sources, identify what is fact and what is opinion, and determine the point of view of each source and how current and authoritative it is. Recognize logical errors and omissions, as well as interrelated concepts, cause and effect, and points of agreement and disagreement. Classify, group, or label the

information and obtain it in the formats that best suit your learning style. Revise and redefine your information problem if necessary.

5. *Interpret the information.* Summarize information in your own words, paraphrasing or quoting important facts and details. Synthesize new information with what you know already. Organize and analyze it in a new way. Does this information address your original problem? Get new information or adjust your search strategy if necessary. Then draw conclusions based on the information you located.
6. *Communicate the information.* What is your conclusion or the resolution to your problem? What audience are you trying to reach, and will your approach be informative, persuasive, or entertaining? What format (written, spoken, or visual) will work best in presenting the information? Create your presentation, providing appropriate attribution and documentation of your sources.
7. *Evaluate the product and process.* How well did you do? What could you or should you have done differently? How can you do better in the future? Ask yourself and others—classmates, teachers, library staff, and parents—how well your final product resolved your information problem and if the steps you took to do so were appropriate and efficient. (p. 3)

But many teachers ask how they can interest 28 different students and how to manage in the face of the unprecedented racial, linguistic, ethnic, and cultural diversity of students. As we noted earlier, mapping the topics provides a graphic representation of the many connecting points within a topic and reveals many different starting points for students. Having a variety of entry points is important for student choice and for engaging students at all levels in work they can honor. Including the librarian as a part of the development of a topic is especially helpful. In addition, if teams of teachers work together on topic development, the teachers can pool their resources, ensuring that the learning possibilities for students will enlarge. For example, in one school, teachers post their theme and topic maps on the wall in the teachers' lounge, leaving Post-Its by the maps so other teachers can add ideas and potential resources. The lounge has become a wall of maps, each inviting the resourcefulness of the entire school community.

Another concern teachers often raise is how to work within existing district curriculum guides, which tend to have broad scope-and-sequence directions, while still maintaining their commitment to pursuing topics in depth. Within a district's scope and sequence, it is possible to generate a topic that engages students' energies and can be pursued with reasonable depth. As an example, one district requires a 2-week unit on immigration. The implication might be to engage in a broad study of immigration, but we can imagine doing the unit using the stories of several individuals, by studying a single town or a single industry, or by learning family stories across several waves of immigration to see the contrasts and similarities. In this way, some important understandings are possible.

Further, we have found in most places that district guidelines have not really kept teachers from doing what they felt was most important. In an extreme case, several teachers in a southern state with heavy state mandates and tests did understanding-oriented teaching work Monday through Thursday and devoted Friday to what they called "Caesar's work." Such a path, although drastic, might be worth considering.

A Word on Assessment

For generative topics to help develop students' understanding, *continuing assessment* is critical. The 1990s language of assessment is familiar: *authentic assessment, performance assessment, documentation, exhibitions of learning, portfolios,* and *process folios.* All these practices grow from a belief that much that has stood for learning does not get close enough to students' growth, knowledge, and understandings. Assessment activities that do not inform teaching practice day in and day out are misdirected and wasteful—doubly so if they do not help students regularly make judgments about their own progress as learners.

Movement toward authentic assessment, performance assessment, and portfolios, however, must include serious reappraisal of the instructional program, the organizational structures, and the purposes that guide curriculum. If coverage remains the goal, performance tasks tend to be too limited. If snippets of knowledge, rather than longer-term projects that produce real works, dominate the day-to-day activities, portfolios become folders of unmanageable and uninteresting paper. If students are not regularly writing across a variety of topics and in a variety of styles for diverse purposes, then promoting self-evaluation has limited value. In addition, if students do not have opportunities to complete work they can honor, performance itself loses its importance. Powerful ideas, powerful curriculum, and different modes of assessment are linked ideas. Without growing discourse about curriculum purposes, student understandings, and ways teachers can foster student learning, assessment measures such as portfolios and exhibitions will not have a long or inspiring history.

In Summary

We, as educators, need to ensure an empowering education for everyone attending our schools. Students need to be able to use knowledge, not just know about things. Understanding is about making connections among and between things; about deep, not surface, knowledge; and about greater complexity, not simplicity. We cannot continue a process of providing a thoughtful, inquiry-oriented education for some and a narrow, skills-based, understanding-poor education for most. We obviously have more to do.

References

Boyer, E. (1993, March). *Keynote address.* Address presented at the national conference of the Association for Supervision and Curriculum Development, Washington, DC.

Cushman, K. (1995, September). Information, literacy, and the essential school library. *Horace, 12*(1), 1-8. (Student research guide portion adapted from "Information literacy: A position paper on information problem solving," available from the American Association of School Librarians, 50 East Huron St., Chicago, IL 60611; telephone 800-545-2433)

Perkins, D., & Blythe, T. (1994, February). Putting understanding up front. *Educational Leadership, 51*(5), 4-7.

Perrone, V., Gardner, H., & Perkins, D. (1996). *Toward a generative curriculum* [Spencer Research Project (Teaching for Understanding) rep.]. Cambridge, MA: Harvard Graduate School of Education.

3

Teaching as Process

Arthur L. Costa
Robert J. Garmston

Influenced by our obsolete industrial paradigm, educators have thought that there was a *content* to teaching that could be observed, counted, and installed. This chapter builds the case for considering the craft of teaching as *process*. We illuminate five fresh assumptions and present the research on teaching as a decision-making process, describing the internal drives that motivate human cognition and action. On the basis of these assumptions, research, and drives, implications for instructional leadership and staff development are drawn.

Toward a New Definition of Teaching: A Historical Perspective

Beginning in the 1960s, a great deal of research energy was devoted to dissecting the act of teaching and task-analyzing it into its component parts. During the 1970s and 1980s, a technological "age of accountability" swept education. During this period, the reductionist orientations driving most of the research attempted to describe excellence in teaching by correlating certain teacher behaviors with student performances.

AUTHORS' NOTE: The source for the concepts presented in this chapter are derived from our 1994 book, *Cognitive Coaching: A Foundation for the Renaissance School,* Norwood, Massachusetts: Christopher-Gordon Publishers. Permission by the publisher to draw on these materials is greatly appreciated.

The view of teaching as a set of mechanistic skills was highly compatible with the existing industrial-technological metaphor in vogue during the 1950s through the 1970s. Teaching was seen as labor in which "management personnel" set standards, directed how the work was to be done, and monitored for compliance. Workers were deemed efficient on the basis of the number of units that they produced in the most efficient and speedy manner. This was the era of the efficiency expert, who studied worker productivity, yield, quantitative measurement, cost cutting, automation, and how to reduce the human variable ("teacher-proof" was a popular term).

The prevailing research paradigm was to identify teachers who produced high achievement on standardized test scores, then observe, describe, and analyze the teachers' classroom behaviors. Exhaustive research was conducted to hold constant the variables while one behavior at a time was isolated and employed: use of silence, response behaviors such as praise and accepting, questioning, and so on (Rowe, 1974).

On the basis of this research, many policymakers believed that if all teachers performed these identified behaviors, then student achievement, as measured by standardized tests, would improve. Process-product correlational studies were amassed and meta-analyzed to prove that when teachers perform certain behaviors, there is, as a result, corresponding effects on student performance. This research has contributed to a massive increase in the fund of knowledge about the essentials of what constitutes the teaching act (Manatt, 1988).

Armed with this knowledge, staff developers, supervisors, and evaluators, believing they could identify, diagnose, and measure excellence in teaching through these behaviors, became proficient at training, counting the frequency of, reinforcing, extinguishing, certifying, and evaluating the performance of specific teaching behaviors that the research "proved" produced student learning. They observed, counted, and categorized the number of questions that the teacher asked at Bloom's (1956) taxonomical levels. They ticked off wait time (Rowe, 1974). They measured the teacher's proximity to certain students and determined the degree to which proximity was distributed to each student (Kerman & Martin, 1980). They counted and certified the presence of seven steps in each lesson design (Hunter, 1984).

With the best of intentions, believing that teachers should perform these research-based behaviors, several states (Texas, Louisiana, North Carolina, Tennessee, and Oklahoma, to mention a few) and numerous school districts installed teacher performance appraisal systems based on this process-product research. Teachers in the state of Texas during the 1980s and early 1990s could be awarded a status of "E.Q.—Excellent Quality" and receive merit pay if they could perform some 65 (the number varied from year to year) state-adopted competencies under the watchful eye of an evaluator (Manatt, 1988).

Through time, however, some problems with process-product research began to emerge, and the research paradigm began to shift. For example, the research is rich with examples showing that when teachers perform a certain behavior, there is a correlation with a specific form of student learning. There are, however, always "outlier" teachers, those who are not performing that behavior yet still are producing the student learning. And even more intriguing, there are teachers who are performing the behavior being studied and not producing the learning. Glickman (1987), from the University of Georgia, concluded, "We have a great deal of knowledge about instructional methodology but we have no *certainty.*" So although we have a great knowledge base about teaching methodology, we have been inappropriately behaving as if that knowledge base were fixed, certain, and universally generalizable.

Shulman (1987) suggests that researchers have been asking the wrong questions for several years. Asking what constitutes good instruction is far too broad. The appropriate type of questions are these: What constitutes good instruction of American history at the 11th grade in a low socioeconomic school? What constitutes good instruction of mathematics at the 3rd grade for gifted students in a high socioeconomic setting? What constitutes good teaching is, therefore, highly dependent on the age of the learner, certain socioeconomic attributes, learner characteristics, and the structure of the discipline.

The National Institute of Education (1974) convened a diverse group of experts on the psychology of human information processing, the anthropology of education, classroom interactional research, and the practical relationship of teaching and produced a report that set a new direction for research on teaching. One panel, chaired by Shulman (1987), reported as follows:

> It is obvious that what teachers do is directed in no small measure by what they think. To the extent that observed or intended teacher behavior is thoughtless, it makes no use of human teacher's most unique attributes. . . . It becomes mechanical and might well be done by a machine. If, however, teaching is done . . . by human teachers, the question of the relationships between thought and action becomes crucial. (p. 15)

Teaching as Process

The renaissance view of teachers is as professionals—efficacious, creative, intelligent, and holonomous. The role of leadership is to enhance that creativity, to empower teachers with greater responsibility and decision making, to sustain their creative capacities, and to provide an environment conducive to continued intellectual growth.

The vast majority of research on teacher cognition has been conducted since 1976 and begins to illuminate some of the contradictory findings from the process-product research. Combined with current understandings of human information processing systems, effective problem solving, human intelligence, and research on brain capacities and functions, these studies provide valuable insights into what teachers think about when they teach, how they think, the relationship to thinking, teaching behaviors, and student learning. This research also offers useful guidance for coaching and staff development systems that support and develop improved instruction and learning.

Through the efforts of a number of researchers, educators are coming to understand that the act of teaching is a highly intellectual process involving continuous decision making—before, during, and after classroom instruction. Jackson (1968) and Coladarci (1959) were among the early theorists who moved beyond teacher behaviors toward a cognitive notion of teaching. We now, finally, accept that the overt behaviors we observe in classroom performance are the results and artifacts of invisible decisions and complex intellectual processes in the teacher's mind.

Five Assumptions Supporting Teaching as Process

1. *All behavior is rational and is the result of internal maps and perceptions.*

What teachers do in the classroom is determined by their perceptions of their role, their knowledge about and repertoire of instructional strategies, and their knowledge of their students and how they learn and the structure of the discipline of knowledge they are responsible for teaching. To install, alter, or refine instructional behaviors, coaches must mediate by inviting teachers to become aware of and to evaluate their own perceptions and cognitive maps of reality.

2. *Teaching is decision making.*

We are coming to understand that the act of teaching is a highly intellectual process involving continuous decision making—before, during, and after classroom instruction. Certain invisible, cognitive skills drive teaching performance. These teacher thought processes influence the teachers' classroom behaviors, students' classroom behaviors, student achievement, and, reciprocally, the teachers' thought processes, theories, and beliefs. The overt behaviors we observe in classroom performance are the results and artifacts of invisible decisions and complex intellectual processes in the teachers' minds (Joyce & Showers, 1988).

As Shavelson (1976) states,

> Any teaching act is the result of a decision, whether conscious or unconscious, that the teacher makes after the complex cognitive processing of available information. This reasoning leads us to the hypothesis that the basic teaching skill is decision making. (p. 402)

These thought processes are influenced by deeply buried theories of learning, beliefs about education and student conduct, and the cognitive styles of teachers. Coaches can raise these deep-structure forms of knowing to a more conscious level so that teachers can elaborate, clarify, evaluate, and alter them.

3. *These invisible cognitive skills can be categorized in four phases.*

Preactive thought occurs as teachers are planning before teaching. *Interactive* thought occurs during teaching. *Reflective* thought occurs as teachers recall and analyze lessons. *Projective* thought involves synthesizing learnings and planning next steps. (These four phases of thought will be elaborated below.)

4. To learn anything well requires the engagement and transformation of the mind.

On the basis of this cognitive perception of teaching, we regard the mediational role of supervisors as a process of engaging, enhancing, and transforming the intellectual functions of teaching. Coaches can fulfill this role by eliciting how and what teachers are thinking as they plan for, execute, evaluate, and construct meaning from their instructional experiences.

If we believe that teaching is an intellectual process of decision making and that the work of teaching is the application of cognitive processes, then the supervision and evaluation of teaching should be enhancement and assessment of decision making. This view, along with the other changes in efforts to restructure schools, constitute yet another paradigm shift in personnel policies and procedures.

5. Professional adults are capable of continual intellectual growth and learning throughout their lifetime.

Beginning teachers may not assume their first teaching assignments as autonomous professionals. And some veteran teachers may experience situations in which their resourcefulness is at a low ebb. Continual teacher growth occurs developmentally and individually through time. Continual intellectual growth is influenced and supported through mediated learning experiences from a variety of sources: from skilled staff developers, graduate course work, reading, collaboration with peers, modeling by others whom the teachers have grown to respect, by the subtle cues emanating from the school culture, and by the new teachers' critical friends and mentors.

Teaching as Process: A Renaissance View

Teachers have implicit theories about teaching and learning that are robust, idiosyncratic, sensitive to their particular experiences, incomplete, familiar, and sufficiently pragmatic to have gotten them to where they are today (Clark & Peterson, 1986). By talking aloud about these internal maps, coaches can cause teachers to examine, refine, and develop new theories and practices. Through supervisory discussions about the reasoning behind their actions and responding to questions about their perceptions and teaching decisions, teachers often experience a sense of professional excitement and renewed joy and energy related to their work. Coaches, therefore, will invite teachers to disclose their thinking and decisions about teaching because it not only energizes teachers but also causes them to refine their cognitive maps and, hence, their instructional choices and behaviors. Furthermore, it creates an image, especially for beginning teachers, of their chosen profession as an intellectually challenging, growth-producing, complex, and dignified profession. Teachers, in turn, will more likely create similar visions of classroom interactions with their students. Some of the cognitive processes that might become the subject of such teacher-supervisory dialogue are described below.

Four Phases of Instructional Thought

Goal-directed teaching consists of four stages: (a) planning for action, (b) monitoring during practice, (c) reflecting on practice, and (d) projecting ahead. *Planning* (the preactive phase) consists of all the intellectual functions performed before instruction. *Teaching* (the interactive phase) includes the multiple decisions made during teaching. *Analyzing and evaluating* (the reflective phase) consists of all those mental processes used to think back on, analyze, and judge instruction. Finally, *applying* (the projective phase) involves constructing meaning by abstracting from the experience, synthesizing new generalizations, and applying them to future situations. Major cognitive functions within each of these phases are described below.

The Cognitive Processes of Planning: The Preactive Phase

Planning may well include the most important decisions teachers make because it is the phase on which all other decisions rest. Planning involves four components (Shavelson, 1976):

1. Anticipating, envisioning, predicting, and developing precise descriptions of students' learnings that are to result from instruction.
2. Identifying students' present capabilities or entry knowledge. This information is drawn from previous teaching/learning experience, data from school records, test scores, and clues from previous teachers, parents, and counselors (Borko, Cone, Russo, & Shavelson, 1979).
3. Envisioning precisely the characteristics of an instructional sequence or strategy that will most likely move students from their present capabilities toward immediate and long-range instructional outcomes. This sequence is derived from whatever theories, beliefs, or models of teaching logic, learning, or motivation that the teachers have adopted. The sequential structure of a lesson is deeply embedded in teachers' plans for allocating that precious and limited resource: time.
4. Anticipating a method of assessing outcomes. The outcomes of this assessment will provide a basis for evaluating and making decisions about the design of the next cycle of instruction.

The human intellect has a limited capacity for handling variables. Miller (1963) describes this as "M-space" or memory space. He found that humans have a capacity for handling and coordinating seven different variables, decisions, or disparate pieces of information at any one time (plus or minus two). When humans approach the outer limits of their capacity, a state of stress begins to set in with a feeling of loss of control. As teachers gain experience, their intellectual energy appears to be invested in techniques and systems to simplify, reduce, and select the number of variables. Certain planning strategies help reduce this stress and should become the focus of the supervisory process.

During planning, teachers envision cues—definitions of acceptable forms of student performance for learning. This simplifies judgments about appropriate and inappropriate student behaviors. The teachers also select potential solutions, backup procedures, and alternative strategies for times when the activity needs to be redirected, changed, or terminated.

Planning causes thought experiments during which teachers can mentally rehearse activities to help anticipate possible events and consequences. This improves the coordination and efficiency of subsequent performance because systematic mental rehearsal prepares the mind and body for the activity and is the main mechanism for focusing attention on critical factors relevant to the task.

When a person thinks about an action, the brain sends impulses to the nerves and muscles in the corresponding locations of the mind and body associated with the action. This is called the Carpenter Effect (Ulich, 1967) and is the scientific basis for the practice of mental rehearsal. Through mental rehearsal, a person learns to direct attention to cues that are most important for performance and, at the same time, to close down the perceptions of distracting external stimuli. During the planning phase, therefore, it is helpful to rehearse entire lesson sequences (Jansson, 1983).

Planning also demands that teachers exercise perceptual flexibility—viewing learning from multiple perspectives. This requires a certain degree of detachment from the instruction to stand off and assume alternative perspectives. Highly flexible teachers have the capacity to view their lessons in both immediate and long-range terms. They not only are analytical about the details of a lesson (the micromode) but also can see connections between a lesson and other related learnings. They know where this lesson is leading and how it is connected to broader curricular goals (the macromode). Less flexible, episodic teachers may view today's activity as a separate and discrete episode, unrelated to other learning events.

Flexible teachers see a lesson from a variety of points of view. Teachers may view the lesson (a) *egocentrically*—from their own points of view, including their goals, teaching strategies, and content background; (b) *allocentrically*—from a student's point of view; (c) *macrocentrically*—imagining how the entire interaction will appear from a mental balcony overlooking the interactions between teacher and students; and (d) *retrocentrically*—envisioning the end or completed product and backing up from that vision to form strategies and steps of how to achieve the vision.

Planning a teaching strategy also requires analysis—both structural and operational. Structural analysis is the process of breaking down the learning of the content into its component parts; operational analysis involves a seriation of events into a logical order of sequence (Clark & Yinger, 1979). To handle this information overload, teachers probably synthesize much of this information into "hypotheses" or best guesses about student readiness for learning. They estimate the probability of successful student behavior as a result of instruction.

Shavelson (1976) believes that of the four phases of teachers' thought, planning is the most important because it sets the standard for the remaining three phases. Also of great value seems to be specifying clear learning objectives. The more clearly teachers envision and mentally rehearse the plan, the greater is the chance that the lesson will achieve its purposes, the more likely teachers will self-monitor their own actions and decisions during the lesson, and the more likely teachers will critically analyze their own lesson during the reflective phase, thereby assuming a greater internal locus of control.

The Cognitive Processes of Teaching: The Interactive Phase

Teaching has been described as the second most stressful profession. This stems from the constant interaction of teachers with students in an environment of uncertainty (Harvey, 1966). Teachers are constantly making decisions that may be subconscious, spontaneous, planned, or a mixture of each. They are probably modifications of decisions made during the planning phase, but now they are carried out on the spur of the moment in the fast-paced interaction of the classroom. Changes may not be well defined or as thoroughly considered as those made during the calmer stage of planning. Teachers have little time to consider alternative teaching strategies and the consequences of each.

Teachers plan in multiple time dimensions: weekly, daily, long range, short range, yearly, and term. Effective teachers relate information from all those time frames as they prepare daily lessons (Yinger, 1977). Several temporal capacities interact constantly with teachers' thoughts and values and influence their moment-to-moment decisions. These may include *sequence*—the seriation or ordering of instructional events within a lesson; *simultaneity*—teaching toward multiple and varied outcomes, strategies, learning styles, and so on at the same time; *rhythm*—pacing the lesson, regulating the tempo and recurrence of learnings; and *synchronicity*—aligning the learning into allotted time constraints and schedules. (For an elaboration of teachers' temporal thought processes, see Costa & Garmston, 1994, Appendix B.)

Keeping a planned strategy in mind while teaching provides teachers a backdrop against which to make new decisions. During the beginning of a lesson, for example, teachers may emphasize structuring the task and motivating students to become curious, involved, and focused. Later in the sequence, teachers may use recall thinking to review previously learned information and to gather data to be considered later. Further into the lesson, teachers may invite higher-level thinking and, finally, tasks for transference and application.

Clark and Peterson (1986) describe the content of teachers' interactive thought related to (a) changing their plans, (b) the influences on those decisions, (c) the cues that teachers read to make decisions, and (d) the relationships between teachers' interactive decisions, teachers' behaviors, and, ultimately, student outcomes. A relatively small portion of teachers' interactive thoughts deal with instructional objectives. A greater percentage of teachers' interactive thoughts deal with the content or subject matter. A still greater percentage of interactive thoughts deal with the instructional process. And the largest percentage of teachers' interactive thought concerns learning and the learner.

Novice teachers may suffer cognitive overload—too many things going on all at the same time—yet skillful teachers respond immediately, intuitively, and spontaneously. Highly conscious teachers are alert to what is going on in the classroom; less conscious teachers continue their lessons regardless of what occurs among the students. Alert teachers search for clues that students are learning—have the students acted on the information, digested it, and made meaning out of it or used it? Are students staring vacantly, or do body language and facial cues indicate attention? Alert teachers constantly observe, question, probe, and interpret students' behaviors to make decisions about moving ahead in the sequence or remaining at the present step longer.

Metacognition in teachers is a critically important capacity to consciously "stand outside and reflect on themselves" as they manage instruction. During a lesson, teachers may conduct an inner dialogue, asking themselves, "Are my directions clear? Can students see the TV monitor? Am I using precise words to make sure that the students are understanding? Should I speed up?" Such self-talk means the teachers are constantly monitoring their own and students' behavior during instruction.

Metacognition also refers to the ability of humans to know what we know and what we don't know. It is the ability to plan a strategy for producing what information is needed, to be conscious of our own steps and strategies, and to reflect on and evaluate the productivity of our thinking. Perkins (1992) has elaborated four increasingly complex levels of metacognition:

1. the *tacit* level, being unaware of our metacognitive knowledge;
2. the *awareness* level, knowing about some of the types of thinking we do (generating ideas, finding evidence, but not being strategic);
3. the *strategic* level, organizing our thinking by using problem solving, decision making, evidence seeking, and other strategies; and
4. the *reflective* level, not only being strategic but also reflecting on our thinking in-progress, pondering strategies, and revising them accordingly.

The metacognitive skills necessary to successful teaching—and what supervisors, therefore, may want to develop—include

- Keeping place in a long sequence of operations
- Knowing that a subgoal has been attained
- Detecting errors and recovering from them by making a quick fix or retreating to the last known correct operation

This type of monitoring involves both looking ahead and looking back. Looking ahead includes

- Learning the structure of a sequence of operations and identifying areas in which errors are likely
- Choosing a strategy that will reduce the possibility of error and will provide easy recovery
- Identifying the types of feedback that will be available at various points and evaluating the usefulness of that feedback

Looking back includes

- Detecting errors previously made
- Keeping a history of what has been done to the present and therefore what should come next
- Assessing the reasonableness of the present and the immediate outcome of task performance

As teachers monitor the classroom for conscious and subconscious cues, they sometimes build up so much information that they disrupt conscious information processing. Flexible teachers restrain their impulsivity by avoiding strong emotional reactions to classroom events. This is an efficient strategy to reserve the limited capacity for conscious processing of immediate classroom decisions.

Flexible teachers have a vast repertoire of instructional strategies and techniques and call forth alternative strategies as needed. In many classes, there is a heterogeneous array of languages, cultures, and learning styles. Each must be dealt with employing different strategies, vocabulary, examples, and techniques. Efficacious and flexible teachers continually add to and draw on their vast repertoire for strategies that may prove effective.

Routines are helpful in dealing with the information-processing demands of the classroom. Routines reduce the need to attend to the abundance of simultaneous cues from the environment. Efficacious teachers develop a repertoire of routine systems for dealing with many classroom management functions (taking roll, distributing papers and books, etc.). They also have systematic lesson designs (for example, spelling and math drills) and teaching strategies (for example, questioning sequences and structuring).

The Cognitive Processes of Analyzing and Evaluating: The Reflective Phase

After teaching a lesson, teachers now have two sources of information: the lesson that was envisioned during planning and the actual lesson as performed. Analyzing involves collecting and using understandings derived from the comparison between actual and intended outcomes. If a great similarity exists between the two, there is a match. But if a discrepancy exists between the lesson that was planned and the lesson that was taught, teachers then generate reasons to explain the discrepancies. Causal relationships between instructional situations and behavioral outcomes are generated and explored.

Teachers can either assume responsibility for their own actions or place the blame on external forces. Teachers with an external locus of control tend to misplace responsibility or situations or persons beyond their control. Efficacious teachers have an internal locus of control. They assume responsibility for their own successes and failures.

Even with this analysis, the cycle of instructional decision making is not yet complete. The learnings must be constructed, synthesized, and applied or transferred to other learning contexts, content areas, and life situations.

The Cognitive Processes of Applying: The Projective Phase

In this phase, teachers construct new knowledge and apply that knowledge to future instructional situations or content. Experience can bring change, but experience alone is not enough. Meaning is constructed when experience is compared, differentiated, categorized, and labeled.

Skillful teachers consciously reflect on, conceptualize, and apply understandings from one classroom experience to the next. As a result of this analysis and reflection, they synthesize new knowledge about teaching and learning. As experiences with teaching and learning accumulate, concepts are derived and constructed. As a result, teachers become more routinized, particularized, and refined. They are capable of predicting consequences of their decisions and are therefore more experimental and risk taking. They expand their repertoire of techniques and strategies to be used in different situations with varying content and unique groups of students. Without this conceptual system, teachers' perceptions of the classroom remains chaotic.

Summary

Teaching is cognitively complex. This chapter has examined some of the cognitive or intellectual processes involved in the four components of the instructional act. The myriad decisions reported here are driven by even more deeply embedded conscious or subconscious beliefs, styles, metaphors, perceptions, and habits. If teachers do not possess these mental capacities, no amount of experience or training will create it. It is through mediation by colleagues, coaches, and a stimulating, cooperative, and trustful environment that these capacities will continue to develop throughout teachers' professional careers. (Feuerstein & Feuerstein, 1991). We are interested, therefore, not in the content of what teachers should know but rather in eliciting, enhancing, and refining the continuous modification of teachers' inner thought processes (Costa & Garmston, 1994).

References

Bloom, B. (1956). *Taxonomy in cognitive domain: A classification of educational goals.* New York: David McKay.

Borko, H., Cone, R., Russo, D., & Shavelson, R. (1979). Teachers' decision making. In D. Peterson & H. Walberg (Eds.), *Research on teaching.* Berkeley, CA: McCutchan.

Clark, C., & Peterson, P. (1986). Teachers' thought processes. In M. C. Wittrock (Ed.), *Handbook of research on teaching* (3rd ed., pp. 255-296). New York: Macmillan.

Clark, C., & Yinger, R. (1979). Teachers' thinking. In D. Peterson & H. Walberg (Eds.), *Research on teaching.* Berkeley, CA: McCutchan.

Coladarci, A. P. (1959, March). The teacher as hypothesis maker. *California Journal of Instructional Improvement, 2,* 3-6.

Costa, A., & Garmston, R. (1994). *Cognitive coaching: A foundation for the renaissance school.* Norwood, MA: Christopher-Gordon.

Feuerstein, R., & Feuerstein, S. (1991). Mediated learning experience: A theoretical review. In R. Feuerstein, P. Klein, & A. Tannenbaum (Eds.), *Mediated learning experiences: Theoretical, psychosocial and learning implications.* London: Freund.

Glickman, C. (1987, April). [Address]. Presentation at a National Curriculum Study Institute for the Association for Supervision and Curriculum Development, Scottsdale, AZ.

Harvey, O. J. (1966). System structure, flexibility, and creativity. In O. J. Harvey (Ed.), *Experience, structure, and adaptability* (pp. 39-65). New York: Springer.

Hunter, M. (1984). Knowing teaching and supervising. In P. Hosford (Ed.), *Using what we know about teaching: 1984 yearbook of the Association for Supervision and Curriculum Development.* Alexandria, VA: Association for Supervision and Curriculum Development.

Jackson, P. W. (1968). *Life in classrooms.* New York: Holt, Rinehart & Winston.

Jansson, L. (1983). Mental training: Thinking rehearsal and its use. In W. Maxwell (Ed.), *Thinking: The expanding frontier.* Philadelphia: Franklin Institute.

Joyce, B., & Showers, B. (1988). *Student achievement through staff development.* New York: Longman.

Kerman, S., & Martin, M. (1980). *Teacher expectation and student achievement (TESA).* Los Angeles: Los Angeles County Superintendent of Schools Office.

Manatt, R. (1988). Teacher performance: A total systems approach. In T. McGreal et al. (Eds.), *Teacher evaluation: Six prescriptions for success.* Alexandria, VA: Association for Supervision and Curriculum Development.

Miller, G. A. (1963, March). The magical number seven, plus or minus two: Some limits on our capacity for processing information. *Psychological Review, 2,* 81-97.

National Institute of Education. (1974). *Teaching as clinical information processing.* Report of Panel 6, National Conference on Studies in Teaching, Washington, DC.

Perkins, D. (1992). *Smart schools: From training memories to educating minds.* New York: Free Press.

Rowe, M. B. (1974). Wait time and rewards as instructional variables: Their influence on language, logic and fate control. *Journal of Research in Science Teaching, 2,* 81-94.

Shavelson, R. (1976). Teachers' decision making. In *The psychology of teaching methods: 1976 yearbook of the National Society for the Study of Education, Part I.* Chicago: University of Chicago Press.

Shulman, L. (1987). Knowledge and teaching: Foundations of the new reform. *Harvard Educational Review, 57*(1), 1-22.

Ulich, E. (1967). Some experiments of the function of mental training in the acquisition of motor skills. *Ergonomics, 10,* 411-419.

Yinger, R. J. (1977). *A study of teacher planning: Description and theory development using ethnographic and information processing methods.* Unpublished doctoral dissertation, Michigan State University, East Lansing.

4

Instruction for Process Learning

Marian Leibowitz

One of the wonders of life is to become a grandparent and to observe the development of young children. While visiting my grandson Benjie when he was 12 months old, I had the opportunity to see the development and support of problem solving. Like many youngsters first learning to navigate, Benjie got himself jammed between the playpen and the wall . . . and, also like most little ones, he let out a loud shriek. My daughter-in-law, quickly assessing the lack of imminent danger, said, "Come on, Benjie, you can do it. You can get out." He made another unsuccessful attempt and let out yet another howl. His mother still did not rush to his rescue. Instead, she said, "Try, Benjie. I know you can do it! Just try it one more time." He explored another way, and, suddenly, there he was—freed. His mother clapped her hands and said, "Hurray! You see—you did it!" I'm not sure he fully understood the magnitude of his persistent problem solving, but her applauding and positive tone of voice obviously conveyed something wonderful had just happened!

About 6 months later, on another visit, Benjie, now 18 months old, was about to go to bed. I heard his mother ask, as she held out two pairs of pajamas, "Which pair of pajamas do you want to wear? Which bottle do you want your milk in?" and so on, providing flexibility through controlled options and alternatives to a 1½-year-old toddler.

The best was yet to come. Once when he was 2 years old, Benjie was about to descend the stairway of a two-story colonial house. In one hand was Mr. Potato Head and in the other—all the parts. His mother, predicting possible disaster, said, "Benjie, remember you need to hold on to the banister." What seemed to be an eternity passed as Benjie kept glancing from Mr. Potato Head to the parts to the banister. Periodically, his mother would remind him of the need to hold on. Suddenly, he had figured it out! He threw all the parts down the stairs and held on to Mr. Potato Head with one hand and the banister with the other. At the bottom of the stairway, he quickly scooped up all the parts and was on his way—a major problem-solving experience in the life of a 2-year-old!

Although the books in this trilogy extol process as content, the current emphasis on process skills in the curriculum should not be viewed as something new. It is instead a more explicit and systematic way of doing what good parents in homes and good teachers in good schools have been doing for many years. If asked "Are you teaching thinking?" most teachers will answer "of course." The specifics of *what* they are teaching will be fuzzy, and there certainly will be little or no connection to what was taught last year or even what is currently being taught in other content areas.

Monitoring student progress in process areas described in these books has been almost nonexistent. Often, the primary group targeted for learning creative and critical thinking, problem solving, and decision making has been those students "validated" as gifted and/or talented. Gifted and/or talented students have also been encouraged to work as "real professionals work." Educators now know that what is good for the gifted is what *every* student should be engaged in.

Processes have now become included as part of the "New Basics," with thinking, communication, and collaboration linked to computer literacy and added to the more traditional three Rs. A number of factors have contributed to this shift:

- The *world of technology* has provided means to easily access information. The task has become how to manage, organize, and make sense out of the information.
- The *rapid pace of change,* with knowledge doubling every 5 years, is altering traditional modes of thinking and functioning. Roles are being redefined and positions created that did not exist 10 years ago, 5 years ago, or maybe even last month.
- *Lifelong learning* moves away from an idealistic vision and becomes more of a necessity because individuals will be forced to engage in continual learning, if only to keep pace with change in their professional work fields and personal lives.
- *Dealing with diversity in thought and ideas* will be a necessity as technology links the globe and every work station becomes a part of a technology network that extends throughout the world.

In *Education and Work for the Year 2000: Choices We Face* (Wirth, 1992), Secretary of Labor Robert Reich is quoted as saying, "We need a formal education that will refine four basic skills" (p. 69):

1. *Abstraction:* The capacity to order and make meaning of the massive flow of information, to shape raw data into workable patterns;
2. *Systems thinking:* The capacity to see the parts in relation to the whole, to see why problems arise;
3. *Experimental inquiry:* The capacity to set up procedures to test and evaluate alternative ideas; and

4. *Collaboration:* The capacity to engage in active communication and dialogue to get a variety of perspectives and to create consensus, when that is necessary. (pp. 69-70)

This chapter will examine and draw implications for Reich's concepts as they apply to classroom instruction.

Abstract Thinking

Recently, in two separate high schools, teachers reported giving assignments that they had given every year:

In social studies: Select a patriot from the years 1700-1840 and do a research paper on his or her life.

In art: Select an artist of your choice and do a research paper on his or her life.

Both teachers reported that the research papers were more accurate in content than ever before, were handed in earlier than usual, and had no grammatical or spelling errors. Soon both teachers realized, however, that both students had accessed information for the assignments by using technology. One felt the students had "cheated" because the intent was for students to engage in a more traditional library task. The issue is not one of students' accessing information in ways not intended by the teacher but questioning the nature of the assignment. The students should be commended for making good use of available resources!

In fifth grade, students in social studies often spend the first 6 weeks of the semester studying explorers. The specifics of each explorer's journey are plotted with extensive geographical detail. The students often do research papers on the life of a selected explorer or build a diorama portraying a scene in the particular explorer's history.

The unifying question for these three examples is this: How appropriate is this assignment at the end of this century? Is the major purpose of teaching and learning simply a reportage of factual information, or might there be more? Beginning with Reich's definition of *abstraction*, let's transform these lessons.

With the intention of having students develop concepts, the teacher may pose such questions as these:

Concept	*Questions*
Patriotism	What do we mean by patriotism? Think about/ hypothesize what characteristics a patriot would need to have. In your learning groups, select someone whom you consider a patriot from the 1700-1840 era. Collect data regarding his or her life. Compare and contrast your data with your hypothesis about what makes a patriot. Compare your data with the data of others in your group. How consistent was your hypothesis as you tested it?

Concept	*Questions*
Art	What is art, and what does it mean to be an artist? Hypothesize what characteristics are needed for someone to become an artist. Select an artist of your choice, research the artist's life, and compare your results with your hypothesis.
Exploration	What do we mean by exploration, and what characteristics does an explorer need? What about modern exploration? Select someone from any field whom you would like to nominate as the Explorer of the Year. Write a letter to the Selection Panel validating how your nominee meets the characteristics that you have established.

Although all three of these lessons included research and data collection, they also had additional outcomes of abstraction. The data were then analyzed, compared, and reflected on to arrive at some conclusions.

Systems Thinking

Let's examine the role of process in content. Students are often expected to develop a product—a report, a diorama, or a presentation to demonstrate what they have learned. What provisions are made to clearly define the expectations, standards, or criteria for the work? For example, how will the students know when the project is complete? How will the students know it is the best it can be? Does the teacher ask for an organizational plan to see how the students are thinking about the assignment? How long might this take? What will be steps one, two, three, and so forth? Does the teacher coach students every step of the way so that by the time they finish the assignment, the students and teacher can identify the key components that led to the presentation of a quality product? Often, it is "Here's the assignment, any questions? It's due in 2 weeks."

I recently observed in a high school when students were presenting their finished products. The lack of skill in process was clear from the tremendous range of presentations. Those who were high achievers and knew how to plan, organize, and raise critical questions for discussion did that intuitively. The lower achievers did not know how and therefore did not complete the work as intended by the teachers. Attention was primarily on the product and not on the process of creating the product.

Systems thinking requires connectedness of content. In most schools, however, each content area is taught in isolation within a designated separate time frame called a schedule. What about the possibility of organizing around integration and using processes as unifiers? Schools need a common vision. Let's focus on problem solving and the same problem-solving model, lexicon of language, as a means of connecting the content in many areas, such as math, science, and so on.

Experimental Inquiry

Science teachers traditionally have students develop hypotheses and then collect data to support or negate the hypotheses. These processes of collecting data, analyzing data, and interpreting data, however, can be included in any content area. For example,

In mathematics: How many different ways can you solve the math problem?
In reading: What could be another ending for the story?
In literature: Why do you think the author selected to end it this way?

An example involves the use of *Dr. DeSoto* (Steig, 1982), a story in which Dr. DeSoto (a dentist and a mouse) tricks the patient (a fox) by gluing the fox's mouth shut so he won't eat him. Second-grade children were asked what other things Dr. DeSoto could have done to save himself. One second grader suggested that Dr. DeSoto could have hired a big animal as his bodyguard and then he wouldn't have to worry. When asked why he thought that hadn't happened, the second grader pondered for a few minutes and then said, "You can't trust anybody but yourself."

Collaboration

Not only could teachers create learning groups composed of students of differing interests, achievement levels, backgrounds, and talents, but also teachers could ask students to examine content from multiple perspectives:

Analyze a story from the point of view of each of the characters.
Examine an event in social studies as an event propelled by diverse perspectives.

I propose not necessarily teaching different content but *teaching content differently.*

We as educators need to examine changes in the world, changes in careers, and professional changes in our everyday lives to identify those process areas that appear to be most relevant. There appears to be agreement that complex thinking, communication, and collaboration will be among the essential process areas for the world as we will know it.

In conceptualizing the development of curriculum and then teaching and learning, the following example might serve as a model to consider:

Curriculum/Instruction

Process	*Content*	*Habits of Mind**
	Example: Social Studies Concept: Representation increases ownership Event: Boston Tea Party	

Process	*Content*	*Habits of Mind**
Thinking: Point of view	Examine diverse points of view: tea owner, colonist, member of Parliament, etc.	Persistence: What evidence would teachers be seeking that students are demonstrating persistence?
Problem solving	Hypothesize what could have been other solutions and why dumping the tea into Boston Harbor was selected	Flexibility of thinking: What would tell teachers that students are flexible in their thinking about the Boston Tea Party?

*Attributes of intelligent behavior (Costa, 1991)

The selection of process areas will largely drive the delivery of content or instructional strategies. Clearly, if collaboration is a goal or standard, then opportunities need to be provided for students to experience a variety of group structures. If complex thinking is a standard, then instructional design needs to promote complex thinking as a means for engaging with content. It becomes necessary for staff, students, and parents to have a clear understanding of what these process goals are and to develop a common language in the attempt to give process goals a prominent role in designing student learning activities.

As schools and school districts identify the key process areas, the following questions need to be considered:

What do we mean by thinking? Communication? Collaboration? Self-direction?

What is our agreed-on definition?

Is it something we value? Why?

If it were happening, what would we see students doing and hear them saying that would tell us that they are able to think, communicate, and collaborate?

What would teachers be doing?
What would administrators be doing?
What would parents be doing to support these process areas at home?

Engaging students, teachers, administrators, and parents in this dialogue produces a common understanding and vision—a shared valuing *or* rejecting of an area. It results in a set of standards, benchmarks, and indicators that could be used to drive instruction, assessment, and curricular design.

For example, if the common vision was that students, at the end of grade 12, would be able to function as *complex thinkers,* what evidence would show that students were engaged in complex thinking? (See Skerritt's chapter, "Process as Content," in the first book in this trilogy, *Envisioning Process As Content.*) Some observable examples of complex thinking behaviors might be students

- Disagreeing with evidence
- Generating many types of ideas
- Raising clarifying questions with peers and with the teacher
- Analyzing information as to the relevancy of the task at hand
- Using multiple resources to check for accuracy of information
- Seeking feedback from peers regarding the clarity of their work

What might teachers do in a school that values complex thinking? Teachers would *themselves* be demonstrating their own complex thinking by

- Articulating their thinking to students
- Reflecting on their work in relation to what worked well or what they learned and how they might do this differently if given another opportunity
- Using multiple resources to check for accuracy of information regarding their own professional practice
- Seeking feedback from peers regarding instructional design and implementation

Teachers would structure activities for students to promote complex thinking by

- Raising complex questions rather than simply asking recall questions
- Coaching students rather than giving all the answers
- Engaging students in self-evaluative opportunities and promoting student goal setting
- Providing opportunities for students to engage in problem-centered learning that teaches for thinking

What about parents? What would be the role of parents in promoting complex thinking? As I described in the examples in the opening of this chapter, parents can provide multiple opportunities for children at a very early age to engage in many diverse thinking activities that are not necessarily academically oriented but that are more appropriate in the less formal environment of a family.

Parents need to be involved not only in the identification of the process skills but also in the definition and teaching of these skills. Students, parents, teachers, and administrators all need to share a common language, set standards for performance based on a clear set of indicators, and model behavior consistent with those valued process areas.

There is no questions that students need to be engaged in content and that quality standards must be established for that content. But in today's world, knowledge of content is only Step 1. The bigger issues are what is done with the content, how the content is processed, how it is analyzed, and what ideas it supports. We are not engaged in a debate about which is more important, content or process. At the present time, one cannot exist without the other. Thinking requires content to think about. Communicating requires information to communicate. It is now time to recognize that content serves as the vehicle for process and that both are *equally* critical.

References

Costa, A. (1991). The search for intelligent life. In A. Costa (Ed.), *Developing minds: A resource book for teaching thinking.* Alexandria, VA: Association for Supervision and Curriculum Development.

Steig, W. (1982). *Dr. DeSoto.* New York: Farrar, Straus & Giroux.

Wirth, A. G. (1992). *Education and work for the year 2000: Choices we face.* San Francisco: Jossey-Bass.

5

A Process-Oriented Paradigm

Implications for Professional Development

Marilyn Tabor

The Lesson of the Stone: A Metaphor

> The stone lay on the shore, comfortably nestled among its fellow rocks, warmed by the sun, brushed clean by the wind, fulfilling its role. Aware of the water nearby, the stone wondered about it but found no simple means to learn more about it. One crisp fall day, the hand of fate lifted the stone, holding it aloft where it glimpsed the world beyond and the vast, seemingly endless sea. Curious, the stone pondered the sea. Hesitant, it wished momentarily to be back in the place that felt more familiar. Suddenly, the stone was flung toward the water, exhilaration and fear surging through it in the same moment. As it touched the top of the water again, again, again, and yet again before finally coming to rest beneath the sea, the stone learned a great truth: Skipping across the surface leaves the sea undiscovered. The water is not known by lying on the shore, nor can the sea be truly understood until it is experienced deeply and profoundly.

So it is with professional development. We do not truly learn unless we deeply explore that which we encounter. Touching the surface lightly and briefly leaves us unable to understand, internalize, or implement new learning.

Overview

"The majority of school districts currently spend less than three percent of their total budget and less than five days per teacher each year" on professional development (Vojtek, 1994, p. 48). Current literature and education initiatives underscore the necessity for and significance of meaningful professional development and support the contention that development efforts must offer richly varied formats and be sustained through time to have impact. It is imperative that professional development be viewed as a continual process that is *never* finished.

Although it is essential to focus professional development on teaching and learning, the impact of the information age with its increasing complexity and rapidly accelerating change makes it impossible to anticipate future knowledge requirements. Darling-Hammond and McLaughlin (1995) contend that

> the success of the nation's reform agenda ultimately turns on teachers' success in accomplishing the serious and difficult tasks of *learning* the skills and perspectives assumed by new visions of practice and *unlearning* the practices and beliefs about students and instruction that have dominated their professional lives to date. (p. 597)

It is therefore crucial that emphasis be shifted primarily from the *what* of knowledge (content) to the *how* of continual learning (process) because a focus on process will facilitate our ability to respond to our changing culture and environment. According to Fullan (1993), "The future of the world is a learning future. . . . Teachers' capacities to deal with change, learn from it, and help students learn from it will be critical for the future development of societies" (pp. vii-ix).

What, then, is necessary in professional development for real learning to take place, for us to be able to construct and embrace changing paradigms, for implementation of the new to occur successfully? This chapter intends three purposes in an exploration of answers to that question:

- The advocacy for the values and perspectives necessary to regard an educational institution as a learning organization and adult learning as a continuing process and perpetual endeavor for both the individual and the organization
- The shaping of the belief that a process-oriented approach is the mind, heart, and soul of significant professional development and essential to the continual renewal and improvement of the organization and its members
- The recommendation that certain pillars are requisite supports of a framework that re-visions dynamic professional development as a process-oriented paradigm

Professional Development Defined

The term *professional development* better captures the essence of the development efforts and conceptual framework needed to meet the demands of the 21st century than does the more familiar term *staff development*. It seems as if we are being flung into the future. Mounting evidence demonstrates that "irresistible forces are currently at work in education" (Sparks, 1994, p. 26), transforming ideas so profoundly that the face of professional development is being changed forever. Called for is an immediate shift away from one-shot or short-term staff development activities and fragmented improvement efforts toward a truer form of professional development, a process shaped by systems thinking with a focus not only on breadth and depth of individual development but also on development of the capacity of the entire organization to solve problems and engage in self-renewal.

Re-visioned professional development is characterized by a wide variety of formats and support practices. There is acknowledgment of the unique concerns, interests, levels of experience, contexts, and cultures within groups, classrooms, and schools. Numerous options and strategies are offered in response to needs: site-based professional development, common planning periods, in-house workshops, peer coaching, multiple forms and levels of collaboration, student work analysis teams, action research teams, study groups, district-sponsored training and institutes, mentor programs, leadership team development, partnerships, professional conferences and seminars, networks, and central office facilitators for site-based processes.

In growth-producing professional development, process is viewed as a system for learning. A process orientation recognizes the importance of setting worthy goals and acknowledges that process is what makes goals achievable. Therefore, great attention is given to planning process carefully and to constant monitoring and adapting to ensure continuous improvement (Bonstingl, 1992). Teachers are viewed as decision makers who flourish in professional development designs that provide "flexibility, personalization, and . . . encouragement to make the new fit their needs" (Valencia & Killion, 1988, p. 7). Formats support teacher engagement in collaborative experiences that are sustained through time and build in reflection related to the learning.

As professional development moves away from traditional models "toward long-term, continuous learning in the context of school and classroom and with the support of colleagues, the idea of professional development takes on even greater importance" (Lieberman, 1995, p. 596). In this context, "learning does not mean acquiring more information, but expending the ability to produce results we truly want" (Senge, 1990, p. 142). In such a vision for the future, the whole purpose of professional development is "to enhance human potential so that every person can achieve a higher standard of attainment, success, or excellence than would otherwise be possible" (Orlich, 1989, p. 2).

Timeless Fundamentals

The ideas proposed in this chapter are predicated on the assumption that certain proven fundamentals of powerful professional development **must** be in place for any development effort to be effective. The following are timeless fundamentals that serve all professional development approaches by supporting a process orientation and facilitating and encouraging continuing learning:

- A focus on teaching and learning
- The application of change theory
- The application of adult learning theory
- The use of proven process elements

A Focus on Teaching and Learning

It is critical that the aim of professional development in an educational organization be the improvement of teaching and learning. Joyce and Showers (in press) contend that

> really fine [professional] development systems do not take place unless policymakers believe there is a link between the investment in [professional] development and the learning of students. . . . [Professional] development must be continuous and focused on the improvement of practice which results in measurable advances in student learning. . . . The key to student growth is educator growth. They happen together; each enhances the other.

In considering the role that professional development can play in re-creating school environments to focus on teaching and learning, Cooper (1991) proposes that

> a shift from the delivery of *mechanical* and *technical* skills to the development of ways to build the *conceptual* skills of practitioners has become necessary. . . . Assumptions must be challenged, learners and learning viewed differently, and questions about production and procedure replaced by questions of belief and meaning. . . . Practitioners must think (conceive) differently about environments; social, economic, and political constraints; themselves; and others—especially students. We must . . . apply new tools to the basic questions of teaching and learning. (pp. 88-91)

For professional development to have a worthwhile and significant impact, its intent must be connected to the most important aspects of teaching, as well as student and adult learning. The most effective professional development will acknowledge new truths:

> Traditional formulations of teaching as technical and managed work, as service and performance are being challenged and replaced by notions of teaching as developmental and thoughtful action and as leadership. Similarly, the traditional views of learning as straightforward and simple acquisition of facts and skills and as assimilation are being reconsidered. New notions of learning are emerging: that learning is production of knowledge, that it is complex and goes beyond facts to thinking and reasoning and learning to learn. (Lieberman & Miller, 1991, p. 106)

The Application of Change Theory

Learning equals change. The work of Hall and Loucks (1978) related to the Concerns-Based Adoption Model continues to be useful in understanding and aligning any professional development endeavor to teacher stages of concern related to adoption of something new or different. This model recognizes that concerns are first at the personal level, then related to management issues, before finally focusing on the impact of the change. The value of the Concerns-Based Adoption Model lies in its attention to teacher concerns because if unaddressed, those concerns impede change efforts. The model also reminds us that change is highly personal. Therefore, the most powerful professional development will have integrated within its design the opportunity for all to become what Fullan (1993) describes as individual change agents committed to purposeful engagement in an educational renewal process.

Learning requires that personal transition occur if any change is to become internalized and operational. An awareness of the personal stages experienced during a change journey enables us to perceive and acknowledge the human response to change and to facilitate movement through each stage (Spencer & Adams, 1990). Furthermore, superior professional development builds in supports for that most challenging portion of personal transition through change that Bridges (1991) terms the *neutral zone,* that place wherein abide discomfort, fears, and/or resistance related to change. The importance of accounting for personal transition through change cannot be underestimated. The demonstration of change is external; the process of accomplishing change is internal. Change is situational; transition is the personal process we go through to come to terms with the new. It is not change that overwhelms us; it is transition. Unless transition occurs, change will not occur. Acknowledgment of change as a process of personal stages is fundamental to successful professional development.

The Application of Adult Learning Theory

The needs of adult learners are complex, influenced by varying concerns, age-related patterns, and developmental stages. Adults have common needs for growth-oriented, rather than deficit-oriented, learning formats and for experiences that are practical, relevant, and related to personal choices, interests, concerns, and contexts (Krupp, 1989). Awareness of age-related transitions and life-cycle issues assists in understanding that growth is the evolution of a life structure through time (Oja, 1991). Levine's (1989) presentation of phase theories and stage theories related to adult development point to the importance of understanding how the individuals with whom we work understand themselves, their world, and others. Oja's summary of developmental stages of thinking and problem solving regarding how adults behave and think while involved in professional development serves as a reminder that challenges and supports within professional development designs should be structured to match adult stages of development in positive, supportive, nonjudgmental ways that acknowledge ever present possibilities for growth and change.

The Use of Proven Process Elements

Quality professional development must be recognized as "a collective set of personal experiences . . . that belies tidy recipes for success. . . . Successful [professional] development considers the learners, the challenge, the reward, and the difference a . . . process can make" (Loucks-Horsley et al., 1987, p. 7). Professional literature describes an abundance of essential process elements that constitute good professional development. Particularly important and worthy of attention are those highly effective, proven processes that link the professional development experience to the expected learning—the methods that engage thinking and facilitate connection making and construction of personal understanding. The following list is a sampling of the most effective processes to consider.

- Setting relevant and precise outcomes that create a focus on teaching and learning
- Accessing and acknowledging prior knowledge and experience as the foundation for personalizing new learning
- Facilitating social learning by means of purposeful dialogue and interactive experiences, as well as personal learning through reflection
- Exploring appropriate research and theory to develop rationale and understanding and then linking it to practice
- Including real-world examples, demonstrations, and/or modeling to create vivid multisensory learning experiences
- Creating an environment and time for action planning and/or implementation practice both during and following professional development experiences
- Supporting implementation and internalization with follow-up in the form of objective feedback, coaching, consultation, and collaborative problem solving

Re-Visioning Professional Development by Means of a Process-Oriented Framework

Dynamic is defined as "having to do with energy or force producing motion, i.e., a dynamic force that produces action or change" (*Thorndike-Barnhart Dictionary*, 1983, p. 652). If professional development is to be a dynamic force in the learning endeavor of teachers and the educational organization, it must be founded on a framework that incorporates process-oriented principles. The following processes are requisite pillars of a framework that re-visions dynamic professional development:

- Making holonomy the overarching goal for professional development
- Creating a systems approach
- Ensuring engagement of the mind

- Placing importance on the "Three Cs"
  - Climate
  - Constructivism
  - Collaboration
- Stressing the "Three Rs"
  - Risking
  - Reflection
  - Research

Making Holonomy the Overarching Goal for Professional Development

An impactful process incorporates the setting of an overarching goal aimed at the global development of participants, in addition to establishing specific outcomes for particular phases of professional development experiences. Perhaps the most powerful overarching goal to set for dynamic professional development is that of increasing personal and organizational holonomy.

The term *holonomy* comes from the Greek: *holos* meaning "whole" and *on* meaning "part." It represents the integration of the parts and the whole. Koestler (1972) coined the term to describe the dual tendency of each of us to preserve our individuality as an autonomous whole while functioning as an interdependent part of a larger system. For example, in a classroom, each teacher is an autonomous individual. Each autonomous teacher, however, is also part of a larger whole and influences and is influenced by the school culture of which the teacher is a part. The overarching goal of increasing holonomy consists of supporting people both in becoming independent and in functioning interdependently as members of a school community.

The sources of holonomy are defined as five states of mind that are catalysts for holonomous behaviors (Costa & Garmston, 1994):

1. *Consciousness:* People who are highly conscious monitor their own thoughts, behaviors, and personal progress toward goals. They know what and how they are thinking and are willingly aware of their actions and the resulting effects.
2. *Efficacy:* People who are efficacious have an internal locus of control and a sense of personal resourcefulness and believe their efforts make a difference. They know they have the capacity to make choices and willingly take responsibility for their choices and decisions.
3. *Flexibility:* People who demonstrate flexibility are able to view through the perspectives of others. They are open-minded, tolerant of ambiguity, and envision a range of options and alternatives. They have regard for diversity and are willing to consider change.
4. *Craftsmanship:* People committed to craftsmanship strive for refinement, precision, elaboration, and mastery. Believing they can continually grow personally and professionally, they willingly pursue learning.

5. *Interdependence:* Holonomous people have a sense of interdependence. They seek collegiality and lend themselves to the achievement of group goals. They know that they benefit from participating with, contributing to, and receiving from others and society and do so willingly.

The findings of Liebmann (as cited in Costa & Garmston, 1994) "support the value of these five dispositions . . . as attributes of vital, effective, growing members of learning organizations" (p. 130). Whether professional development centers on improvement of instructional practices, development of curriculum, revision of assessment approaches, or other important teaching and learning initiatives, the learning of all involved is enhanced by an overarching focus on holonomy.

The result is the development of educators who are consciously more intentional about instructional decisions and demonstrate greater optimism and perseverance in the face of challenging goals and circumstances. There is the emergence of an improved ability to engage in creative problem solving and to view situations from the perspective of students, parents, and colleagues. Refinement and elegance in performance become sought-after outcomes, as does thoughtful self-monitoring of progress. Teachers place greater value on working together toward common goals and drawing on the resources of others. When holonomy is the overarching goal of professional development efforts, educators become more effective at teaching and learning, at participating in a learning community, and at contributing to the building of a self-renewing organization.

Creating a Systems Approach

A systems approach and the concept of holonomy feature an integration of parts and whole, a necessary connection among goals, people, departments, locations, programs, and resources so that both professional development and the daily business of schooling are built on a foundation of important interrelationships within the organizational culture. "The primary concept associated with school culture . . . is that of a system. A system is an entity comprising many elements or components that interact in a positive manner so that the system functions effectively" (Orlich, 1989, p. 172).

In a system, value is placed on the ways one teaching-learning theme is connected to another, how the selection of one small focused action can produce significant improvements, and how all parts of the system can be integrated to form a unified, dynamic whole. Senge (1990) addresses systems thinking and the development of a learning organization in this way:

> Systems thinking is a discipline for seeing wholes. It is a framework for seeing interrelationships rather than things, for seeing patterns of change rather than static "snapshots." . . . Systems thinking is needed more than ever because we are becoming overwhelmed by complexity. (pp. 68-69)

Systems interaction can either stimulate or retard learning (Orlich, 1989). Too often, staff development has been a series of episodic events, each of which may be of value but none of which fulfills the potential possible when framed within the greater scope of an interrelated system. "Because educational leaders typically have not thought systemically, reform has been approached in a piecemeal fashion" (Sparks, 1994, p. 27). The work of Senge, Roberts, Ross, Smith, and Kleiner (1994) vividly impresses upon us the value of systems thinking as we consider a learning organization and the capacity development of its members: "Learning in organizations means the continuous testing of experience and the transformation of that experience into knowledge—accessible to the whole organization, and relevant to its core purpose" (p. 49).

Thus, dynamic professional development capitalizes on a systems approach—the fact that any part of the system has significant effects on other parts. When viewed in this manner, professional development is far more than a series of topics or disjointed improvement efforts; it becomes a multifaceted process that is fundamental to the growth and self-renewal of the whole system. It serves as one of the most essential and vital elements of a learning organization's infrastructure, encompassing both individual and organizational development.

Ensuring Engagement of the Mind

Berliner views good teaching as thoughtful practice (Brandt, 1986). In his work identifying characteristics of expert teachers, he found that those who are expert think differently from those who are not. Expert teachers organize knowledge into meaningful structures, have strong pattern-finding skills, can process several sources of information simultaneously, and develop mental road maps. Of greatest significance is his finding that thought processes are behind sound instructional decisions and form the critical components of effective teaching (Costa & Garmston, 1994, p. 35).

Learning implies the ability to change mental models (Caine & Caine, 1993). Obviously then, for professional development to make a valuable impact, significant attention must be paid to the thinking that is related to teaching and learning. It is not enough to focus on new and more effective classroom practices or current innovations. Accompanying any such effort must also be an emphasis on teacher thought related to how, why, and when to apply new practices, as well as thinking about the diverse daily contexts in which the practices will be applied. According to Guskey (1994), "reforms in education today succeed to the degree that they adapt to and capitalize on the variability of complex and diverse contexts" (p. 43). In other words, the most effective professional development will be shaped by processes that encourage teachers to think about their own values, norms, structures, situations, and resources as they construct new paradigms, make choices, and determine actions.

In addition, a definite link exists between the thoughtful performance of teachers and the thoughtful performance of their students. As a result, there is a greater payoff for both teachers and students when time is given to the thought processes related to teaching and learning. The imperative that professional development engage the minds of teachers is underscored with exquisite simplicity by Glickman (1986):

> I believe that the development of teachers' ability to think about what they do should be the aim of [professional] development . . . and I

> believe that teachers who do not think for themselves will not be able to help students think for themselves. . . . Research is fairly conclusive that successful teachers are thoughtful teachers. . . . Furthermore, the research is clear that thoughtful teachers stimulate their students to be thoughtful. (p. 6)

Placing Importance on the Three Cs

Climate

To achieve results, professional development must be viewed as a process, not an event (Loucks-Horsley et al., 1987). When we plan an event, we pay great attention to the climate or ambiance that is to surround it. A process is continuous, however, and we often tend to give less attention to the climate we create for something that takes place over time than one we create for a single event. The effect of a positive climate on the success of professional development is too important to be taken for granted. The presence of three components greatly enhances the possibilities for positive learning: safety, regard, and trust.

Safety. MacLean's (1978) triune brain theory suggests that under perceived personal threat, the brain downshifts by resorting to deeply entrenched, primitive responses and moves into a "fight or flight" mode of survival, interfering with creativity and with the higher-level thinking functions that are crucial during learning (Hart, 1983). When people feel intimidated by the task or the environment, or feel that competence is at risk, the ability to construct new learning is greatly diminished. Positive social interactions and emotional well-being are critical to feelings of safety (Caine & Caine, 1991). A climate in which it is safe to be oneself, ask questions, challenge ideas, express differences, and experiment with new competencies is vital to the ability to learn and do the best thinking.

Regard. The *Thorndike-Barnhart Dictionary* (1983) defines *regard* as "showing thought, consideration, or esteem for" (p. 1742). This term describes an attitude that recognizes the worth of each person, a quality essential in professional development. The word *respect,* although seeming to reflect the same attributes, unfortunately is often a by-product of authority. *Regard,* on the other hand, appears to originate from a belief system that places true value on every person. When we experience regard as an element in the climate surrounding professional development, we all are treated in such a way that our uniqueness, individual styles, and prior knowledge are valued, thereby encouraging and motivating our learning and implementation efforts.

Trust. Professional development is ultimately a relationship among learners, and "trust is a vital element in all sorts of relationships" (Costa & Garmston, 1994, p. 36). Although safety and regard can be established rather quickly, trust is a relationship that develops through time. Trust takes many forms when applied to a professional development setting: trust in oneself as a learner, trust in fellow learners, trust in the environment, and trust in the whole process of professional development. A climate that promotes the development of trust also encourages inquiry, experimentation, and problem solving. Such an atmosphere nurtures the construction of personal meaning and pursuit of self-modification, the very essence of learning.

Constructivism

Engagement of the mind presupposes that we are involved in constructing our own new understandings as we continuously create and reconstruct knowledge. There can be no prescribed set of procedures or solutions transmitted to teachers because such an approach would imply that a generalized, decontextualized list would be good for all time and all situations (Peterson & Knapp, 1993). Within a constructivist model of professional development, teachers are regarded as individuals, not as duplications of a standardized ideal. Teachers build their own personal meanings and solve dilemmas encountered in their own ways. "Deep understanding occurs when the presence of new information prompts the emergence or enhancement of cognitive structures that enable us to re-think our prior ideas" (Brooks & Brooks, 1993, p. 15). A re-visioned professional development program founded on a constructivist philosophy is designed so that adult learners discover, internalize, reshape, and/or transform information by constructing their own new or revised cognitive structures.

Regrettably, successful implementation of what is learned as a result of professional development experiences is not accomplished as often as teachers would like. Implementation is far more likely to occur, however, when we engage in personal construction of the knowledge base needed to understand, embrace, and internalize conceptual shifts, especially when that knowledge base is contextualized within our specific situations. Building professional development programs on a constructivist foundation supports our construction of understanding and does much to increase the possibility of achieving successful implementation.

Collaboration

In reference to the previous discussion of holonomy, one of the five states of mind that acts as a catalyst for the development of holonomous behavior is interdependence. Although there are points in the learning curve when individual reflection and personal work are absolutely necessary, the most effective professional development acknowledges the deep need for interconnectedness with others and includes a balance between the thinking and learning work that is done individually and that which takes place with the support of colleagues. Lieberman and Miller (1991) refer to studies conducted by Little and Rosenholtz that develop convincing rationale for viewing teaching as collaborative work. Unfortunately, teachers frequently feel isolated and find it difficult to change their instruction and their approach to curriculum when they cannot have professional discussions with peers or when they are in the midst of uninterested colleagues (Wasley, 1991).

Although Little's (1982) findings substantiate that collegiality and experimentation are essential aspects of the culture of an effective school, Sergiovanni

(1992) contends that "the culture of most schools is characterized by norms of privatism and isolation, which keep teachers apart" (p. 88). There is, therefore, a tremendous need to create a more collaborative culture and strong sense of community in professional development endeavors. Experience has demonstrated that extraordinary results can be produced in social settings where educators engage in professional dialogue about new ideas, explore similar and contrasting perspectives with colleagues, gain insights from considering the thinking of others, and solve common problems and issues. Furthermore, collaboration in schools generates greater productivity in improvement efforts, resulting in significantly different learning opportunities for students (Joyce, 1990).

Of the many forms of collaboration, one of the most valuable is coaching. Change is relationship intensive and is nurtured by long-standing connections and commitments with colleagues. Coaching provides support during the risk-taking associated with change. Joyce and Showers (1983) view it as a critical component to successful implementation of new learning for teachers. One model of coaching in particular does much to foster collegial relationships. That model is Cognitive Coaching, a dynamic and growth-producing form of coaching founded on constructivist principles. Cognitive Coaching engages educators in a nonjudgmental process wherein "specific strategies are applied to enhance one another's perceptions, decisions, and intellectual functions" (Costa & Garmston, 1994, p. 2).

Despite its importance, collaboration is not easily accomplished. In addition to contextual limitations such as time, scheduling, and insufficient financial resources, educators themselves present a challenge. Many implementation efforts have failed because of the mistaken assumption that we naturally and automatically know how to work together effectively. Without established norms for collaboration that support collegial effort, existing habits of unskillful behavior become covert norms that may unintentionally produce a negative influence on implementation efforts. The following is an example of highly effective norms that facilitate collaboration (Baker & Shalit, 1994):

- Pausing to listen attentively and allow time for thinking
- Probing/inquiring with questions to promote thinking, personal connection making, and decision making
- Paraphrasing to acknowledge, summarize, and clarify individual and group ideas
- Putting ideas on the table and pulling ideas off the table to move the group forward and reduce blocking
- Paying attention to self and others to acknowledge multiple perspectives and differing beliefs and preferences
- Presuming positive intentionality to create a climate of trust
- Pursuing a balance between advocacy and inquiry to gain information and clarify positions

According to Fullan (1993), "without collaborative skills and relationships it is not possible to learn and to continue to learn as much as we need in order to be agents for . . . improvement" (p. 17). In schools that become places of professional development, it is known that teaching is a collective enterprise (Rosenholtz, 1989), and it is assumed that teachers will have stimulating, meaningful interactions with colleagues in supportive environments focused on improvement.

Stressing the Three Rs

Risking

Risk-free learning is an oxymoron because the act of learning implies some sort of change, and "to challenge the status quo is to take a risk" (Valencia & Killion, 1988, p. 4). "To change or to try something new means to risk failure, and that is both highly embarrassing and threatening to one's sense of professional pride" (Guskey, 1994, p. 44). It is a given that professional development can have no impact if those involved are unwilling to take the risk implicit in learning.

Establishing an expectation for risking in a professional development setting parallels what teachers expect of students in the classroom. Just as the most effective classroom programs support students in their learning risks, the most successful professional development encourages risk taking by providing a wide range of support options, determined by asking the adult learners to identify their own needs and the supportive conditions under which they would most like to work (Levine, 1985). It is therefore critical that professional development efforts address openly both the need to take learning risks and the provision of necessary supports that create a safe-to-risk learning context and experience.

Reflection

Real change takes place when educators act as reflective practitioners, have time to reflect on what they are learning, confront assumptions and ways of doing things, and solve problems presented by new information. Reflective practitioners value taking time to think about their work, about what they are doing and why, and about what they might do differently. The process of reflection requires learning what questions to ask, how to ask them, and what to do with the information that results from asking questions (Richert, 1991). Reflection facilitates the cognitive restructuring process required to integrate new learning with former habits and old patterns of thought (Oja, 1991) and offers the opportunity to fashion new knowledge and beliefs.

The act of reflection has certain important attributes: a focus on real problems, an action orientation, an investigation of multiple perspectives and courses of action, consideration of the consequences of actions, and the application of a spiral, rather than a linear, process (Hannay, 1994). There are also different types of reflection for different purposes (Killion & Todnem, 1991):

- *Reflection on action* after actions and thoughts are concluded
- *Reflection in action* while thinking and action is taking place

- *Reflection for action* to plan or prepare for the future

Even if individuals are not naturally reflective by nature, the practice of reflection is something that they can and need to learn. Quality professional development creates opportunities for reflection by committing time to the practice and by designing structures wherein reflection can be personalized, be centered on real concerns and issues, and take a dynamic rather than static form (Hannay, 1994). Acknowledging the need for variety in professional development, the most growth-producing formats demonstrate a balance between reflection engaged in by the individual and reflection that is a part of a collaborative process.

Research

Just as professional development is being redefined for the 21st century, so too is the view of *research* being modified and expanded. It cannot be argued that research should be used to inform effective practice; neither can it be disputed that those who might profit most from the research findings (the teachers) are often those for whom the research is least user-friendly. Malouf and Schiller (1995) document that "research knowledge only sporadically finds its way into educational practice, even when the research has produced substantial knowledge related to problems of real-world importance" (p. 414).

Perhaps the problem is that research models tend to disregard practice. "In all professions *except* teaching, practitioners are expected to interact with and contribute to the development of their profession's knowledge base" (Sagor, 1992, p. 3). Unfortunately, both research and practice knowledge can be problematic.

> Research knowledge ignores particularities of persons and places in order to be generalizable, but at the risk of applying to nothing in particular. Local knowledge is immediate and more tangible, but it can be incomplete and runs the risk of blind and rigid insularity. (Malouf & Schiller, 1995, p. 416)

It is important, therefore, to view research knowledge and practice knowledge as complementary systems, both necessary to the improvement of teaching and learning. Research should be used to inform teachers when making decisions but not used as required rules. According to Shavelson (1988),

> Professional competence lies in the translation of scientific theories and "facts" into practical, goal-directed actions. . . . Practice must involve the art of translating scientific knowledge into actions applied to novel situations, even constructing new knowledge on the spot from experience when surprising situations arise. (p. 6)

Inquiry is one process for blending research and practice knowledge. Educators improve by means of inquiry practices that are based on collecting and analyzing data, trying out new approaches, evaluating and modifying them, and then trying them again. The primary task is to translate what is being learned from inquiry to what happens in the classroom (Kent, Austin, & Kaufman, 1989).

Another process that is gaining increasing respect is that of action research. "In action research, teachers identify instructional problems, determine what current evidence is available for solving these problems, propose changes that might be more successful, implement changes, and finally, judge the success of their endeavors" (Glickman, 1986, pp. 15-16). There are two major guidelines: What is studied must concern the teaching/learning process and must also be within the teacher's scope of influence (Sagor, 1992). Action research is a powerful form of professional development and is central to the restructuring of schools (Holly, 1991). It is a process that redefines the teacher's professional responsibilities to include the role of researcher and

> is based on the assumption that school change is most effectively promoted from within by teachers themselves through careful and systematic study of their teaching practice. . . . This process results in an improved sense of professionalism and efficacy, and increases the likelihood that teachers will become change agents by increasing their role in decision making. (Bennett, 1994, p. 34)

One of the most important goals of professional development is to support enlightened decision making. Through reflective practice and inquiry-based action, teachers can use disciplined inquiry and action research to evaluate values and actions (Lieberman & Miller, 1991). "Educators should not go about blindly doing what research says. Rather, research . . . findings should be used as conceptual tools to enlighten decision making" (Sparks & Simmons, 1989, p. 126).

Making the Vision a Reality

"Effective organizations are characterized by a deep sense of purposefulness and a vision of the future" (Costa, 1991, p. 4). Re-visioning professional development is simple, but it is not easy to bring the vision to life. The simplicity of such a view lies in knowing that educators must do things differently if professional development is to be a continuing, relevant, and growth-producing experience that leads to more than insignificant changes on the periphery of practice. It is not easy because such an undertaking requires imagination, courage, limitless persistence, and a commitment to a process-oriented paradigm.

To bring the reality about, it is necessary to assume the responsibility for seeing that professional development is regarded as crucial and indispensable to the accomplishment of our central purpose: the preparation of students for a productive and contributing role in a changing world. We must embrace the belief that our work needs redefining to include not only *what we do* each day but also *how we learn* each day to improve our practice.

To support the reality calls for demonstrating that we understand "The Lesson of the Stone" by making professional development a deep, profound, process-based learning experience for both the individual and the organization itself. This can be accomplished by practicing what Morris (1994) calls "components of a successful mind-set" (p. 24):

- A clear conception of what we want, a vivid vision, a goal or set of goals powerfully imagined
- A strong confidence that we can attain our goal
- A focused concentration on what it takes to reach our goal
- A stubborn consistency in pursuing our vision, a determined persistence in thought and action
- An emotional commitment to the importance of what we are doing and to the people with whom we are doing it

Guided by a spirit of collegial interdependence that coexists with the valuing of individuals and their uniqueness, the advocacy of educators for a process-oriented approach is fundamental to dynamic professional development. Our confidence in the powerful results to be achieved by re-visioning professional development must be communicated to all members of school communities—students, teachers, administrators, parents, boards of education, businesses, and government officials. If such communication includes our passionate commitment to making adult learning and renewal a perpetual endeavor, the potential impact is limitless. As we make re-visioned professional development a priority in education, we also create the gift of an invaluable contribution to an improved future.

References

Baker, W., & Shalit, S. (1994). *Exploring norms and structures that enhance our working together to improve schools: A training syllabus.* Oakland, CA: Group Dynamics Associates.

Bennett, C. K. (1994). Promoting teacher reflection through action research: What do teachers think? *Journal of Staff Development, 15*(1), 34-38.

Bonstingl, J. J. (1992). *Schools of quality: An introduction to total quality management in education.* Alexandria, VA: Association for Supervision and Curriculum Development.

Brandt, R. (1986). On the expert teacher: A conversation with David Berliner. *Educational Leadership, 44*(2), 4-9.

Bridges, W. (1991). *Managing transitions: Making the most of change.* Reading, MA: Addison-Wesley.

Brooks, J. G., & Brooks, M. G. (1993). *In search of understanding: The case for constructivist classrooms.* Alexandria, VA: Association for Supervision and Curriculum Development.

Caine, G., & Caine, R. (1993, Fall). The critical need for a mental model of meaningful learning. *California Catalyst,* 18-21.

Caine, R., & Caine, G. (1991). *Making connections: Teaching and the human brain.* Alexandria, VA: Association for Supervision and Curriculum Development.

Cooper, M. (1991). Stretching the limits of our vision: Staff development and the transformation of schools. In A. Lieberman & L. Miller (Eds.), *Staff development for education in the '90s: New demands, new realities, new perspectives* (pp. 83-91). New York: Teachers College Press.

Costa, A. L. (1991). *The school as a home for the mind.* Palatine, IL: IRI/Skylight.

Costa, A. L., & Garmston, R. J. (1994). *Cognitive coaching: A foundation for renaissance schools.* Norwood, MA: Christopher-Gordon.

Darling-Hammond, L., & McLaughlin, M. W. (1995). Policies that support professional development in an era of reform. *Phi Delta Kappan, 76*(8), 597-604.

Fullan, M. (1993). *Change forces: Probing the depths of educational reform.* Bristol, PA: Falmer.

Glickman, C. D. (1986). Developing teacher thought. *Journal of Staff Development, 7*(1), 6-21.
Guskey, T. R. (1994). Results-oriented professional development: In search of an optimal mix of effective practices. *Journal of Staff Development, 15*(4), 42- 50.
Hall, G., & Loucks, S. (1978). Teacher concerns as a basis for facilitating and personalizing staff development. *Teachers College Record, 80*(1), 36-53.
Hannay, L. M. (1994). Strategies for facilitating reflective practice: The role of staff developers. *Journal of Staff Development, 15*(3), 22-26.
Hart, L. (1983). *Human brain, human learning.* New York: Longman.
Holly, P. (1991). Action research: The missing link in the creation of schools as centers of inquiry. In A. Lieberman & L. Miller (Eds.), *Staff development for education in the '90s: New demands, new realities, new perspectives* (pp. 133-157). New York: Teachers College Press.
Joyce, B. (with Bennett, B., & Rolheiser-Bennett, C.). (1990). The self-educating teacher: Empowering teachers through research. In B. Joyce (Ed.), *Changing school culture through staff development* (pp. 26-40). Alexandria, VA: Association for Supervision and Curriculum Development.
Joyce, B., & Showers, B. (1983). *Power in staff development through research on training.* Alexandria, VA: Association for Supervision and Curriculum Development.
Joyce, B., & Showers, B. (in press). *Student achievement through staff development: Fundamentals of school renewal* (2nd ed.). White Plains, NY: Longman.
Kent, K., Austin, J., & Kaufman, B. (1989). Continuous improvement: Context and support. In S. D. Caldwell (Ed.), *Staff development: A handbook of effective practices* (pp. 84-91). Oxford, OH: National Staff Development Council.
Killion, U. P., & Todnem, G. R. (1991). A process for personal theory building. *Educational Leadership, 48*(6), 14-16.
Koestler, A. (1972). *The roots of coincidence.* London: Hutchinson
Krupp, J. A. (1989). Staff development and the individual. In S. D. Caldwell (Ed.), *Staff development: A handbook of effective practices* (pp. 44-56). Oxford, OH: National Staff Development Council.
Levine, S. L. (1985). Translating adult development research into staff development practices. *Journal of Staff Development, 6*(1), 6-17.
Levine, S. L. (1989). *Promoting adult growth in schools: The promise of professional development.* Boston: Allyn & Bacon.
Lieberman, A. (1995). Practices that support teacher development. *Phi Delta Kappan, 76*(8), 591-596.
Lieberman, A., & Miller, L. (1991). Revisiting the social realities of teaching. In A. Lieberman & L. Miller (Eds.), *Staff development for education in the '90s: New demands, new realities, new perspectives* (pp. 92-112). New York: Teachers College Press.
Little, J. W. (1982). Norms of collegiality and experimentation: Workplace conditions of school success. *American Educational Research Journal, 19*(3), 325-340.
Loucks-Horsley, S., Harding, C. K., Arbuckle, M. A., Murray, L. B., Dubea, C., & Williams, M. K. (1987). *Continuing to learn: A guidebook for teacher development.* Andover, MA, and Oxford, OH: Regional Laboratory for Educational Improvement of the Northeast and Islands and National Staff Development Council.
MacLean, P. D. (1978). A mind of three minds: Educating the triune brain. In *The 77th Yearbook of the National Society for the Study of Education* (pp. 308-342). Chicago: University of Chicago Press.
Malouf, D. B., & Schiller, E. P. (1995). Practice and research in special education. *Exceptional Children, 61*(5), 414-424.
Morris, T. (1994). *True success: A new philosophy of excellence.* New York: Berkley.
Oja, S. N. (1991). Adult development: Insights on staff development. In A. Lieberman & L. Miller (Eds.), *Staff development for education in the '90s: New demands, new realities, new perspectives* (pp. 37-60). New York: Teachers College Press.
Orlich, D. C. (1989). *Staff development: Enhancing human potential.* Boston: Allyn & Bacon.
Peterson, P. L., & Knapp, N. F. (1993). Inventing and reinventing ideas: Constructivist teaching and learning in mathematics. In G. Cawelti (Ed.), *Challenges and achievements of American education: 1993 yearbook of the Association for Supervision and Curriculum Development* (pp. 134-157). Alexandria, VA: Association for Supervision and Curriculum Development.
Richert, A. E. (1991). Using teacher cases for reflection and enhanced understanding. In A. Lieberman & L. Miller (Eds.), *Staff development for education in the '90s: New demands, new realities, new perspectives* (pp. 113-132). New York: Teachers College Press.
Rosenholtz, S. (1989). *Teachers' workplace: The social organization of school.* New York: Longman.

Sagor, R. (1992). *How to conduct collaborative action research.* Alexandria, VA: Association for Supervision and Curriculum Development.

Senge, P. M. (1990). *The fifth discipline: The art and practice of the learning organization.* New York: Doubleday/Currency.

Senge, P. M., Roberts, C., Ross, R. B., Smith, B. J., & Kleiner, A. (Eds.). (1994). *The fifth discipline fieldbook: Strategies and tools for building a learning organization.* New York: Doubleday/Currency.

Sergiovanni, T. J. (1992). *Moral leadership: Getting to the heart of school improvement.* San Francisco: Jossey-Bass.

Shavelson, R. J. (1988). Contributions of educational research to policy and practice: Constructing, challenging, changing cognition. *Educational Researcher, 17*(7), 4-11.

Sparks, D. (1994). A paradigm shift in staff development. *Journal of Staff Development, 15*(4), 26-29.

Sparks, G. M., & Simmons, J. M. (1989). Inquiry-oriented staff development: Using research as a source of tools, not rules. In S. D. Caldwell (Ed.), *Staff development: A handbook of effective practices* (pp. 126-139). Oxford, OH: National Staff Development Council.

Spencer, S. A., & Adams, J. D. (1990). *Life changes: Growing through personal transitions.* San Luis Obispo, CA: Impact.

Thorndike-Barnhart dictionary. (1983). Chicago: Field Enterprises Educational Corporation.

Valencia, S. W., & Killion, J. P. (1988). Overcoming obstacles to teacher change: Direction from school-based efforts. *Journal of Staff Development, 9*(2), 2-8.

Vojtek, R. O. (1994). Twenty-five years in organization development: A conversation with Richard Schmuck and Philip Runkel. *Journal of Staff Development, 15*(1), 46-50.

Wasley, P. A. (1991). The practical work of teacher leaders: Assumptions, attitudes and acrophobia. In A. Lieberman & L. Miller (Eds.), *Staff development for education in the '90s: New demands, new realities, new perspectives* (pp. 158-183). New York: Teachers College Press.

6

Enhancing Transfer

Robin Fogarty

Introduction

Yes, process instruction enhances transfer. In fact, process instruction *is* transfer; it's what transfer of learning is all about. Process instruction turns a singular activity into a lifelong strategy; it changes an event into a meaningful framework, a set of dates into an era, and a string of words into a schema of thought. Process instruction is the difference between a novel study and a genre study, between a solitary element and a discernible pattern, between episodic learning and conceptual understanding. Process instruction is epitomized in the Chinese proverb, "Give a man a fish, and you feed him for a day. Teach a man to fish, and you feed him for a lifetime."

Now, that is not to say that when process is the content of instruction, there is no subject matter content. To the contrary, the subject matter takes on a different, yet crucial, role. The content becomes the vehicle for thought, communication, and craftsmanship. History, literature, mathematics, sciences, the arts, and technology become the vehicles that carry the skills, operations, and dispositions of process instruction. The content provides the organizing center for thoughtful, active, and purposeful learning. After all, the goal of transfer involves both the transfer of a conceptual knowledge base as well as the transfer of skills, operations, and dispositions.

Thus, we must teach students to fish in different waters and diverse cultures if we are to help them fish for a lifetime. As an accomplished pianist once commented, "You're really an expert when you are able to transfer your skill to any piano. It sounds silly, but it is the difference between a skillful performer and an expert performer." Just as pianos differ, experience in life differs, also. It differs with an unending string of challenges, changes, and the unknown, which is precisely why process instruction must drive the content. The processes go with us everywhere. They transfer to the myriad situations of life.

Students must be equipped not only with the *what* but also with the *how* to become productive problem solvers, mindful decision makers, and craftsmen of pride, with freedom to flex and feel the flow and efficacy.

Defining Transfer

Some are unequivocal about the definition of transfer. "If learning means reconstructing previous knowledge or skills, then it is indistinguishable from transfer. That is to say, no transfer—no learning" (Ben-Hur, 1994b, p. 1). "All learning is for transfer; all learning is transfer" (Fogarty, Perkins, & Barell, 1991, p. xi). Others define it a bit more didactically: Transfer means learning something in one context and applying it in another. For example, when people learn to drive a car, they can usually drive any car. This learning can be moved not only from one car to another but also to a different context, such as a self-haul rental truck. This type of transfer is known as *near, low-level transfer*—transfer that is almost automatic.

When the same people decide to enroll in flight school, some things from driving instruction, such as reading gauges, making judgments, and sequencing steps, automatically transfer. Yet there are many things about driving a car that just won't apply to flying a plane. Moving from the context of driving a car to the context of piloting a plane is considered *remote transfer.* It is not automatic. It requires, instead, mindful abstractions, and, in this case, further information and skill training.

Experts seem to agree about this natural dichotomy in the concept of transfer. The following list shows several researchers' terms for the two types of transfer.

Researcher	*Simple Transfer*	*Complex Transfer*
Fogarty (1989)	Simple	Complex
Wittrock (1967)	Near	Far
Joyce & Showers (1983)	Horizontal	Vertical
Perkins (1986)	Automatic	Mindful
Salomon & Perkins (1988)	Low road	High road
Hunter (1971)	Similar	
Beyer (1987)		Cued
Sternberg (1984)	Spontaneous	Guided and scaffolded
Feuerstein, Rand, Hoffman, & Miller (1980)	Practiced	Mediated

In addition, Gagne (1968) refers to the types of transfer as *vertical* and *horizontal,* and Glick and Holyoak (1987) refer to them as *general* and *procedural.* Although these are similar to the other words, this terminology lends itself to the discussion of content-oriented and process-oriented transfer. Content-oriented transfer, of course, concerns the use and application of a knowledge base, conceptual learning, principles, and laws, whereas process-oriented transfer manifests itself in the transfer of skills, operations, dispositions, and attitudes. Both are necessary; both are coveted; both can be shepherded and mediated with notable results.

Although it is important to be aware of the labyrinth of intricacies surrounding the issue of transfer, it is easiest to understand this concept in its most simplistic definition. Transfer is "portable" learning—learning that is relevant and applicable in diverse contexts.

Discovering the Theory Base

Historically, transfer seems to have evolved through three distinct phases. Perkins's (1986) Bo Peep theory represents the standard instructional practice: "Leave them alone and they'll come home wagging their tails behind them" (p. 25). In other words, teach the content and give students practice that is both immediate and spaced through time, and the transfer of learning is sure to follow. For example, by teaching students about the digestive system and giving them practice in recognizing, drawing, and labeling the elements of the digestive tract, it is presumed that this factual content information somehow transfers into relevant application. It may also be presumed that students who learn about the digestive system also somehow transfer the concept of systems, the art of scientific drawings, and the skill of sequencing, simply by working with the content. Although there is some possibility of the first presumption occurring as a result of varied practice, there is slim possibility of the second type of transfer occurring. Unfortunately, Little Bo Peep will most likely lose her sheep. In fact, the transfer is so lacking and so rare that transfer has become what Perkins calls the "black sheep" of education: If it doesn't work, if we can't seem to get the transfer we want, then let's just not talk about it.

Historically, it was believed that Latin, geometry, and the like train the mind. In the early 1900s, however, Thorndike (1903, 1906) and others presented convincing evidence that suggested that "training the faculties" did not transfer in generalized ways. Thus, they advocated learning that encompassed identical elements for the two situations. Training would be specific, and transfer would occur.

Diametrically opposed to that view, Polya (1957) advocated the position that a general, generic, heuristic approach to problem solving in math was the key to the transfer of learning in diverse settings. Here, the arguments for transfer from specific, similar contexts versus transfer from generalizable heuristics are cast. Unfortunately, buried within the embers of the fading controversy is one illuminating fact. Neither side—context-bound, specific training or generalizable principles and rules—shows overwhelming and convincing evidence of transfer.

Fortunately, the transfer embers, close to becoming forgotten ashes, have recently been stirred by the winds of curricular change. A number of voices are focusing on the transfer issue again, igniting sparks for discussion and careful scrutiny. Although the controversy surrounding "transfer-as-context-bound" or "transfer-as-generalizable" remains a somewhat unresolved issue, agreements about transfer of learning do show evidence of promise for the educational community.

Although teaching Latin does not seem to transfer for a more disciplined mind, it is now agreed that the reason for this may be that Latin has not been taught to cultivate transfer. And, although teaching general heuristics such as steps to math problem solving do not seem to transfer into steps to problem solving in the writing process (even though transfer had been expected), intricate and powerful implications have emerged from work in both areas.

In essence, current transfer researchers suggest that when teachers pay attention to transfer in contextual learning situations, transfer does occur. It also occurs when general, bare strategies are accompanied with self-monitoring techniques. In both context-bound teaching and a general heuristics approach, transfer must be mediated or shepherded.

Thus, there is Perkins's (1986) Good Shepherd theory that states that when transfer is provoked, practiced, and reflected on, it is fairly easy to get. With the Good Shepherd theory comes an increased interest in teaching and mediating for transfer (Feuerstein et al., 1980).

Discussing Mediated Transfer

In working with teachers in the area of shepherding transfer, Fogarty, Perkins, and Barell (1992) have found a simple framework to be helpful. It is called, for lack of a better term, the "three somes:" There are *somethings* that we *somehow* want to use *somewhere* (Figure 6.1).

Figure 6.1 illustrates that there are "somethings" to transfer. These include the more obvious things such as content, knowledge, principles, and conceptual learning, as well as the more universal processes that encompass the microskills, operations, attitudes, and dispositions.

Exactly where might this "something" transfer? Within the content? Across other subject matter lessons? Or into life situations? Determining the "somewheres" ahead of time, or anticipating future applications, also has an impact on the shape of the lesson.

Once the "somethings" are sifted out and the "somewheres" of transfer are targeted, the center of the diagram in Figure 6.1 illustrates the "somehows" or transfer options that are available. To get the desired transfer, Salomon and Perkins's (1988) reference to low-road, automatic transfer, and high-road, abstracted transfer suggests two mediation strategies for transfer, which they label *hugging* and *bridging*. *Hugging* means teaching to meet the resemblance conditions for low-road or automatic transfer. *Bridging* means teaching to meet the conditions for high-road transfer by mediating the needed processes of abstraction and connection making (Perkins & Salomon, 1988). Either way, simple

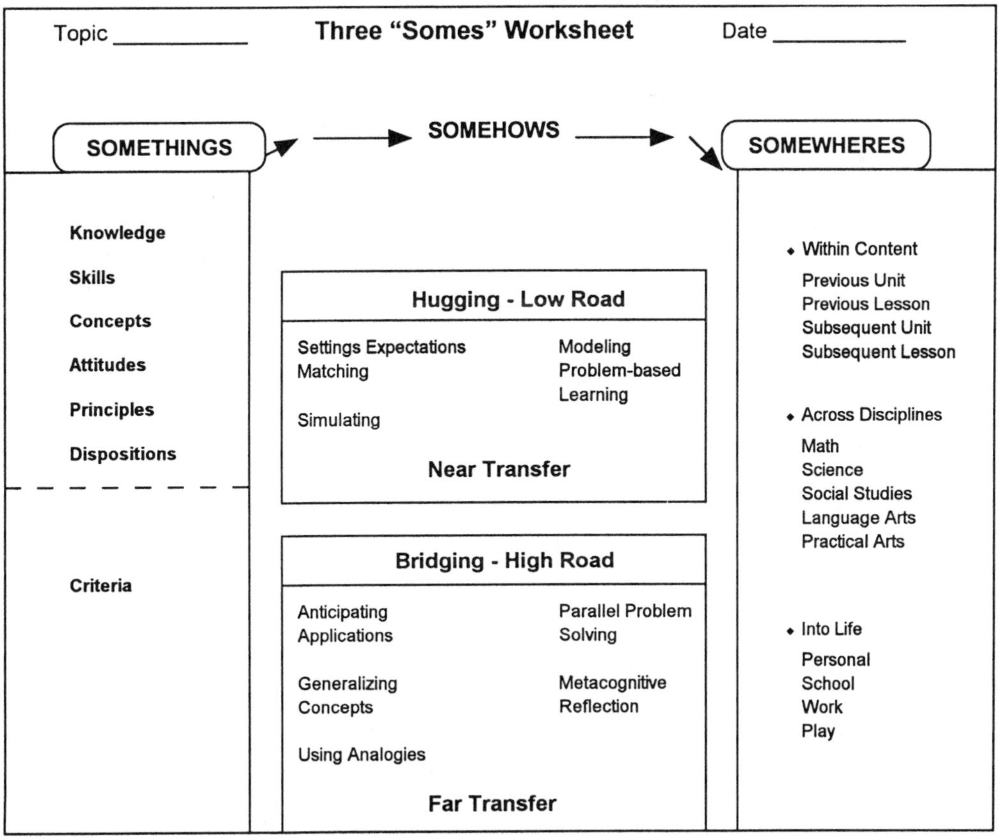

Figure 6.1. The Three "Somes"

SOURCE: From *The Mindful School: How to Teach for Transfer,* by Robin Fogarty. © 1992 by IRI/Skylight Training and Publishing, Inc., Arlington Heights, IL. Reprinted with permission.

hugging strategies of explicit mediation foster the transfer of learning. The difference in learning when transfer is targeted is dramatic.

In history class, the difference is between learning a bunch of dates and learning the bigger lessons from history, such as war strategies, economic trends, and political positioning; in math, the difference is between learning to compute by multiplying numbers and embracing the concept of multiplicity and transferring it to planning a vegetable garden; in science, the difference is between learning about the water cycle and learning about the concept of life cycles, such as photosynthesis and the cycle of locusts; in art, the difference is between learning about Picasso and cubism and learning about risk taking, originality, and criticism; in literature, the difference is between reading *The Old Man and the Sea* and understanding Hemingway's (1952) importance as an American voice of the time.

When transfer is shepherded and mediated, the bigger picture is revealed. With this enhanced view, learners are more likely to understand the overriding context and, in turn, move that learning to new and different contexts.

Describing How to Track Transfer

It follows that with this increased attention to transfer, there is also a focus on the results. Can transfer actually be tracked? One schema for scouting for transfer is depicted in Figure 6.2. This metaphorical model delineates whether transfer of learning is occurring.

Using the metaphor of birds, Figure 6.2 describes six situational dispositions, or levels of transfer: overlooking, duplicating, replicating, integrating, mapping, and innovating. As learners transfer, they move through the various levels. They may dip in and out of a level, or they may move sequentially through the levels, from the top of the chart to the bottom. Although most learners experience all levels at one time or another, depending on their past experience, prior knowledge, and propensity for learning the new ideas, each situation is different, and each learner is unique. The transfer or mediation for transfer varies accordingly.

To operationalize the model for tracking transfer, a T-chart format is employed. What does transfer look like? What does it sound like? How do we know it is occurring? Knowledge of transfer and its hypothesized levels creates conditions for it to occur.

Delineating the Effects

With definitions in hand and an understanding of transfer—what it looks like and how it works—the question of how process instruction enhances transfer leads to an intriguing analysis. Process instruction seems to enhance transfer in five distinct ways: It *decontextualizes* learning through generalizations, *crystallizes* learning for deep understanding, *recontextualizes* learning for purposeful use, *energizes* learning with active involvement, and *personalizes* learning for internalization.

Decontextualized Learning: What's the Big Idea?

Scenario: Prior to a lesson introducing the Periodic Table of Elements, the teacher deliberately targets the skills, operations, and dispositions of process instruction as well as the content to make explicit the relevance to students for later transfer.

Physics teacher: [Points to a dilapidated and yellowed Periodic Table of Elements hanging above the black lab table] You will be responsible for knowing the contents of this table.

Tim: [Rolls eyes and mumbles to himself] I'm never gonna use this stuff ever again. What a waste. How am I ever gonna memorize all this?

Physics teacher: Some of you are probably thinking, "When am I ever going to use this?"

Tim: [Sits up with a start, waiting for the punch line]

SITUATIONAL DISPOSITIONS FOR TRANSFER

Bird Model	Transfer Disposition	Looks Like	Sounds Like
Ollie the Head-in-the-Sand Ostrich 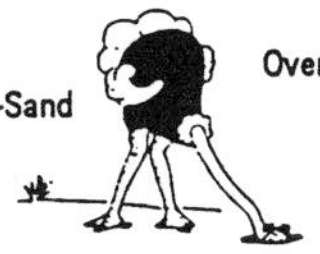	Overlooks	Persists in writing in manuscript form rather than cursive. (New skill overlooked or avoided.)	*"I get it right on the dittos, but I forget to use punctuation when I write an essay."* (Not applying mechanical learning.)
Dan the Drilling Woodpecker 	Duplicates	Plagiarism is the most obvious student artifact of duplication. (Unable to synthesize in own words.)	*"Mine is not to question why—just invert and multiply."* (No understanding of what she/he is doing.)
Laura the Look-Alike Penguin 	Replicates	"Bed to bed" or narrative style. "He got up. He did this. He went to bed." or "He was born. He did this. He died." (Student portfolio of work never varies.)	*"Paragraphing means I must have three 'indents' per page."* (Tailors into own story or essay, but paragraphs inappropriately.)
Jonathan Livingston Seagull 	Integrates	Incorporates newly learned French words into essay. (Applying: weaving old and new.)	*"I always try to guess (predict) what's going to happen next on T.V. shows."* (Connects to prior knowledge and experience; relates what's learned to personal experience.)
Cathy the Carrier Pigeon 	Maps	Graphs information for a social studies report with the help of the math teacher to actually design the graphs. (Connecting to another.)	From a parent: *"Tina suggested we brainstorm our vacation ideas and rank them to help us decide."* (Carries new skills into life situations.)
Samantha the Soaring Eagle 	Innovates	After studying flow charts for computer class, student constructs a Rube Goldberg type invention. (Innovates: invents; diverges; goes beyond and creates novel idea.)	*"I took the idea of the Mr. Potato Head and created a mix-and-match grid of ideas for our Earth Day project."* (Generalizes ideas from experience and transfers creatively.)

(Fogarty, 1994)

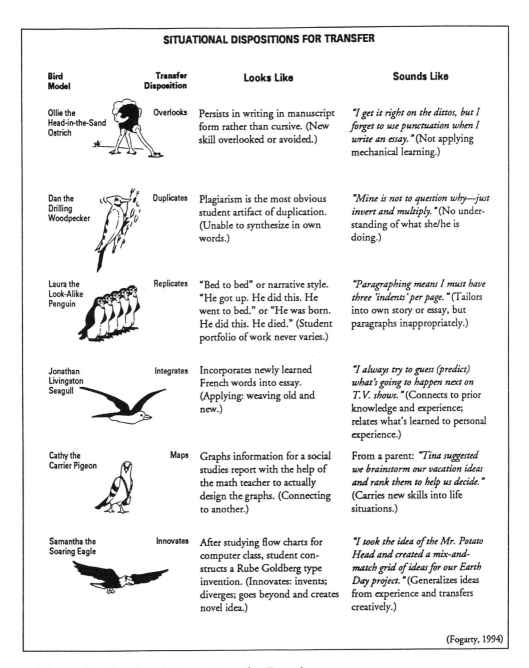

Figure 6.2. Situational Dispositions for Transfer
SOURCE: Fogarty, 1994, p. 293.

Physics teacher: Well, for those of you who are plotting a career using the sciences, it's quite clear that the scientific knowledge contained in the chart will be invaluable to you. But what about those of you who already feel that the sciences will not be a life pursuit? Let's talk a little about how learning this table might benefit you in other ways. Let's look at what might transfer for you besides the science content. Any ideas?

Renee: I was thinking that maybe the chart itself might serve as a model for gathering information. Grids and matrices are useful tools to organize data. I use them in social studies a lot.

Physics teacher: That's pretty perceptive. How many of you have used a matrix to sort or depict information? [Three hands go up] What else?

José: The symbols on the chart remind me of Greek letters and other symbols we use in math. So I guess the idea of decoding symbolic language may be useful in other situations.

Physics teacher: Quite so! I agree with you. The use of symbols is something we encounter throughout life. Just look at the international road signs. What else?

Rosa: Probably because I'm so involved in art, I think the thing that is most interesting—and maybe most universal for the future use of this Periodic Table of Elements—is the pattern in the chart. There are patterns in everything, and these patterns help us understand and remember things.

Tim: [Now sitting on the edge of his seat] Yeah—and I've been thinking, too. Just figuring out how these elements are related to each other might help me see connections in other things. Once I find a way to get this in my head, I'll be able to connect lots of things.

Physics teacher: I'm amazed at your ingenuity. Great thinking. Now, do we agree, at least mildly, that this Periodic Table of Elements is worth my teaching and worth your learning?

When process instruction becomes the content of instruction, transfer is enhanced because learning is decontextualized (Feuerstein et al., 1980); skills, operations, and dispositions are easily extracted from original contexts through generalizations and a focus on the "big ideas." Learning more readily targets relevant life skills as subject matter content becomes the vehicle for learning. For example, while studying about disease and the relationship to health and wellness, students learn the critical skills of cause and effect, comparing and contrasting, and drawing conclusions. The curiosity they experience drives continued and persistent inquiry, and they gain insight into the interdependence of all things. These are all processes they can take away with them. Knowledge, facts, and information are naturally the products of this learning, but perhaps more important, the students' tools of critical thinking are honed and their habits of mind begin to take shape.

Decontextualized learning "chunks" learning into discernible patterns that reveal universal attributes. These generalizable chunks are often mediated through analogies in which the generic pattern is uncovered and analogous ideas are slotted in, thereby chunking learning for future use (Perkins & Salomon, 1988). Decontextualized learning is fostered when process is the content because procedural learning is more neutral, or context free. For example, steps to problem solving are quite easily mediated toward generalizations that transfer to varied contexts: Solving a "tower problem" is a typical strategic problem-solving technique in which an analogous situation is recognized and the solution mitigated according to previously learned procedures.

Crystallized Learning: Diamonds Are Forever

Scenario: Teachers plan an interdisciplinary unit work to reframe it so the learning targets deep understanding and skillful transfer.

Ms. Whitney: I'd like to use Canada as the topic for our next unit. It would be easy to bring in a number of disciplines. What do you think?

Mr. Rodriguez: Instead of using Canada as our topic, why not use the idea of "neighbors to our north?"

Ms. Whitney: I like that, especially because the Mexico unit usually follows this one. We can easily dovetail the two. Get it? Our neighbors to the south!

Mr. Rodriguez: In fact, our study of both can focus on the concept of "neighbors."

Ms. Whitney: Yes! And we can target "communication" as a key to cultural understandings and to understanding our next-door neighbors, too.

Mr. Rodriguez: Wow! I'm really excited about these two units, now. It'll be so clear to the kids. By tying the units together with the concept of neighbors, the skills of communicating and getting along with others are crystallized.

Ms. Whitney: Yep! They'll have these skills forever.

When process instruction becomes the content of instruction, transfer is enhanced because learning is crystallized. It is understood, as previously discussed, that skills, operations, and dispositions are taught through the vehicle of subject matter content. Students think well, with skill and grace and rigor, when they have something to think about; they work collaboratively and exemplify team skills when they are engaged in a project that requires cooperation; and they organize information when they have an abundance of data to manipulate. Thus, if students work with the subject matter content in wholesome, project-oriented instruction, in which these very processes are the focus and transfer of learning, all learning is crystallized. Not only is content learning enhanced and deepened, but the processes, skills, operations, and dispositions are, in turn, crystallized (Ben-Hur, 1994a).

In essence, understanding is deepened as students induce learning from specific situations and subsequently apply it and use it in other situations. For example, as students are immersed in a problem-based learning scenario concerning Columbus's voyage and the near mutiny on board, they use skills of analysis, conflict resolution, responsibility, and leadership, as well as generate ideas. Also, they learn about the historic moments, the concept of exploration, and the implications of the event. Not only do they gain insight into the knowledge base of the subject matter under scrutiny, but also they gain insight into the processes that undergird the learning of that knowledge base.

The crystallization of ideas elaborates, or "fattens," the ideas, and, at the same time, the crystallization process distills or "narrows" the learning until it is "crystal clear." Process instruction provides an opportunity for this crystallization to occur both in the use of skills, operations, and dispositions and in the extrapolation of the knowledge base itself.

Recontextualized Learning: When Am I Ever Gonna Use This?

Scenario: By asking students to think back to an experience or to project ahead to a possible application, the teacher helps students recontextualize the learning with a focus on a worthy disposition or habit of mind.

Literature teacher: In *The Old Man and the Sea,* Hemingway [1952] presents an impressive characterization of a man who perseveres against tremendous odds. Take a moment to think back to a time in your life when you used your willpower to stick to something and see it through. [Pauses for a minute or two of silence] Now, share your stories with a partner.

Dennis: [Turning to Louisa] Once, when I was really little, I climbed a tree, and when I was trying to get down, I slipped and ended up clutching on to this branch. I had to hold on really tight for a long time while my brother went to get the ladder. It seemed like forever.

Louisa: I remember once when I forced myself to finish my social studies project because it was due the next day. I had to paint this salt-and-flour relief map. It was a lot of fun when I started—but boy did I get sick of it. I think that was hard to do—just like the old man's struggle with the marlin.

Literature teacher: Now, go to your logs and think to the future. Write a sentence or two about how this ability to persevere will help you in another class. For example, when will persevering help you in math class or in the science lab? Be specific. Target an upcoming assignment for another subject area that is going to take a lot of willpower and "stick-to-itiveness" to get it done. Try to think about how you can use this persevering attitude in other places. See if you can transfer it to another subject.

Rodney: [Writes the following in his log] The algebra problems are really hard for me, right now. If I don't give up so easily—if I stick to them longer, like the old man—maybe I can get through them.

Recontextualizing learning involves moving learning from one context to a new context. When process instruction becomes the content, transfer is enhanced as the skills, operations, and dispositions become portable as they are carried from one situation to the next and as they are recontextualized into meaningful application and use.

Recontextualized learning often requires mediation toward future applications (Feuerstein et al., 1980). Recontextualization, however, once realized, prolongs episodic learning; it generates relevant connections and ensures the longevity of learning. Recontextualized learning is a necessary step in transfer. It is the moment of meaning that occurs as the learners intentionally or unintentionally use skills, operations, and dispositions in similar or novel contexts.

One example of recontextualizing learning involves mindful abstraction, or bridging, of learning (Perkins & Salomon, 1988). A group of middle school students are expected to use "argument and evidence" to write a persuasive speech. The content of the argument, open to personal choice, encompasses issues of politics, economics, human rights, and the environment. Although the content of each speech is certainly one focus of importance, the process of arguing and providing evidence to support the argument is another critical focus of learning.

Although the content of the arguments may have transfer power, argument and evidence as an analysis technique is a highly portable process. Argument and evidence moves easily to proofs in math, to hypotheses and conclusions in science, to court cases in government class, and even to artistic criticism in literature class. Argument and evidence is recontextualized in each. Although the recontextualization of argument and evidence may require some mediation to move from science to math to literature, the process appears to have universal qualities that expedite transfer through recontextualization. In summary, recontextualized learning guarantees that the learning lives on—that it survives in other forms, tailored to the new context.

Energized Learning: Beyond Pour and Store

Scenario: Struggling with the challenge of inert learning, one teacher appeals to his principal with an idea to energize his lessons.

Mr. Jefferson: [To his principal] What would you think of starting a school newspaper?

Miss Thorpe: Hmm. I hadn't really thought about it. Tell me more.

Mr. Jefferson: Well, I'd like to energize the writing by making it more significant.

Miss Thorpe: Yes, a school paper does give purpose to student writing.

Mr. Jefferson: I could team up with Ms. Jacobs in the computer lab to produce a quality product that we'd be proud of.

Miss Thorpe: Actually, I've been looking for a way to communicate with parents. This might serve several purposes.

Mr. Jefferson: It would certainly motivate my kids; it's the catalyst we need.

Miss Thorpe: Let's do it! Let me know how I can help.

Process instruction enhances transfer because it fights the inert knowledge syndrome; it shifts from the pour-and-store model of learning the facts, data, and information of subject matter content to the dynamics of process instruction itself. It shifts toward the fluid use of skills, the management of operations, and the fueling of dispositions as students use, apply, and transfer these behaviors to varied and relevant situations.

Energized learning moves learners from the "nobody taught me" refrain to the idea that they are the "generation of information and thereby can be engaged in the processes of discovery and creativity" (Ben-Hur, 1994a, p. 30). Energized learning is epitomized in process instruction because the *how* is highlighted, rather than (or along with) the *what*. Students are led into active engagement in the steps and procedures of accomplishing something, rather than merely knowing of that something's existence. Inert knowledge, passive learners, and docile thinkers are instructional concerns that seem to disappear when process becomes content and is energized with action (Bransford, Sherwood, Vye, & Riser, 1986). For example, process instruction energizes learning even in the simplest of illustrations. Reading a chart of information and memorizing it for later recall form inert knowledge. Taking a survey, analyzing the results, and charting the data, on the other hand, constitute energized learning. The first scenario dictates passive learning, whereas the second creates active involved learning; one is content focused, the other is process focused.

When learning about coins in a process-oriented manner, youngsters are involved in using them to purchase items in their classroom store. Not only are the students cognizant of the value of the coins and why they are used, but also they are immersed in a simulation of appropriate use. Students are immersed in sets of skills and various operations—problem solving and decision making—as well as the employment of the dispositions of efficacy and interdependence. The dynamics of the interaction become as important as the content of the interaction. Learning is fluid and flexible and changing. It is activated and energized with vigor. Process instruction lends power to learning because students use their capacities for action and involvement.

When process instruction energizes the learning into powerful, dynamic, and ever changing ideas, transfer is, in turn, enhanced. Once learning is in motion, it moves easily from one situation to the next. Process instruction, by its very nature, is mobile; it moves skills, operations, and dispositions into diverse circumstances. In summary, process instruction is energized learning, and energized learning is portable, transferred learning.

Personalized Learning: Gotcha!

Scenario: One teacher personalizes a lesson about the Revolutionary War by bridging it to the lives of her students.

Ms. Talbot: Let's label the strategies that the colonists used when they were in conflict with their mother country.

Lupe: One thing they did was throw the tea overboard.

Ms. Talbot: Yes. That strategy is called violence or revolt.

Tony: Some colonists left. They moved west toward the frontier to escape the unrest.

Ms. Talbot: That might be called avoidance.

Susie: The colonists refused to buy the tea because of the tax.

Ms. Talbot: Right. That would be considered boycotting. Now, let's personalize these strategies. Pretend you hate to eat peas, but your mom insists on giving you a large helping of peas. You are now, similar to the colonists, in conflict with your mother. Think about the strategies you might use.

Jim: I'd throw a temper tantrum—my own personal riot.

Ms. Talbot: That would be the revolt strategy of violence.

John: I'd go to my room and pout.

Ms. Talbot: That might be called avoidance.

José: I'd wait her out. I'd hope the phone would ring and that she'd get preoccupied. Then I could sneak out.

Ms. Talbot: Oh! A boycott! Notice how the strategies of conflict resolution are similar in historical contexts and in personal situations.

Process instruction enhances transfer because it personalizes learning. As the focus shifts toward skills, operations, and dispositions as content, students grasp the universal aspects and at the same time adapt the processes to a personal style. For example, while students learn a generic methodology for problem solving, each develops a set of procedures particular to his or her own problem solving. One student may examine both sides by comparing and contrasting ideas, whereas another may prefer to gather multiple solutions before analyzing any of them.

Personalization is simply the way to fingerprint the technique or series of techniques that seem to work best for each individual. It is the unending tailoring necessary for students seeking the perfect fit for productivity and progress in their own endeavors. The personalization process is critical to the enhancement of transfer because it helps learners internalize learning in deeply significant and personally relevant ways.

The personalization process builds individuals' capacities not only for relevant, immediate transfer but also for long-term use. This allows learners to tap into their resource banks throughout their lives. Learners are better able to recall and initiate appropriate behaviors if and when they are tagged with a personal reference point or telling label.

The skill of prediction may be labeled by some persons in their repertoire of strategies as "guessing" or "intuiting" outcomes on the basis of gut feelings. Others may refer to the same microskill of prediction as "forecasting" and rely in personal ways on the analysis of information to make predictions. Although differences between the two are subtle, they do, however, suggest the powerful role of personalization in the transfer process.

Process instruction, when more fully personalized, moves from tacit, implicit behaviors to aware, explicit actions. The tailoring process fosters metacognition (Brown, 1978). By understanding one's personal interpretation of craftsmanship as a feeling of pride in the completed task, the individual is more likely to explicitly transfer that disposition to multiple situations in life. For example, pride in craftsmanship may occur early in life. An individual may create a model airplane and have craftsmanship reappear later in a more abstract form of pride in a well-crafted argument.

Delivering the Power of Process Instruction

In summary, process instruction enhances transfer in a number of subtle ways. In what Glick and Holyoak (1987) call general schemata, process instruction *decontextualizes* learning through generalizations. It also *crystallizes* learning by deepening understanding. In yet another view, process instruction fosters transfer by *recontextualizing* learning through meaningful applications. It *energizes* learning and fights inertia through active involvement, and it *personalizes* learning through adaptations and tailoring.

Process instruction, as discussed extensively in this trilogy, is a key to enhancing transfer. After all, when we ask ourselves, "What will kids need to know and be able to do 25 years from now?" we are asking what learning needs to transfer into their adult lives. Without a doubt, they will need to know how to think, how to get along with others, how to solve problems, and how to make mindful decisions. At the same time, it seems that learning about learning, adopting a posture of inquiry, acquiring a sense of efficacy, and achieving a conscious state of flow (Csikszentmihalyi, 1990) are also desirable goals for learners. To achieve those goals, we must push them to the edge:

> Come to the edge, he said.
> They said: We are afraid
> Come to the edge, he said.
> They came
> He pushed them . . . and they flew.
>
> *Guillaume Apollinaire, cited in Ferguson, 1980, p. 293*

References

Ben-Hur, M. (1994a). *On Feuerstein's instrumental enrichment: A collection.* Palatine, IL: IRI/Skylight.

Ben-Hur, M. (1994b, December). *Thoughts on teaching and transfer.* Paper presented at IRI/Skylight Consultant Conference, Chicago, IL.

Beyer, B. (1987). *Practical strategies for the teaching of thinking.* Boston: Allyn & Bacon.

Bransford, J., Sherwood, R., Vye, N., & Riser, J. (1986). Teaching thinking and problem solving: Research foundations. *American Psychologist, 41*(10), 1078-1089.

Brown, A. L. (1978). Knowing when, where, and how to remember: A problem of metacognition. In R. Glaser (Ed.), *Advances in instructional psychology* (Vol. 1, pp. 77-165). Hillsdale, NJ: Lawrence Erlbaum.

Csikszentmihalyi, M. (1990). *Flow: The psychology of optimal experience.* New York: Harper & Row.

Ferguson, M. (1980). *The aquarian conspiracy: Personal and social transformation in the 1980s.* Los Angeles: J. P. Tarcher.

Feuerstein, R., Rand, Y., Hoffman, M. B., & Miller, R. (1980). *Instrumental enrichment.* Baltimore: University Park Press.

Fogarty, R. (1989). *From training to transfer: The role of creativity in the adult learner.* Unpublished doctoral dissertation, Loyola University of Chicago.

Fogarty, R. (1994). *The mindful school: How to teach for metacognitive reflection.* Palatine, IL: IRI/Skylight.

Fogarty, R., Perkins, D., & Barell, J. (1991). *The mindful school: How to integrate the curricula.* Palatine, IL: IRI/Skylight.

Fogarty, R., Perkins, D., & Barell, J. (1992). *The mindful school: How to teach for transfer.* Palatine, IL: IRI/Skylight.

Gagne, R. M. (1968). Learning hierarchies. *Educational Psychologist, 6*, 1-9.
Glick, M. L., & Holyoak, K. J. (1987). The cognitive basis of knowledge transfer. In S. M. Cormier & J. D. Hagman (Eds.), *Transfer of training* (pp. 9-46). San Diego, CA: Academic Press.
Hemingway, E. (1952). *The old man and the sea.* New York: Scribner.
Hunter, M. (1971). *Teach for transfer.* El Segundo, CA: TIP.
Joyce, B., & Showers, B. (1983). *Power in staff development through research and training.* Alexandria, VA: Association for Supervision and Curriculum Development.
Perkins, D. (1986). *Knowledge as design.* Hillsdale, NJ: Lawrence Erlbaum.
Perkins, D., & Salomon, G. (1988, September). Teaching for transfer. *Educational Leadership, 46*(1), 22-32.
Polya, G. (1957). *How to solve it.* Princeton, NJ: Doubleday.
Salomon, G., & Perkins, D. (1988). Rocky roads to transfer: Rethinking mechanisms of a neglected phenomenon. *Educational Psychologist, 24*(2), 113-142.
Sternberg, R. (1984, September). How can we teach intelligence? *Educational Leadership, 42*(1), 38-48.
Thorndike, E. (1903). *Educational psychology.* New York: Lemke & Buechner.
Thorndike, E. (1906). *Psychological review.* New York: Appleton-Century-Crofts.
Wittrock, M. (1967). Replacement and nonreplacement strategies in children's problem solving. *Journal of Educational Psychology, 58*(2), 69-74.

7

New Technologies

New Learning?

Timothy Melchior
Gwen Gawith
John Edwards
Michael Keany

Consider this recent experience of a high school principal. In the morning, as the principal walks the school hallways, he finds a junior seated on the floor by his locker with a notebook computer on his lap. When the principal questions him about sitting in the hallway, the student explains that he uses the hallway outlet near his locker to save his battery. He is writing a persuasive essay for his English teacher after extracting and copying some statistics from a program in the school's Writing Center. When he finishes, he needs to use some CD-ROMs for his course work and then review some SAT vocabulary using a computer program in the Media Center. He then cavalierly says to the principal that in the afternoon, he plans to access the Internet. While he sits in the hallway, he is thoroughly focused on the 6-pound marvel in his lap.

The Context for a New View of Curriculum

Sophisticated, new technologies are now common in schools, and their educational potential is extraordinary. Decades ago, the promise of technology caused major corporations to forecast their management of schools and even their control of the school's curriculum, but this revolution never came to pass in the form in which it was cast.

Ironically, although there have been many attempts to bring about change in education, new technologies are now driving major changes in schools, especially in instruction and curriculum. Why? Because new technologies firmly challenge traditional instructional practices, such as teaching as telling and learning as remembering, and because teaching and learning now take place increasingly by means of technology both in the school and in the home.

Today, it has even become common to believe that technology is the end and not the means. In addition, the highly sophisticated entertainment and design features of new technologies, as Postman (1985, 1992) and Roszak (1986) argue, can be not only informative but also manipulative of human brain functions.

New technologies pose highly complex challenges for educators. As a result, educators must familiarize themselves with the new technologies, understand their implications and limitations, and, above all, teach their students how to use the new technologies to enhance the quality of their learning.

Thornburg (cited in Betts, 1994) makes this basic point:

> To me, technology's not the driving force for education. If we allow technology to be the engine, we're going to end up being quite disappointed. We make a mistake if we just bring a bunch of technology into a room and then think that an excellent educational program is going to materialize. We need to look at the child and base our decisions on how kids learn. (p. 22)

Technological and Information Literacy

A central question needs to be examined. Is technology the artifact or the process? The term *technology* tends to be used as a catchall for the media, the machines, *and* the cognitive processes that make use of the technologies. Papert (1993), the creator of LOGO, writes about "the potential synergy of two trends in the world":

> One of these trends is technological. The same technological revolution that has been responsible for the acute need for better learning also offers the means to take effective action. Information technologies, from television to computers and all their combinations, open unprecedented opportunities for action in improving the quality of the learning environment, by which we mean the whole set of conditions that contribute to shaping learning in work, in school, and in play. (p. viii)

Papert continues, "The other trend is epistemological, a revolution in thinking about knowledge. . . . The powerful contribution of the new technologies in the enhancement of learning is the creation of personal media capable of supporting a wide range of intellectual styles" (pp. viii-ix).

Papert is suggesting that we should question the traditional view of curriculum as the sum total of learning experiences provided for the child, and he calls for a new and more effective focus. "It is often said that the world is entering the information age. This coming period could equally be called the age of learning." (Papert, 1993, p. viii)

A more effective focus in Papert's age of learning is a curriculum that addresses how, not what, children learn and how new technologies can assist in this effort. Here the focus is no longer on students' learning by being immersed in what educational technology can provide but rather on students' developing information literacy, which is directly related to processes, such as how students find, use, select, reject, and interpret information critically.

Two types of literacy are required: technological literacy and information literacy. The former is learning to operate the machine; the latter is learning to use and interpret the information to which the machines provide access. In essence, what technology and information imply for learning should be the focus for all curricular decisions and for all instructional design.

Gibbon (1987) highlights the importance of information literacy:

> The principal addition to the curriculum called for by the arrival of the Information Age is a new emphasis on information itself. Students must learn to analyze critically its various forms and their characteristic uses, to recognize the ways in which opinion and behavior can be influenced by information, to search out needed information from the multiple sources available, to evaluate the quality of information, and to use the various media for effective communication. (p. 3)

New technologies are pervasive, especially personal computers (PCs). Students everywhere have access to sophisticated media and software, and they are learning keyboarding, computer applications, spreadsheets, word processing, programming, and other computer functions. Indeed, many students are more technologically literate than many of the faculty members who teach them.

In addition, today's students, in their schools and in their homes, have access to global information networks. Access to these networks, so rich in information, presents students and their teachers with new sets of complex problems. For example, when students had access to two or three sets of print encyclopedias, the need to discriminate and make decisions was not great. But when students can easily access five laser discs, three databases, and hundreds of periodicals on CD-ROMs, the challenge is both what to select and what to reject. Rejecting information has not been a traditional focus in education. This is one of a number of new process skills that students will need in the learning age. Kay (1991) states:

> In the near future, all the representations that human beings have invented will be instantly accessible anywhere in the world on intimate, notebook-size computers. But will students be able to get from the menu to the food? Instant access to the world's information will probably have an effect opposite of what is hoped: Students will become numb instead of enlightened (p. 100).

Some Questionable Assumptions

One pervasive myth is that the technologies themselves teach important, complex skills, but process skills and thinking skills are not acquired by osmosis from machines. They need to be identified, taught, modeled, and reinforced by capable teachers. A second myth is that the more sophisticated the media, the more sophisticated is the thinking that has gone into its development.

There are also questionable assumptions about information. It is easy to assume that information is the answer, that information is enough, that better answers are provided through more information, and that more information means more learning. Information, however, simply is not the answer to better learning.

Another assumption is that teachers teach better than the technology, such as PCs. What are the educational limits of PCs and their software? This provocation can be examined in this way. In 1950, Alan Turing (see Johnson, 1986, p. 44), the famous British mathematician, posed the Turing test, which raised the question of whether or not a computer could think. He proposed a test conducted by a judge who communicated by Teletype with a human and computer, in separate rooms, both hidden from the judge's view. The judge's task was to discern which was which, but if the judge could not tell the difference, the answer would be self-evident.

A new form of the Turing test would put a teacher and a computer in separate rooms and have the judge discern in which room resided the teacher. The implicit questions for the judge to explore are these: What are the instructional differences between a teacher and a computer? What can a teacher provide that a computer cannot? These questions present complex issues for educators.

As an illustration, courses of study traditionally have been content based, but computer software can provide the same information in a readily accessible and, at times, richer and more interesting format. In addition, this software can be accessed 24 hours a day by modem. It is a tireless, unemotional resource that is student responsive, student controlled, and more educationally economical because it demands no salary, no benefits, and no negotiations. Teachers can see a computer system either as a tough instructional competitor or as an empowering educational ally. Therefore, teachers need to differentiate between those things that humans do well and those better facilitated by technology. Simply stated, teachers can and must free themselves to work more creatively and productively with their students by giving up those things better done through technology.

The image underpinning traditional curriculum is of a whole class working on teacher-directed learning. The real joy of educational technologies is that they allow a rich variety of interactions between learners and machines, so now teachers can and should design learning opportunities that acknowledge the open-ended, learner-driven nature of the encounter between learners and machines.

There are two bottom lines implied here. One, teachers now have no choice but to be mediators of the learning environment because they cannot successfully compete with the computer as a resource for delivering data, information, and even concepts and for building routinized skills. Two, control of the traditional curriculum is going, going, gone. Teachers, departments, schools, and school districts can no longer control curricula as they have in the past. With the growth of technology, the teaching of specific, prescribed courses of study that are textbook driven and that are based on course outlines sitting on administrators' shelves with a concomitant emphasis on content and information is no longer viable.

Once students are empowered to pursue personal, enriched learning experiences, the curriculum becomes divided in myriad ways. A powerful conceptual and process core remains, and this needs more definition and focus from teachers.

Process Skills for the Learning Age

Research, for example, Brumby (1982) and Perkins (1992), has shown that current schooling facilitates the ability to regurgitate large masses of information and little else. Although learning taxonomies, such as that of Bloom (1956), mention many of the processes that are important, few of these objectives have been translated into educational practice (Goodlad, 1984).

For teachers to facilitate learning by their students of necessary process skills requires that the teachers have both technological and information literacy that embodies a mastery of the new skills required and an understanding of skill acquisition. As Dreyfus and Dreyfus (1986) point out, novices rely on rule-governed behavior. To move beyond this state of operation, students must amass their own personal, practical knowledge (Butler, 1994). The secret for teachers is first to provide students with the support and structure needed in the early stages of skill acquisition and then to provide them as well with the process skills and freedom to learn for themselves.

Many process skills needed are already taught in schools, but they are not necessarily taught directly, much less consistently, through a common vocabulary combined with adequate development and reinforcement. Some process skills that do not receive strong emphasis in many classrooms at the present time include these:

Process skills for selecting and using information

- Knowing when and how to select and reject data and information
- Being able to place information along a continuum ranging from so-called hard objective data to opinion or even rumor
- Being able to use flexibly a range of communication media, as well as the ability to translate from one to another
- Forming mental concepts or images of things not experienced from electronic data
- Asking powerful questions and recognizing that different questioning strategies elicit different qualities of response/information

Metacognitive process skills

- Applying modern learning theory and brain theory to learning how to learn
- Overcoming impulsivity
- Learning to make thinking processes more explicit through reflection
- Learning self-analysis combined with peer analysis of work rather than relying on teachers for such analysis

Process skills for personal management of thinking

- Applying both generalizable and domain-specific thinking skills, including creative, lateral, generative, critical, and logical approaches
- Turning data and information into knowledge by analyzing, synthesizing, and interpreting
- Accepting that there is more than one definition of a problem and more than one solution
- Learning to tolerate ambiguity and lack of certainty (Melchior, 1994b, 1994c),
- Moving from polarities, such as yes/no and right/wrong, to continua (Melchior, 1994a)
- Learning to interact with and use the ideas and thinking of others

These process skills need to be set within range of important contexts such as the ethical dimensions of knowledge, the social skills for generating and sharing knowledge, the attitudinal skills to facilitate learning and sharing, and an appreciation of the balance between knowledge and ignorance in human functioning. Needed are students with the knowledge and process skills to use technology as a tool, rather than unskilled students trying to use it as a crutch.

Gawith (1992) uses the term *cognitive technology* to encompass the mental means whereby students are taught to form mental concepts and harness their experience to imagine and create a future world for themselves. Imagination is crucial in such development. "Technology becomes a human means by which imagination is harnessed to truly flexible, interactive, responsive reading, thinking, problem solving, writing, and learning." (p. 8)

Designing Curriculum for Learning

Although education professionals may be quite knowledgeable about methods and models of teaching (Joyce, Well, & Showers, 1992), we have barely explored models of learning. We currently function with learning models that emphasize exposure to information and concepts and practice in routinized skills. A challenge for teachers is to explore the implicit assumptions and theories that underlie the current practices. This needs to be accomplished within a context that acknowledges the challenges, potentials, and limitations of a technology-enriched curriculum.

> I believe that if we are to have new forms of learning, we need a very different kind of theory of learning. The theories that have been developed by educational psychologists and by academic psychologists in general are matched to a specific type of learning—the school type. As long as these ways of thinking about learning remain dominant, it will be hard to make a serious shift from the traditional form of school (Papert, 1993).

Schools tend to overemphasize the value of information and misunderstand the subtleties and complexities of learning. Although information can be provided by humans and/or machines, it is what people accomplish with the information that counts. By itself, information is inert. Although computers may sort, categorize, and classify information, they do not create concepts. What people do with information is what matters, and that often involves functioning without clarity and certainty. As de Bono (1994) says, "Analysis of information will allow us to choose from among our standard ideas but will not create new ones. Information by itself is not enough. It is only concepts that give value to information" (p. 219).

An undue emphasis on information also raises ethical issues, such as the production of information collages from CD-ROMs. Recently one of us, as an exercise, wrote a 68-page article on Burkina Faso, a newly emerged African nation. The article contained maps and charts, comparisons of economic indicators, and information on culture, religions, and political systems. The article was reviewed by faculty members and judged to be an effective, comprehensive article. Yet the author put it together electronically in 38 minutes and acknowledged that he knew little more about the country than when he had begun. Such abuses of the technology are emerging in the proliferation of academic publications that are mixes and matches of previous publications. This practice is already evident in schools in which students have ready access to educational technologies.

Traditional lesson plans remain teacher driven, a whole set of experiences planned to meet the needs of individual children. Typically, they do not tap the rich cognitive potential that can come from effective use of technologies, yet trawling the Internet does not necessarily get one very far. Therefore, teachers are crucial as facilitators of targeted use of technology. This involves teaching the process skills, modeling their uses, and helping students design their own learning and harnessing their cognitive skills to the technological opportunities to meet learning objectives that are important to them. Simply stated, it is designing learning, not lessons.

Important Issues for Teachers

One challenge for teachers is that many individuals, students and adults alike, desire information, answers, and certainty. The computer as an information processor fulfills this need. The danger is that technology-based schools can mindlessly feed this mind-set. Educators can lose sight of the meaning of the word *educate*—to lead out—and replace it with a reverence for information and technological systems that minimizes the importance of human thought and the human condition. Care must be taken that students remain aware that the human brain is a biological entity and that the computer is a machine and a surrogate resource for the human brain.

In addition, a strength of human thinking is that it is ultimately driven by perceptions and concepts that often lack clarity, certainty, and adequate information. As Searle (1984) cogently argues, a computer can simulate student thinking but cannot duplicate it. Similarly, the neuroscientist Gazzaniga (1992) maintains that neural tissue, not technology, "feels" the world and that consciousness or "felt states" demand that humans see, talk, share, and desire to understand and learn. Machines do not.

Another issue is related to this same challenge. Many individuals believe that clarity through thinking is a linear progression, a gradual escape from ignorance and confusion, and that the solution for most problems resides in the availability of adequate information. Information, however, is driven by and filtered through beliefs, values, needs, and concepts and is rarely pure. Therefore, information has a context, and the implicit assumptions about information and its alleged objectivity need to be questioned. Unfortunately, students often blindly pay obeisance to information, and they are especially vulnerable in a technological age. Teachers need to be aware of these complex issues and to teach accordingly. Rudduck (1991) offers a view of the current situation:

> Many teachers during professional training have not acquired the intellectual tools they need to view knowledge as problematic. Many pupils find it hard to conceive of questioning adults after years of regarding knowledge as something that lies between the covers of the textbook or that exists in the teacher's mind. In short, the classroom has not generally been an arena for the exercise of critical thinking. (p. 34)

Conceptual growth comes in stages, and it includes dissonance and confusion. Students and teachers do not grow conceptually unless existing perceptions and concepts are challenged and unless they spend time wallowing in the domain of uncertainty. They need to see confusion as a positive means for cognitive growth because most issues in life are filled with ambiguity.

Sternberg (1993) recently posed the question of whom you would rather captain your starship, Kirk or Spock. Or whom would you rather teach your child? The two answers to this question (Kirk, the humanistic, flexible, best-intentioned leader, or Spock, the cool, supremely logical, computerlike humanoid) beg for a third answer, a combination of both.

And so it is with schools. We need Kirk, the teacher, and Spock, the computer. The metaphor is complete when we remember that Spock is a member of Kirk's staff—a resource for Kirk's planning, problem solving, decision making, exploring, and designing. Therefore, Kirk is an appropriate symbol for the teacher. The teacher is aware of available resources and how to use them, is aware of issues and objectives, and plans ahead for the mission of the Enterprise.

And what is the teacher's mission? It is not just to teach information and concepts and develop fundamental skills but, more important, to help students to manage ambiguity, to grow conceptually from concrete to abstract thinking, and to understand what and how they are learning.

The question is how to achieve this. Student understanding is not simply a matter of taking in information with clarity. Many students will not naturally become more abstract conceptualizers and more effective, more critical, and more creative thinkers. Growth in abstraction, thinking, and understanding requires student-teacher interactions through time, combined with conceptual explorations and development, inquiry, applications, transfer, and tasks that require students, as Perkins (1993) says, "to perform in a variety of thought-demanding ways" (p. 29) with a topic, situation, or provocation.

As de Bono (1993), Perkins (1993), and Edwards (1994) contend, if teachers want students to grow in these dimensions, direct instruction in process skills, thinking skills, conceptualizing, and understanding must be regularly provided and reinforced. Research on the teaching of thinking, such as Edwards's, suggests the great potential in teaching students to think directly rather than as a by-product of learning academic disciplines. This raises the fundamental issue of how teachers can facilitate the infusion of these skills, once learned, throughout the curriculum (O'Brien, Stapledon, Edwards, & Diamond, 1994). Therefore, teachers, like Kirk, need to be problem solvers, decision makers, and, above all, mapmakers who help the students orient themselves to their unknowns, explore new territories, and use and exchange information about their learnings, their realities, their hopes, and their fantasies.

We can conceive new models of learning on the basis of what we have learned from how computers operate, what they can and cannot do. Computers are programmed to have direction and move in the direction of clarity, not ambiguity. As de Bono (1969) long ago argued, only the human brain can deliberately change perceptions, change patterns, invent concepts, and tolerate ambiguity. This view is supported by Papert (1993), who says, "The basic kind of thought is intuitive: Formal logical thinking is an artificial, though certainly enormously useful, construct: logic is on tap, not on top" (p. 167).

Although it may be comforting for teachers to know that a computer expert such as Papert sees the limitations of logic and of the computer, the challenge for teachers is to know how to tap the strength of both teachers and computers and to build appropriate bridges. Teachers also need to be aware of the limitations of logic and to learn how to teach new thinking tools, process skills, and learning models.

The many new foci for teachers suggested here have strong implications for teacher training and retraining. For experienced teachers, much of this will develop naturally from their felt needs in the face of new technologies. Changes in both areas will require time and understanding. Changes also require a supportive political climate based on an awareness in the community of the need for continuing change in schools and teacher training institutions. To be done effectively, this needs both appropriate funding and support from business and the wider community.

In Summary

Our professional challenge as educators is to give students the information and technological literacy skills to make the best possible use of technology. Because we do not fully appreciate the power of the children or the technology, we tend to focus on information and the technology as the end, not the means. We need to help students explore the power of their own minds and celebrate the human condition and human learning.

The bottom line is that computers, computer networks, and sophisticated technologies are changing and challenging schools for the better. Education has come a long way from the time when individuals such as Abe Lincoln wrote ciphers on the back of a coal shovel by the fire. In today's schools, it would be impossible for Abe to become a Westinghouse scholar without the use of computers and related technology. New technologies abound in schools, and they will continue to grow in value as a major instructional resource. They present educators with many challenges because they provide new freedoms for both students and teachers and because they open up the curriculum. The new age of learning is on an inexorable march because it is a new freedom for both teachers and students, and as we have seen in the latter part of the 20th century, freedom just seems to have a tendency to prevail.

References

Betts, F. (1994). On the birth of the communication age: A conversation with David Thornburg. *Educational Leadership, 51*(7), 20-23.

Bloom, B. (1956). *Taxonomy in cognitive domain: A classification of educational goals.* New York: David McKay.

Brumby, M. (1982). Medical students' perceptions of science. *Research in Science Education, 12,* 107-114.

Butler, J. (1994). From action to thought: The fulfillment of human potential. In J. Edwards (Ed.), *Thinking: International interdisciplinary perspectives* (pp. 17-22). Melbourne, Australia: Hawker Brownlow.

de Bono, E. (1969). *The mechanism of mind.* New York: Simon & Schuster.

de Bono, E. (1993). *Teach your child how to think.* New York: Penguin.

de Bono, E. (1994). *Parallel thinking: From Socratic thinking to de Bono thinking.* London: Viking.

Dreyfus, H. L., & Dreyfus, S. E. (1986). *Mind over machine.* New York: Free Press.

Edwards, J. (1994). Thinking education and human potential. In J. Edwards (Ed.), *Thinking: International interdisciplinary perspectives* (pp. 6-15). Melbourne, Australia: Hawker Brownlow.

Gawith, G. (1992). Imagination technology. *English in Aotearoa, 18,* 7-12.

Gazzaniga, M. (1992). *Nature's mind: The biological roots of thinking, emotions, sexuality, language, and intelligence.* New York: Basic Books.

Gibbon, S. Y. (1987). Learning and instruction in the age of information. In M. A. White (Ed.), *What curriculum for the information age?* Hillsdale, NJ: Lawrence Erlbaum.

Goodlad, J. (1984). *A place called school: Prospects for the future.* New York: McGraw-Hill.

Johnson, G. (1986). *Machinery of the mind: Inside the new science of artificial intelligence.* New York: Times Books.

Joyce, B., Well, M., & Showers, B. (1992). *Models of teaching* (4th ed.). Boston: Allyn & Bacon.

Kay, A. (1991). Computer networks and education. *Scientific American, 265*(3), 138-148.

Melchior, T. (1994a, July). *Counterpoint thinking: Connecting learning and thinking in schools.* Paper presented at the Sixth International Conference on Thinking, MIT, Cambridge, MA. (Published 1995 in *Inquiry: Critical Thinking Across the Disciplines, 14*(3), 82-90, by the Institute for Critical Thinking, Montclair State University, Upper Montclair, NJ)

Melchior, T. (1994b). The disparate nature of learning or team teaching is not enough. In S. Dingli (Ed.), *Creative thinking: A multifaceted approach* (pp. 67-79). Msida: Malta University Press.

Melchior, T. (1994c). What is an effective thinker? *Cogitare, 8*(1), 1, 3 (Newsletter of the ASCD Teaching Thinking Network). (Reprinted 1994 in *In Transition, 11*(3), 28, by the New York State Middle School Association)

O'Brien, J., Stapledon, A., Edwards, J., & Diamond, P. (1994). An implementation of CoRT-I, -IV and -V in a large secondary school. In S. Dingli (Ed.), *Creative thinking: A multifaceted approach* (pp. 51-66). Msida: Malta University Press.

Papert, S. (1993). *The children's machine: Rethinking school in the age of the computer.* New York: Basic Books.

Perkins, D. (1992). *Smart schools: From training memories to educating minds.* New York: Free Press.

Perkins, D. (1993). Teaching for understanding. *American Educator, 17*(3), 8, 28-35.

Postman, N. (1985). *Amusing ourselves to death: Public discourse in the age of show business.* New York: Penguin.

Postman, N. (1992). *Technopoly: The surrender of culture to technology.* New York: Knopf.

Roszak, T. (1986). *The cult of information: The folklore of computers and the true art of thinking.* New York: Pantheon.

Rudduck, J. (1991). *Innovation and change: Developing involvement and understanding.* Milton Keynes, UK: Open University Press.

Searle, J. (1984). *Minds, brains, and science.* Cambridge, MA : Harvard University Press.

Sternberg, R. J. (1993). Would you rather take orders from Kirk or Spock? The relationship between rational thinking and intelligence. *Journal of Learning Disabilities, 26*(8), 516-519.

8

Using Technology to Combine Process and Content

Stanley Pogrow

I resent the debate on whether the focus of curricula should be content or process. This is the wrong question. It is as wrong to focus on process as content as it has been wrong to focus on content as content. Educators need to get out of the either/or mentality. Today, education needs a far more sophisticated conception of curriculum that simultaneously combines both process and content in a highly synergistic fashion. We need to figure out ways to systematically use a process approach to teaching and learning that actually increases the learning of content—both new and traditional forms of content. The best state-of-the-art curricula should be designed not only to develop new skills but also to produce even higher levels of traditional skills and outcomes.

It is, of course, much more difficult to design curricula that can produce both process and content learning. This chapter reports on a new, process-oriented, technology-based approach to curriculum that appears to do a more effective job of teaching content, even as it changes students' perceptions of the content and increases problem-solving skills.

Introduction

Most conceptions of how to use visual technology such as computers involve either direct presentation of information or use as a tool to enable students to do something. Examples of direct presentation are computer-assisted instruction

(CAI) and integrated learning systems (ILS) approaches. An example of use as a tool is word problem processor software. This chapter will describe a new approach to using computers—Learning Drama, a process approach to using computers that is designed to teach content more effectively.

I first developed the Learning Drama approach 16 years ago as the basis for a new type of program for students who are educationally disadvantaged that was a pure thinking skills approach. All supplemental drill was eliminated, and the students were treated as though they were bright students attending an expensive private school. This program, which has come to be known as HOTS (Higher Order Thinking Skills), has spread to 2,000 school in 49 states. HOTS, a process approach to developing thinking skills, has spread because of its ability to simultaneously increase problem-solving skills, social confidence, and standardized test scores for educationally disadvantaged students. It has also been able to increase cooperative problem-solving skills and standardized test scores in gifted students.

Although HOTS is a process approach to developing general thinking skills in educationally disadvantaged students, the Learning Drama approach is now also being extended to the development of math problem-solving skills for all students. My staff and I have spent the past 6 years extending Learning Drama techniques to develop a 2-year mathematics curriculum with the support of the National Science Foundation. This 2-year curriculum, called SUPERMATH, starts with arithmetic and extends into algebra. This is the first application of Learning Drama techniques to teaching content from a process point of view. SUPERMATH is currently being piloted with a wide variety of students ranging from gifted to educationally disadvantaged. The goals of SUPERMATH are to simultaneously increase math content knowledge, math problem solving, and interest in math.

This chapter will describe Learning Drama techniques and report findings from large-scale research experiences. The findings suggest that the techniques form a powerful process learning environment capable of producing a wide variety of cognitive gains—including even higher levels of content learning. And, because many of the ideas on how to develop the Learning Drama approach came from research on the effective conditions for instructional television, the conclusions are applied to the use of any visual media.

The Conventional Curricular Approach to Using Computers

Research is disclosing little overall effect from the use of computers under conventional approaches to using them with educationally disadvantaged and other students beyond the third grade and finds that computers may even widen learning gaps.[1] Conventional approaches to using software rely on its explicit content goal to produce learning. For example, to teach students how to calculate and use averages, the teacher would use software explicitly designed to provide practice in that content goal. Such software would be expected to independently increase the students' knowledge of calculating and using averages. The only curricular concern would be to coordinate the use of that software with the learning objective of the school's content. This is usually referred to as integrating computers into the curriculum.

CAI and ILS approaches to using computers use the explicit goal of software to teach content. Although CAI is usually associated with drill and practice, the new computer tools, such as word processors, spreadsheets, and simulations, generally end up being used as CAI because the goal of the software is expected to produce content learning. Word processors are expected to increase students' writing ability, and a simulation of chemical titration is expected to enhance students' knowledge of the specific chemical reactions that are modeled. Content learning is presumed to occur when students successfully use the software.

The belief that successful use of software can produce substantial amounts of learning has so dominated the use of computers since their inception that there are virtually no articles on alternative curricular approaches to using them. If one believes that computers can enhance learning by simply integrating software into the curriculum, there is no need or incentive to rework the curriculum or change instructional approaches. Nor is there any reason to develop alternative, more sophisticated, curricular approaches. Unfortunately, integrating literal content uses of software into the curriculum has generally failed to help students who are educationally disadvantaged—except at the earliest grade levels. Nor has there been any evidence that the use of word processors has enhanced the quality of writing.

There are also logistical problems with relying on the explicit goal of software. First, the approach is simply not practical. Matching software goals to the ever increasing number of curricular objectives and negotiating with all the different vendors are logistical nightmares. The more objectives that students need help with, the worse the logistics. At the same time, ILSs, which do incorporate a wide range of objectives, are expensive and are built largely around prosaic activities.

The second problem is that literal use of software misunderstands the fundamental learning problem when it is applied to students who are educationally disadvantaged. CAI and ILS incorrectly assume that the fundamental learning problem of educationally disadvantaged students is that they have not internalized specific content concepts because they have not had enough practice using them. The explicit goal approach of using software assumes that providing additional computer-based practice increases the chances that the concepts will be internalized. Experience with the HOTS program has determined that the root cause of the learning problems of educationally disadvantaged students in grades 4 to 7, however, is probably something else—inadequate metacognitive skills. (A simple definition of *metacognition* is the ability to consciously apply and test strategies when solving problems and engaging in normal thinking activities such as reading comprehension.) As a result, although explicit content goals of software can probably provide some useful help in the earliest grade levels with simple concepts that need to be memorized, such as multiplication tables, it is of little value in developing more complex concepts later on.

The use of tool software has not been successful either. The call to "use the computer as a tool" is about as useful as giving someone a hammer and saying, "Use this tool to build a house." Obviously, if someone knows how to build a house, the hammer will help. If someone is an accomplished writer, a word processor will help. Someone who is not accomplished at cognitively demanding tasks will receive little benefit from direct use of a computer tool. In addition, even if a more sophisticated use of a tool or simulation program does provide experience in a process approach, such occasional experience is not likely to produce any substantial change in problem-solving ability.

Approaches to using computers that depend on the literal goal of software cannot substantially enhance cognitive functioning. CAI, ILS, and tool approaches, which have the potential to be process based, can help only those students who already spontaneously construct linkages and understandings, that is, those students who already have high levels of problem-solving skills.

A Learning Drama Approach to Using Software

The Learning Drama approach to using computers combines two of the oldest pedagogical traditions, Socratic dialogue and drama, with the newest forms of technology and learning theory. These elements are combined via a highly detailed and creative curriculum and intensive teacher training.

The six key characteristics of Learning Dramas are as follows:

1. Instead of using the goal of the software to teach concepts, the learning occurs indirectly from the process of engaging in special conversations developed around dilemmas encountered while learning to use the software. The explicit goal of the software has nothing to do with the content that is taught or learned.
2. There is virtually no discussion of technical issues about how to use software. Students are expected to figure that out on their own from textual clues. Discussions focus on ideas designed to develop key thinking skills.
3. Dramatic techniques are used in the lessons to heighten the students' curiosity and motivation.
4. The activity has to engage the students; failure to use content or strategies appropriately has negative consequences from the point of view of the students.
5. There is a rich and systematic discussion environment for a significant portion of each period. The questions that teachers ask in the curriculum are designed in accordance with key principles from cognitive psychology.
6. Teachers are trained how to systematically probe student answers in a Socratic manner to produce understanding. (Socratic questioning is teaching by asking questions as opposed to teaching by presenting information.)

In Learning Dramas, the explicit goal of the software is viewed only as a motivator or a visual setting to entice the students' interest and provide them with something they want to achieve. The explicit goal is an interesting objective for students to achieve. Learning, however, comes from building Socratic conversations around other aspects of the software. Words and concepts in the menus, instructions and activities on the screen, and dilemmas encountered while trying to develop a strategy for successful use of the software provide opportunities to invent questions and sophisticated, interactive conversations that enable students to practice key thinking or skill activities—regardless of whether such questions help students achieve the goal of the software.

As students use the software, issues arise related to the processes of using the software. These can be talked about and summarized as "using the computer as a metaphor for life." Much as parents use life experience to engage their children in conversation about the events of the day, Learning Dramas use the process of learning to use software as an opportunity to talk about ideas. Instead of parents asking, "What happened in school today?" the teacher asks, "What happened when you tried your strategy of guessing middles to find the missing creature?" In both cases, student answers set the stage for follow-up probing.

The dinner table conversation of parents produce major gains in cognition. How is that possible, given its ad hoc nature that it takes advantage of life's events as they occur as opposed to a preplanned linkage to formal content or even formal learning objectives? It appears that the sustained and consistent process of communicating about ideas and problem resolution produces a wide variety of social and cognitive benefits, if such conversation is oriented toward the development and questioning of ideas.

Learning Dramas do the same. They involve continuing, sustained conversations between the students themselves and students and teacher about what they see happening around the process of using software. Specific content objectives are built indirectly into these discussions. Situations are created in the curriculum wherein it is important to talk about the content as a means to resolve a dilemma in trying to use the software successfully.

Suppose, for example, that a teacher wanted students to learn how to calculate and use averages. Instead of using software designed to teach how to calculate an average (a CAI or ILS approach), a teacher using a Learning Drama approach finds a piece of software of interest to the students and around which a situation could be created that would require the use of averages. Any program that produces a numerical score and requires the use of a strategy can be used. The Learning Drama scenario is as follows:

> Teachers would tell the students: "Yesterday, you got some good scores but also some poor ones. That means that you were guessing. If, on the other hand, you have a good strategy, you will get good overall scores." After students played the game a few times, teachers would then tell students: "An *average* tells you how good your overall score is and, therefore, how good your strategy is." Teachers would then quickly show students how to calculate an average and have students go back to playing the game. Thereafter, the teacher would discuss with students whether their averages were improving and what strategies they were using to get better averages.

Tying the content objective of calculating an average to an interesting problem-solving activity using software intended to "teach" something else seems to produce greater understanding and retention with just a small amount of discussion than continued CAI or ILS practice with software whose explicit goal is to teach how to calculate an average. In addition, as students read clues and talk about their strategies, they are practicing reading comprehension and metacognition, developing their reading and thinking skills even as they are learning content.

In HOTS, the questions can arise from textual clues or the need to resolve information on the screen. In SUPERMATH, the computer is used to present either a setting around which dilemmas arise or a setting that provides a mental model for some reasoning task. A mental model is a way of thinking. Conversations are developed, and content is introduced around the resolution of the dilemmas or on how to extend the mental model to solve mathematical problems. Examples of each will be provided in the curriculum section later in this chapter.

To produce substantial amounts of learning, however, the conversations cannot just be talk for the sake of talking or thinking for the sake of thinking. To produce a variety of cognitive gains, as well as content learning, the conversations have to model key thinking skills in a consistent way. In addition, like the conversations of parents, these conversations have to be sustained during an extended period. Unlike the conversations of parents, however, the conversations cannot be completely ad hoc because specific learning and problem-solving objectives are desired. A detailed curriculum is needed to maintain the consistency of the conversations. In addition, a model of how to probe student answers needs to be developed, and a teacher needs to be trained in how to Socratically probe student responses. Indeed, it is the probing behavior of the teacher (or parent) that determines whether the conversation is a problem-solving process or a lower-level exercise.

For the Learning Drama approach to work, all the above elements must be in place. The following sections describe how the curriculum is designed.

Designing Learning Dramas to Develop General Thinking Skills

To develop general thinking skills for the HOTS program in ways that were likely to transfer to overall academic and emotional growth for Chapter 1 students, information processing theories of cognition suggested that the following key cognitive operations were the ones on which to focus:

Metacognition: Consciously applying strategies to solve problems

Inference from context: Figuring out unknown words and information from the surrounding information

Decontextualization: Generalizing ideas from one context to another

Information synthesis: Combining information from a variety of sources and identifying the key pieces of information needed to solve a problem

Learning Dramas turn these concepts into fun for both the students and teacher. The curriculum develops these thinking skills in the following ways.

Metacognition is produced by constantly asking students what strategy they used for solving a problem. This includes how they knew the strategy was a good one, what strategies they found that did not work, how they could tell if they did not work, and how they could predict what a better strategy might be (and to try it), and so on.

Inference from context is initiated in two ways. The first technique is to have students read interesting stories on the computer that combine text with graphics. Teachers then heighten student involvement by introducing the setting of the story in a dramatic fashion—such as warning the students that they will encounter many dangers in the story. The dramatic element builds high levels of engagement—a prerequisite for thinking to take place.

The story chosen must also have words in key places that students do not understand. (It does not matter which words or whether the words are in the students' regular curriculum.) Students are then told that every time they come to a word they do not understand, they should (a) write down the sentence in which it appears, (b) circle the word, and (c) call the teacher over and make a guess about what the word means. They are also told to make a prediction of what will happen next in the story. (Twist-a-Plot stories are best.) The next day, the teacher lists the sentences on the board and asks students to explain what they think the circled words mean from the reading and pictures and why they think that. The conversations begin, and student answers are probed. These rich conversations model prediction comprehension processes that good readers spontaneously engage in and provide experience in information synthesis and metacognition, as well as in inference from context.

The second technique for inference from context is to build inference questions around unknown or ambiguous words in the instructions. Teachers constantly ask students to figure out what the unknown words mean, along with the strategy they used for figuring it out. The visual clues make it easier initially for students to build up confidence in their inference skills. Inference then becomes a normal part of learning how to use any piece of software.

Decontextualization occurs in two ways. The first is by using words in the software that students are familiar with from their everyday experience and having them make predictions about what they are likely to do in the context of that program. For example, the graphics program Dazzle Draw has a menu choice called *flood fill.* Students are asked to predict what will happen if they make that choice on the basis of what they know about the word *flood.* Students then go to the computers to test their predictions. (*Flood fill* fills an area of the screen with the color they chose.)

The second, and more powerful, decontextualization technique is the use of a series of concepts that are discussed across many contexts (software programs). For example, perspective is discussed when flying a hot-air balloon, when writing a story from the perspective of an object when using a word processor, and when discussing how a character in a computer-based story is viewing a given situation. Students are then asked about how the use of the content in the current piece of software is the same and different from its use in the prior program(s).

Information synthesis occurs by creating situations in which students have to use information from a variety of sources, or several different types of information, to answer a question. Curriculum is developed by taking a piece of software that will be of interest to students (games and adventure stories are always good) and inventing a series of questions that will provide practice in the above cognitive processes and that will link to concepts discussed around other pieces of software. For example, in the popular simulation Oregon Trail, the explicit goal is for students to reach Oregon along the old Oregon Trail that pioneers used. Students have to budget food and supplies appropriately to make it safely through a variety of problems such as attacks, bad weather, and floods that the computer throws at them.

The curriculum will pose such questions as, "From what perspective are you looking at the wagon?" (decontextualization of the use of *perspective*), "What could the *yoke* of an ox be?" (inference from context), "What strategy did you use to reach Oregon?" (metacognition), and "Is anyone who traveled the trail alive today?" (information synthesis). These questions are incidental to the goal of reaching Oregon. They are based on words or phrases in the instructions. The questions are asked to initiate discussions that provide practice in the four key thinking skills. The quality of discussions about the answers to these questions is far more important to the learning process than is the quality of the software or successful use of the software. (Indeed, the newer, technologically jazzy version of Oregon Trails is not as good for Learning Dramas as is the old, black-and-white classic version.[2]) This focus on discussions around tangential questions that model key thinking processes distinguishes Learning Dramas from CAI or ILS.

Although using the explicit intention of technology to create a setting around which to invent other types of learning seems counterintuitive, the success of this approach has also been demonstrated by Dr. John Bransford (1989) at Vanderbilt University. He used laser disc technology to show a segment of Indiana Jones jumping across a pit (i.e., to set an interesting visual context that was familiar to students), followed by a discussion of the physical forces and mathematics that make such an act possible. He found that using technology to provide visual settings to set a context for a follow-up discussion was a more effective way to teach math than using the technology, or even one-on-one instruction, to teach the math.

Learning Dramas must have drama that engages and intrigues the students. Thinking cannot be developed unless students are absorbed in the task. In Learning Dramas, teachers often wear costumes, tell jokes, and so on. In addition, much as a good stage drama involves the audience in the situation and emotion of the story and characters, teachers create situations to get students emotional about the tasks in which they are involved. Such emotion deepens the learning process.

Every piece of software has unintended uses that a clever curriculum can use to construct dramatic situations. For example, in a popular program called Wordmaster, students have to turn a pointer to match words on the screen. Students must match words quickly to win. A word on the bottom indicates the matching rule. The intended CAI/ILS use of the software is a vocabulary drill and practice program.

In the Learning Drama use of Wordmaster, the teacher switches the rule for matching words without telling the students. When students suddenly discover that they are not being successful, their enthusiasm turns quickly to feelings of outrage about how it is the computer's fault for not working. The teacher calmly explains that the computer is working perfectly and the information they need is available. When finally convinced that things are not going to work, they start to look at the screen carefully and notice that the word on the bottom is now *synonym*. Students then make the adjustment, get good scores, and feel proud of themselves. The next day, the teacher engages them in a conversation about the importance of words in understanding what the rules are, and how students cannot develop strategies until they have first read the available information carefully or, in the case of the classroom, listened to the information provided by the teacher. This is learning in the context of high drama, with excitement turning to despair, then once again to excitement, and joy. The literal use of the software becomes secondary to students experiencing a deeper and more important type of learning.

From that day forward, the students never forget about the importance of rules and are attentive during future discussions about rules. Letting students experience and discover on their own the importance of concepts in dramatic situations is more effective than adults lecturing them. Research has demonstrated that interaction about ideas in socially meaningful situations is critical to their internalization (Vygotsky, 1978). Choreographing situations that generate passion about new ways to think about ideas leads to powerful forms of learning. (A more detailed description of the structure of the HOTS Learning Drama environment is contained in Pogrow, 1990b. Since its publication, there have been some enhancements to the techniques.)

Extending Learning Drama Techniques to Teaching Math Content

SUPERMATH is a 2-year Learning Drama curriculum that starts with fractions and decimals and takes students into the basics of algebra. SUPERMATH has all the basic process characteristics of the HOTS system. The curriculum, however, has been modified to support the special needs of developing content knowledge. SUPERMATH has several key goals. The first is to show that a Learning Drama process approach can be designed that produces higher levels of content learning and retention than do direct instruction (either traditional or computer-based) approaches. The second goal is to show that if educationally disadvantaged students are first exposed to the HOTS general thinking environment, they will then do as well as regular students in an academic content course in which they are mixed together. The final goal is to see whether a more visual and dramatic approach to mathematics can increase students' interest in the subject. As this is being written, the first pilot of students having 2 years of SUPERMATH has been completed.[3]

SUPERMATH develops and decontextualizes a core of strategies/problem-solving skills, concepts, and skills that are fundamental to pre-algebra and algebra. Students are constantly asked to choose from among a small set of strategies and problem-solving skills to make inferences and to justify the use of that strategy. Key examples include (a) visualization by imagining and drawing, (b) estimation, (c) comparison with similar problems that are familiar and simpler, (d) looking for patterns by either examining the answers of several related problems or changing one variable at a time, (e) making a proportion, and (f) language parsing. Examples of key general mathematical concepts that are abstracted whenever possible include (a) approximation, (b) general versus specific, (c) interaction, (d) reversibility, and (e) validity.

Students continue to encounter these skills, concepts, and strategies in diverse software environments and settings. Students, therefore, continually discover many different uses of the same skills and concepts. For example, angles are used in a golf game and then also discussed as headings in the Voyage of the Mimi, a science software program involving a sailing adventure in the Gulf of Maine. Angles are also discussed while designing a home using an architecture program in the geometry unit. In each case, teacher-led conversation discusses how the use of angles in a given context is the same as and different from the use in other contexts, along with how algorithms derived in one could be used in the other. By experiencing the constant abstraction of a limited set of strategies and concepts through time, at-risk students begin to develop decontextualization skills/tendencies.

In SUPERMATH, the computer is used not to present mathematics but rather to present settings. For example, in one program one week, students may be driving a Corvette through San Francisco, and in another, they will travel to Mars and go to a burger stand. The settings are designed so that they either (a) provide a mental model that enables students to learn a formerly unintuitive math concept in a highly inferential way or (b) are an excuse to introduce a dilemma that can be overcome only through the use of mathematics. Examples of each use of software follow.

An example of taking advantage of a dilemma to introduce math is when students are playing computer golf and discover that the unit length they are working with does not let them get the ball in the hole. After initial consternation at their ballooning scores, students begin to realize that they must use fractions or decimals to adjust the unit length of their shots. In addition, while their scores continue to get better as their estimation skills improve, the students still cannot get the holes-in-one the curriculum expects to get an A for the activity. Students then begin to realize that they need to measure to have a chance for an A, and the teacher uses that realization as the opening to show them how to use a protractor to measure the angle of their shots, which together with a ruler makes the formerly impossible task relatively simple. This then leads in the curriculum to a discussion of the relative advantages of estimation versus measurement. In the meantime, students will have gained experience in the skills of measuring angles and calculating decimals and the concept of approximation.

Another example of taking advantage of a dilemma to introduce math content involves a computer program in which students drive a Corvette through San Francisco. When students are asked to determine how long it will take to get from one place to another, they discover that their map of San Francisco has no scale. Students then have to use the car as a measuring tool to begin to estimate distances and scale. On the basis of the questions and tasks contained in the curriculum, students begin to intuitively discover (a) how to relate rate, distance, and time and (b) how to determine the scale from the speed of the car and use the resultant scale to estimate the amount of time it would take to travel to different points. Students also test their estimated distances resulting from the model with the actual distance. This leads to a discussion of the sources of inaccuracies, as well as of the expected accuracy of models and the conditions under which the degree of accuracy is important. In this way, a highly motivating program designed for entertainment becomes a context for discovering and integrating a rich set of mathematical concepts and content objectives.

Software settings are also used to enable students to create a mental model of math concepts in their heads from which they can make mathematical inferences. For example, students seldom understand why subtracting a negative number is the same as adding a positive number. Rationalizations from adult experiences do not make sense to students; it is usually taken as an article of faith by students, who then apply the "adult" rules. As an alternative, a simulation called 3-Smile Island has been developed. In this simulation, students try to keep a nuclear reactor from exploding by using an injector and vacuum cleaner to bring the radioactive "positons" and "negatons" inside the reactor into balance. Students then intuitively come to see how vacuuming negatons (which is the model for subtracting negative numbers) has the same effect as injecting positons (adding positive numbers). Students then infer how to extend their experience with balancing opposite quantities from their mental model of operating the reactor to represent the process with just numbers and signs. From that point, they can infer and articulate the rules for adding signed numbers.

Another concept that is difficult for students to understand is why 3.2 is bigger than 3.199. There is no way to explain this concept so that it is intuitive to most students. As a result, teachers usually impose a rule whereby students look to the right of the decimal place for the first largest digit they encounter. This teaches students that math is a subject in which adults impose arbitrary rules that they must follow.

The alternative provided by SUPERMATH is for students to play a computer game in which they search for a crooked decimal through the "hood." The hood is a series of homes with several types of addresses. All students are told throughout the game is that the addresses get larger as they move to the right. In this game, students first search a series of houses with addresses ranging, for example, from 3.1, 3.2, 3.3, and so on, to 4.0. Students then discover that the decimal has escaped into an alley between two of the buildings, for example, 3.3 and 3.4. Students must then enter a possible address for the alley, for example, 3.35. Students then encounter nine garbage cans with two decimal place addresses and discover that the crooked decimal has escaped between the garbage cans to one of nine mouse holes. The mouse holes will then have a three-place decimal address, such as 3.354. They then capture the crooked decimal.

In the coordinated curriculum, students then apply this game to solving problems such as which is bigger, 3.2 or 3.199? Students then use the game as a mental model to respond, "3.2 is bigger because 3.199 is in the alley between 3.1 and 3.2, and therefore 3.2 is to the right of 3.199." After students have used their mental model to solve a series of such problems, the teacher then asks them to find a pattern to their answers and come up with a rule to explain to a friend, who does not have access to their decimal game, how to solve such problems. Students end up inferring the rule about comparing decimals place by place to the right of the decimal point.

The most significant mental model incorporated into SUPERMATH solved the biggest problem in teaching math: word problems. A new genre of software was created to help students visualize how to convert language to mathematical representation. This new genre of software is called *word problem processors.* A word problem processor helps students construct a mental model of how language is translated into mathematics by enabling them to communicate with a creature stuck inside the computer. Students first construct a series of sentences forming a story—a story that turns out to be a word problem. Students then present their story to the creature for its reaction.

Having students write word problems is not new. Having an entity that can react to the language, however, is new. Simulated artificial intelligence techniques have been used to provide the creature with the ability to interpret a constrained set of language expressions on an inexpensive personal computer. The creature can judge if problems are valid, valid but trivial, or invalid. (The teacher can override the creature's judgment.) If problems created by the students are judged to be valid, the creature provides the solution. If the problems are judged to be invalid, students are given clues as to what the difficulty is. Students then revise their problem. The teacher continually asks students to analyze why the creature is judging and solving their problems the way it does.

By constantly trying to figure out and explain the creature's reactions to their language, students start to "understand" in their own way the transformation between language and mathematics and are able to use comprehension strategies to solve problems when the solution is not presented. As students progress through the levels of word problems, the sophistication of the language in the stories they create increases, as does the math.

In addition to providing students with a sense of ownership of the stories/problems they create, word problem processors provide students with a chance to experience how rules and language drive the resultant mathematics and problem structure. The interaction wherein the teacher constantly asks students to analyze how the creature reacts to their language causes students to construct hypotheses about the relationship between the language of problems and the associated mathematics. These hypotheses are revised as new problems and solutions are generated.

When students are given later opportunities to solve problems created by each other, they intuitively first look for the underlying structure of the language and think of how the creature would have reacted to the language. How students visualize the creature as reacting to the language structure eventually becomes how students themselves look at the problems. Solving word problems becomes a process of social interaction and behavioral analysis (i.e., analyzing the behavior of the creature). The frequent use of the mental models teaches students (a) that math is inferential, (b) that there are rationales for the rules, and (c) that they can figure out the rules on their own.

The visual and interactive computer-based settings enable SUPERMATH to treat math content as a means to solve other ends that are of interest to students. For example, geometry is introduced to help students design a dream home and appraise gems, and ratio is introduced to help students analyze classical art. Applying mathematics to other problems that are important to students is a more natural way to learn mathematics that better models how it is used in the real world. The fantasy nature of many of the settings helps intrigue students and lead them to associate mathematics with highly creative endeavors.

Once students have engaged in the process of inferring concepts and problem-solving strategies from the settings, they then practice the techniques using either textbooks or a mathematics CAI program to automate the skill. The process stage is thus converted to a skill practice phase. In addition, although the specific mathematical content is learned indirectly in the computer settings via a process approach, the content covered in the SUPERMATH curriculum is comprehensive.

The sophisticated SUPERMATH curriculum is able to combine both process learning with full content coverage because once the students have a mental model or see a real need for the concept, learning becomes much more efficient. In addition, multiple objectives are covered in each lesson. For example, the rules for signed numbers are developed along with discussions of reciprocals, with both indicating forms of inverses. Each lesson usually covers at least three or four content objectives. Such integration helps students see the relationships among mathematical concepts and the multiple representation of mathematical situations. The simultaneous discussion of multiple concepts increases retention and understanding. At the same time, more research is needed to determine the optimal mix of process to direct content learning.

Using a process approach to increase the learning of content is a highly ambitious goal. Achieving such a goal requires the use of state-of-the-art technology with state-of-the-art pedagogy and a highly sophisticated curriculum to blend the elements together in a manner that is consistent with learning theory. Although it is not uncommon for other curricula to have an occasional unit that integrates a highly creative and motivating approach, the SUPERMATH curriculum maintains a consistently high level of creativity in presenting mathematics in ways that will motivate and interest the vast majority of students. In addition, the sophisticated cognitive architecture, wherein concepts at each of the levels of the development model are constantly abstracted across different settings, ensures that the mathematics are learned in ways that promote understanding and the ability to apply the concepts, along with developing their ability to generalize and enjoy mathematics. As a result, SUPERMATH has great potential for bringing an understanding of the value and beauty of mathematical thought to a wide range of students who are currently not interested in mathematics or who simply are unable to understand the significance of the concepts.

Implementing Socratic Dialogue Techniques

Even the best curriculum provides only the potential for appropriate forms of conversation to exist. Although the curriculum provides the questions to initiate the conversations, teachers' follow-up questions and reactions are even more critical. Teachers must react to student questions and answers in ways that maintain the types of ambiguities that guide students to construct meaning on their own. If teachers do not question or probe student responses appropriately, the most sophisticated curriculum and software become rote learning activities.

The single most misunderstood factor about the use of technology with most students (particularly those who are educationally disadvantaged) is that *producing sophisticated learning is a function of the sophistication of conversation that surrounds the use of the technology—not the sophistication of the technology.* That was true of television, it is true of calculators and lab experiments (McPartland & Wu, 1988), it is true of computers, and it will be true of the next generation of shiny boxes—no matter how powerful or how many flashing lights they have.

Although many articles on technology point to the need to "teach as a process," they never provide a system for doing so. Rhetoric is not sufficient. Observation of student-teacher conversation and interaction during a long period identified the key types of interactions that occur between teacher and student in the development of understanding. This led to the development of a specific system of Socratic techniques for dealing with each key situation. This system has been refined for more than a decade.

A major component of Learning Dramas is training teachers in Socratic dialogue techniques. Teachers have to learn (a) how to be guides rather than providers of information, (b) how to listen to student answers for understanding (rather than for right or wrong answers), and (c) how to probe student responses to help the students construct their own understanding.

Becoming skilled in Socratic dialogue is not easy. It takes a week of practice to train even good teachers to start to become Socratic. Teachers spend a week teaching lessons from the curricula to each other. During the week, each teacher encounters each of the key dialogue situations many times. At the end of each teaching, there is a debriefing on whether the appropriate Socratic strategy was used in the situations encountered. Tying the learning of the techniques to specific experiences is as important for teachers as it is for students.

The practice and feedback enable teachers to become metacognitive about their teaching, that is, how to listen to what they are doing and consciously reflect on their own as to the appropriateness and inappropriateness of how they handle a given situation. The hardest situation to learn to deal with is when students give logically correct but unexpected and inconvenient answers. Although good teachers can implement the techniques effectively immediately, they report that it takes a year of monitoring themselves before the techniques become automatic.

Are Learning Dramas Effective?

The use of Learning Dramas requires purchasing software, using it in unintended ways, developing curriculum around such unintended uses, and then training teachers in advanced pedagogical techniques. Why go to such trouble? Are the results worth it?

The advantage is that this approach has been demonstrated to be more effective than literal use of software or non-technology-based interventions. Research submitted to the National Diffusion Network in the U.S. Department of Education found that HOTS not only increased thinking and social confidence of educationally disadvantaged students in grades 4 through 7 but also doubled national average gains on both standardized reading and math tests. When one teacher compared the use of the HOTS techniques against a commercial CAI drill and practice program in two of her groups, HOTS students did better in reading and math on the vendor's own test. In addition to basic skill gains, almost 15% of HOTS students are currently making honor roll—suggesting that students are transferring the cognitive development to the learning of content.

More recent comparisons show even more powerful effects. A recently completed dissertation (Darmer, 1995) measured the cognitive development of HOTS students in gains in reading comprehension, metacognition, writing, components of IQ, transfer to novel tasks, and grade point average. Of the 12 measures developed, HOTS students went up substantially in all and outperformed a control group of students in all comparisons. (Indeed, the control students in a traditional Chapter 1 program in the same school declined in reading and grade point average performance.) This suggests that the effects of the process approach were so powerful that it produced transfer to gains in both content learning and problem solving. Indeed, the effects are so powerful that they show up both on traditional standardized tests as well as on alternative assessment. The Learning Drama approach used in HOTS has proved to be the most effective large-scale intervention for educationally disadvantaged students in grades 4 through 7.

Data on SUPERMATH are being collected. Data from the first-year sites show students making consistent gains on standardized test scores, with most of the gain coming from the problem-solving section of the test. Scores increased despite a dramatic reduction in drill and practice activities. Indeed, close to 75% of the activities are inferential. As a result, the Learning Drama approach is able to stimulate formal content learning to such a degree that the growth is reflected on even traditional scores. It also appears to provide a way to construct a highly creative curriculum with a great deal of depth while also maintaining needed content coverage.

One of the pilot sites provided an opportunity to examine the cumulative and inclusionary effects of providing both HOTS and SUPERMATH to students who are educationally disadvantaged. In this school in Denver, Colorado, Chapter 1 students were placed in HOTS in the sixth grade and were then placed into the second year of HOTS as seventh graders, along with a heterogeneously grouped class of SUPERMATH. Some of the students had pretest math scores in the 90th percentile, and some of the HOTS students were below the 12th percentile. The HOTS students held their own in SUPERMATH and made substantial test score gains. As one of the students noted, "It was neat to see how our thinking strategies could help in math." The high-performing students stayed high. Especially important was the bonding that occurred between the low-performing students who had a weak math background but who had more experience in explaining ideas and representing them on the computer and the high-performing students who had a good math background but did not feel comfortable representing their ideas.

To be effective, Learning Drama activities must be maintained through time for substantial cognitive development to occur. The activities must also be targeted at appropriate grades for different types of students. It also appears that it takes at least half a year before students start to feel comfortable with the inferential nature of SUPERMATH. Although average to high-performing students can start right into SUPERMATH, it is critical that educationally disadvantaged students must first be in a general thinking program such as HOTS for 1 to 2 years to internalize a general sense of being reflective. Educationally disadvantaged students placed directly into SUPERMATH find it overwhelming to try to simultaneously develop both a sense of reflection and a sense of how to reflect about mathematics.

Interviews with students at the end of 2 years of SUPERMATH reveal that the experience substantially increased their interest in math and their ability to explain mathematical ideas. Students clearly preferred this process approach to learning math content. Girls and boys were equally enthusiastic.

Why Are Learning Dramas So Effective?

How can using computer software in ways that it wasn't intended produce substantial gains in content learning without extensive linkage to the curriculum or text? The effectiveness of the Learning Drama approach is that it alleviates the primary cognitive problems inhibiting learning. My research revealed that the lack of content knowledge of educationally disadvantaged students in grades 4 through 7 was not the problem but a symptom. The real problem was that they did not seem to know how to deal with unstructured types of learning, generalizations, and ambiguity. They seemed incapable of dealing with more than one concept at a time, having a conversation about ideas, thinking with general principles instead of specific examples, and thinking ideas through. They viewed each piece of information as a discrete entity that applied only to the context in which it was learned. They did not seem to understand how to generalize or even that they are supposed to generalize. They did not know how to work with ideas or even know what understanding is.

That at-risk students do not understand "understanding" is not their fault. Nor is it an indicator of a problem with their intellect or a function of their race, ethnicity, or economic class. Rather, it probably results from the adults in their lives not modeling the thinking processes for them. Such modeling has typically been done through sophisticated conversation at the dinner table and in school. Such conversation, however, is increasingly rare. Most students who are at risk have literally never had opportunities to construct meaning on their own—not in the home or in school. In school, these students are generally told what to do. In my observation of classroom processes, one is struck by how little conversation exists in classrooms—even in small group settings.

The absence of adequate interaction with adults leads to a profound understanding deficit. So what is the solution? Learning Dramas are able to develop a sense of understanding by modeling the same techniques that good parents use at home to create a sense of understanding. Children develop a sense of understanding by experiencing how adults react to various forms of their ideas. In U.S. culture, the primary mechanism for passing on that instinct is conversation. In essence, Learning Dramas are dinner table conversation in school. The key is to replace what was missing and what caused the understanding deficit to evolve in the first place—general thinking conversations in which adults probe youngsters' attempts to construct meaning.

As children engage in sophisticated conversation daily in the Socratic environment within Learning Dramas, they start to imitate the form of conversation used by their teacher with each other. The increase in the sophistication of the students' verbal social interactions appears to parallel a growth in general cognitive functioning, and an intuitive sense of understanding emerges. (The finding that a sophistication in the use of language presages growth in cognitive development is similar to findings by Vygotsky, 1978.)

Learning Dramas are powerful because developing a sense of understanding simultaneously produces multiple types of learning. Once students understand what it means to understand ideas, they seem to spontaneously construct the types of understandings that enable them to learn all content better—the first time it is taught. This is probably what accounts for the gains in content learning and the high percentage of students making honor roll. Learning Dramas have helped reveal how intellectually bright educationally disadvantaged students really are and that instead of dumbing down the curriculum, educators should be spending more time figuring out how to make parts of it more sophisticated and interesting (Pogrow, 1990a).

The use of visual settings in SUPERMATH to either develop mental models of concepts or resolve dilemmas overcomes two key inhibitors to learning math: an inability to visualize the concepts and an inability to connect the concepts to a significant (to students) application.

Visual devices such as televisions and computers offer several advantages over books as vehicles for stimulating Socratic conversations and Learning Dramas. In addition to motivational effects, interactive visual devices such as computers provide (a) a way of mixing different learning modalities together and providing students with the flexibility to draw on the modality, be it graphic, tactile, or listening, with which they initially feel comfortable; (b) a dynamic way for students to test ideas at the speed at which they can think of them, with immediate feedback; (c) feedback whose interpretation is critical to understanding the correctness of answers and strategies; and (d) a private environment in which uncertain students can first test their ideas before having to discuss them publicly. At the same time, the ultimate goal of Learning Dramas is to transfer these skills to nonvisual media and develop students who love to read and discuss books and ideas.

Conclusions

Technology advocates and researchers may have missed the fundamental point about the significance of technology in education. They often seem more interested in putting a television or computer in every classroom, training all teachers, and proving that the technology can produce learning by themselves. Unfortunately, this has led to simplistic patterns of use that cannot possibly enhance learning in most students (Pogrow, 1988). To what extent technology is responsible for the learning gains reported in the HOTS program, I do not know, and, frankly, I do not care. All that matters is that the combination of techniques and technology used in Learning Dramas produces high levels of learning.

The inability of visual technology by itself to produce learning in students who are educationally disadvantaged, however, does not mean that it is not a valuable tool in the construction of learning. The research does mean that the obvious way to use technology with educationally disadvantaged students is not the best way!

Any piece of software can be used either as CAI/ILS or as part of a Learning Drama. The difference is as simple (or complicated) as what is talked about when the software is used and how teachers talk and listen to students. Instead of using computers as a tool, Learning Dramas use computers as a metaphor for life, a setting that creates opportunities and excuses to talk about ideas. Experience has shown that the Learning Drama approach, although counterintuitive, produces dramatic improvements in learning in a wide range of students.

Computers are powerful potentials that require more, not less, sophisticated forms of curricula and pedagogy. Without new and more creative forms of curricula and sophisticated models of teaching and teacher training, technology will be of little help in solving the most intractable education problems. When all the elements come together, however, as they do in carefully developed Learning Dramas, the effects are powerful.

The roots of this work are drawn from the research on the effects of television on learning and have been extended to another visual device, the computer. I suspect that most of the conclusions in this article will be equally valid for the next generation of visual technology.

The systematic and powerful learning processes inherent in the Learning Drama environment produce a wide range of learning gains, from cognitive development to higher levels of traditional content acquisition. This demonstrates that a process approach can be designed which produces even higher levels of content learning than direct instruction does. At the same time, developing Learning Dramas requires extensive amounts of time, creativity, and training. Let's stop wasting time and energy engaging in irrelevant debates and research questions and make the kinds of professional and policy commitments to producing new and more powerful forms of Learning Dramas. The knowledge on how to proceed is there. Is the will there?

Notes

1. Research reviews of the effectiveness of CAI, such as Bangert-Drowns, Kulik, and Kulik (1985) and Niemiec and Walberg (1987), found that the major effects from CAI have been demonstrated at the early elementary grade levels and then decline rapidly thereafter. Haller, Child, and Walberg (1988) found that metacognition (without technology) has twice the effect as CAI. Finally, Hativa (1988) found that when both high- and low-performing students use CAI, the technology widens learning gaps.

2. The new version of Oregon Trail is far more elaborate than the older version. It uses color graphics and provides many more decision-making situations. Unfortunately, its potential for metacognition is much less because it takes an hour for students to find out if they have successfully reached Oregon, and there is no time left in the period to discuss whether a strategy did or did not

work for getting to Oregon. This illustrates how advances in software can actually be detrimental to the development of key thinking activities.

3. Information about the HOTS and SUPERMATH programs can be obtained by writing Dr. Stanley Pogrow, c/o Education Innovations, 2302 East Speedway, #114, Tucson, AZ 85733.

References

Bangert-Drowns, R., Kulik, J., & Kulik, C. (1985, Summer). Effectiveness of computer-based education in secondary schools. *Journal of Computer-Based Instruction, 12*(3), 59-68.

Bransford, J. (1989, Fall). Learning with technology: Theoretical and empirical perspectives. *Peabody Journal of Education, 64*(1), 5-26.

Darmer, M. A. (1995). *Developing transfer and metacognition in educationally disadvantaged students: Effects of the higher order thinking skills (HOTS) program.* Unpublished doctoral dissertation, University of Arizona, Tucson.

Haller, E., Child, D., & Walberg, H. (1988, December). Can comprehension be taught? A quantitative synthesis of "metacognitive" studies. *Educational Researcher, 17*, 5-8.

Hativa, N. (1988, Fall). Computer-based drill and practice in arithmetic: Widening the gap between high- and low-achieving students. *American Educational Research Journal, 25*, 366-397.

McPartland, J., & Wu, S. (1988, July). *Instructional practice in the middle grades: National variations and effects.* Baltimore: Johns Hopkins University.

Niemiec, R., & Walberg, H. (1987). The comparative effects of computer-assisted instruction: A synthesis of reviews. *Journal of Educational Computing Research, 3*(1), 19-37.

Pogrow, S. (1988, April). The computer movement coverup. *Electronic Learning, 7*, 6-7.

Pogrow, S. (1990a, January). Challenging at-risk students: Findings from the HOTS program. *Phi Delta Kappan, 71*, 389-397.

Pogrow, S. (1990b). *HOTS (Higher order thinking skills): A validated thinking skills approach to using computers with students who are at risk.* New York: Scholastic.

Vygotsky, L. S. (1978). *Mind in society: The development of higher psychological processes.* Cambridge, MA: Harvard University Press.

9

Teaching Science Literacy and Critical Thinking Skills Through Problem-Based Literacy

Robert J. Swartz

It is estimated that 90% of the students who take middle and high school science courses will never engage in professional work that is directly related to science or technology. Despite this, there is a powerful rationale for teaching science to all students. We live in a world in which we cannot spend even one day without having to relate actively to science. Not only do we constantly read and hear about scientific discoveries, but also we routinely use scientific information in our lives, from basic information about the conduction of heat to more sophisticated information about electricity and weather systems. The contact we have with claims that grow from scientific works that others do about health and safety is, in many cases, even more pervasive. And we are continually interested in making our lives easier through the use of various technologies. Science instruction has a powerful rationale when it is geared to providing students with

AUTHOR'S NOTE: The research for this chapter was funded in part by a grant from the National Science Foundation (ESI-9452805). A version of this chapter was presented at the 1996 Conference on Multiple Intelligences in Jerusalem, Israel, sponsored by the Branco Weiss Institute for the Development of Thinking.

basic literacy so they can make the best use of this information and understand the application of new technological advances in their own lives.

Despite these pragmatic needs, traditional science instruction aims at preparing young learners to enter scientific professions and occupations. Standard science curricula from middle school on emphasize the technical science content and scientific research skills that are appropriate to meet the needs of preprofessional training in science. How do educators begin to meet the needs of that other 90% while still preparing future scientists and technologists?

To be science literate in the world of the 21st century, individuals certainly must understand the essential concepts of science, know the principles at play when these concepts are applied, and have access to key information about how the everyday world works when these principles play themselves out. But scientifically literate persons must also have and use good thinking as they apply their scientific understanding to their lives. They must have the ability to identify and use scientific knowledge appropriately to make wise choices and to solve problems encountered in their personal and professional lives effectively. Furthermore, they must be able to make judicious critical judgments about the reliability and accuracy of information that is passed off as scientifically based. People who are science literate do not simply give out what they know about scientific concepts in a quiz-show context. Scientifically literate persons make skillful use of science while working through the everyday, although sometimes complex, thinking tasks encountered in both personal and job-related contexts.

Science can be of great benefit to us all. No matter how much science we learn, however, those benefits are lost if we do not use it well as we think through the issues and routine tasks that call for its application. Both basic science content and the problem-solving/critical-thinking skills involved in scientific thinking that are needed to use this content well in everyday contexts are equally important to teach in courses geared to science literacy. (See also Chapter 10 by Young in the first book of this trilogy, *Envisioning Process As Content: Toward a Renaissance Curriculum.*)

The Methods of Science in Everyday Life

The demand to use good scientific thinking in our lives is sometimes reflected in assessment items designed for all students. Insofar as it is, the use of these assessment items recognizes the need for instruction in science literacy. Here, for example, are two precollege assessment items from a state testing program, based on one of the key standards of scientific research—the need to control variables if the data from an experiment are to be used to support a judgment that one thing was the cause of another. It is important to note the contexts of application of this concept in two everyday situations.

1. A person wants to determine which of two spot removers is more effective. Describe in detail an experiment the person might perform to find out which spot remover is better for removing stains from fabrics.

2. A television commercial shows two shirts with "ring around the collar" being washed in two washing machines but with different soap, soap A and soap B. After the wash is over, the person who has washed the shirts takes each out. The shirt washed with soap A still has ring around the collar. The other one does not. The person says that this shows that soap B is better for removing dirt than soap A. Is there anything you want to find out before you accept this conclusion? If so, what? If not, do you accept this conclusion as it is? Why?

These examples differ. The second one involves assessing someone else's claim that is advanced as scientific and is supposed to be based on a viable experiment. The first involves designing an experiment through which a similar claim can be supported, although this case is about spot removers, rather than laundry soap.

Applying good scientific standards to the claim about the soaps immediately raises a red flag: Simply knowing that the ring around the collar disappeared when washed with soap B may make it seem easy to say that soap B is better, but this information is not enough on which to base that judgment. Students also have to consider the other variables that could be causing this difference and determine if they were controlled. For example, students might question water temperature. Was one shirt washed in cold water (soap A) and the other in hot water (soap B)? Perhaps a larger quantity of soap B was used as opposed to soap A. Were the initial stains identical? Was soap B used as a pre-stain remover, therefore having more time to soak into the fabric than was given to soap A? Did the machines run for the same length of time? And so on. When all such variables are held the same (controlled), students who apply the standards of good causal thinking know that it is reasonable to say soap B is superior in performance to soap A; when the variables are not controlled, they know that the claim is not yet justified.

The many factors that might cause a difference besides the soap are not usually addressed in a commercial of this sort. Scientifically literate observers, therefore, should adopt the attitude that there is insufficient data presented to determine if soap B is better than soap A for removing ring around the collar. This is, of course, not the way the manufacturers of soap B want viewers to respond. The ability to be science literate, however, can help students be wise consumers.

The processes of scientific thinking addressed here are fundamentally those of problem solving imbued with standards of judgment that require sufficient empirical evidence before ideas and claims being considered are taken as worthy of acceptance. Although teaching for science literacy will not involve students in complex technical work in which they use the problem-solving methodology of the empirical sciences, nonetheless, it is of great importance for students to learn to apply these methods to appropriate contexts in their lives.

Figure 9.1 shows a model that emphasizes important questions to ask in scientific problem solving—questions not unlike those to ask in doing any type

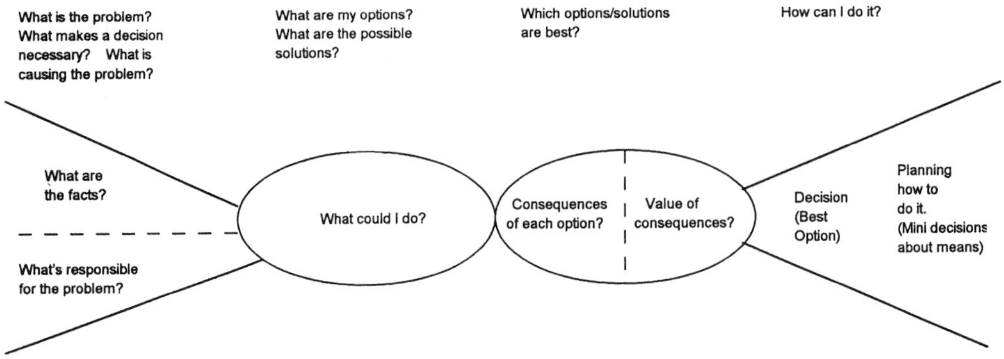

Figure 9.1. The Decision-Making/Problem-Solving Process
SOURCE: Swartz & Parks, 1994, p. 8.

of problem solving. What we need to add to this model to give it a distinctively scientific flavor are the following:

1. The types of problems grappled with are characteristically problems relating to the behavior of things in the natural world.
2. The standards of critical thinking incorporated into this model are standards whereby acceptable judgments must be supported by credible and publicly accessible data or evidence derived from observation and well-constructed experimentation.

For example, when we diagnose the *causes* of a problem, we should develop hypotheses that we judge reasonable only on the basis of observable evidence and only when we know the variables that provide competing causal possibilities are controlled, if the data are derived from an experiment, or otherwise accounted for. (In a similar fashion, predictions about future outcomes should be based on and supported by data about past patterns of events that indicate a strong likelihood that the predicted outcome will occur. Predictions that are just guesses and are not well supported cannot be claimed to be scientifically based.) If we raise questions about the empirical data behind "scientific" judgments and are prepared to accept these judgments only if they are based on sufficient supportive data, we are using standards of critical thinking that are at the hard core of scientific thinking.

Our lives are full of examples such as those flagged in the two assessment items. Each time we turn on the television, we are bombarded with advertising that appeals to the senses and not necessarily to the mind. Scientifically literate persons, although not professional scientists, must exercise the same type of thinking in which scientists engage. The difference is simply in the nature of the problem to be solved. Most of us wrestle with more commonplace examples as we strive to be successful in the world in which we live. Scientists usually grapple with highly technical problems that require a base of more technical information. The thinking and the critical standards employed, however, are fundamentally the same in both cases.

Problem-Based Learning

Problem-based learning has its historical roots in preprofessional medical education. Its application to other content areas and to K-12 education is a relatively recent innovation. In the 1970s and 1980s, on the basis of an original project at McMaster University in Canada, projects were established at many medical schools in which, from the outset, students were plunged into diagnostic situations in which they needed understanding of body functions and disease mechanisms that they did not necessarily have. (Perhaps the best known of these projects is the Pathway Program at Harvard Medical School.) Faculty mentors guided them to find the information they needed to make plausible diagnoses and to prescribe treatments that were likely to succeed. During their investigations, students had recourse to getting some of the information they needed from textbooks. They also had the full resources of the medical school library as well as of staff members who had the pertinent knowledge. In problem-based learning, students must search for the information they need while working on complex medical problems. They learn to identify good sources of this information. This creates a culture similar to that in which medical professionals find themselves outside the traditional educational arena.

These projects contrast sharply with more traditional learning situations (e.g., in an anatomy course) in which students are given the information to be learned detached from such diagnostic contexts and asked to learn it so that they can pass their exams. In such courses, students are usually not called on to apply what they know to various professional situations. When students' learning is detached from applications, few immediate opportunities are provided for assessment of their understanding of and ability to use what they are learning in their courses. At best, in traditional preprofessional programs such as medical school, internships and practical experiences come toward the end of the students' education. By that time, much of what they have learned has become dormant and must be rediscovered. Hence, the conceptual adaptations that occur when students do apply their knowledge rarely occurs. Their knowledge tends to be cursory and unused. It often becomes difficult for students to even recognize those situations in which the applications of what they have learned would be of benefit.

Learning through problem-solving, therefore, has a second great advantage over learning from textbooks and classroom lectures. Problem-based learning creates a rich atmosphere in which one of the fundamental mechanisms of learning and understanding can play itself out: learning as an active constructive process that connects concepts and ideas with the contexts of application.

In summary, proponents of problem-based learning claim students learn how to get information they need when they don't have it and learn to understand the relevance of this information to real problems. These two results are not so readily obtained when students learn information in traditional courses. As a result, problem-based learning eliminates the need for additional training in applying what has been learned, an educational experience that many preprofessional schools have found necessary to provide prior to the completion of students' studies.

Two Examples of Problem-Based Learning in Science

Just as problem-based learning has shown great promise in preprofessional medical education, it can provide a powerful strategy for a wide range of other forms of preprofessional science education. More relevant to this chapter, however, is the insight that it can also provide an equally powerful strategy for teaching for science literacy. The difference is that problem-based learning used as a strategy for preprofessional science education concentrates on problems faced by professional scientists. When the goal is science literacy, on the other hand, the problems chosen should be examples of everyday problems, the solutions to which also require an understanding of basic concepts and principles in science—concepts and principles that we would expect every scientifically literate person to understand and be able to use.

Science instruction that aims at literacy and uses a problem-based learning model is exemplified in the work of an 11th-grade science and mathematics team, Roy Wilson and Patsy Patricelli from Gulfport High School, Gulfport, Mississippi, and a group of 6th-grade teachers from Ligon Middle School, Raleigh, North Carolina, with Rita Hagevik as their group leader.

Wilson's and Patricelli's students are concerned about a troublesome situation in one of the schools in their district. People are constantly complaining about the noise level in the cafeteria. The students have been asked by the school to develop some initial recommendations for what can be done about this situation.

Hagevik's students are in a similar situation. They are taking on the role of colonists fleeing from the British, who have overrun the area, during the Revolutionary War. They have found a cave in which they hide, realizing that they are likely to have to stay in the cave for a long time. They can forage for food at night, but any exit during the day would lead to certain capture and probably death. The cave, typical for that region of North Carolina, has a river running through it, contains passages created by cracks in the granite that forms the mountain in which it is located, and is peppered with stalactites and stalagmites.

These two classroom situations form the start of problem-based curricular units. They were designed to make solving authentic problems the locus for learning. The 11th-grade example combines the science and mathematics of sound, the characteristics of waves, and graphing sinusoidal waves. The 6th-grade unit was on heat, light, sound, rocks, and minerals. Both units are good examples of how science instruction can be reshaped as instruction for science literacy.

These two groups of teachers designed this unit as part of a broader project to determine the feasibility of teaching students standard science content through solving authentic problems. The two projects were established to test whether a problem-based approach to learning content would have two primary results: (a) Students would learn and understand the same content at least as well as they do in the same time they would need to cover this content through standard textbook/lecture approaches; and (b) students would be better able to use the information learned through the problem-based model compared with information learned through the more traditional mode of learning. The hypothesis was that each of these questions would be answered in the affirmative.

Teaching Critical Thinking Skills in These Problem-Based Units

The teachers involved in these projects had a third goal, however, which is not usually incorporated explicitly into problem-based learning projects. They wanted to use problem-based learning as a vehicle for direct instruction in the problem-solving and critical and creative thinking skills and processes that are as important for science literacy as is the science content students learn. Such direct instruction was complemented by an emphasis on the students' metacognitive reflection regarding the way they solve problems to guide and improve their processing skills. And finally, these activities were accompanied by the guided application of the strategies taught to a variety of other problem situations.

The hypothesis of each group of teachers was that although students acquire some problem-solving strategies as they solve problems, direct instruction and practice is far more effective in helping students learn how to engage in important thinking processes well. In these units, the thinking processes are those already mentioned that are involved in solving problems scientifically.

The approach used by both groups of teachers to teach students scientific processing skills was the *infusion of direct instruction in critical and creative thinking* into the content students were exploring in their problem-based learning units. Five specific types of thinking were incorporated: Problem solving/decision making and the component processes of causal explanation, prediction, comparing and contrasting, and determining the reliability and accuracy of sources of information. The emphasis was on how to engage in these types of thinking carefully and skillfully. Guided by the teachers, students developed a set of important focus questions to be raised and for which quality answers were sought as they engaged in these specific thinking processes. The learners were then provided opportunities to apply these questioning strategies by using them to think through aspects of what they were learning.

For example, the students developed the overarching questioning strategy for problem solving/decision making (Figure 9.1) as they faced problems to solve in the unit. This questioning strategy was applied and its effectiveness was considered as students faced problems to solve. Modification of the existing questions usually took place, or additional questions were added as a result. They did the same for causal diagnosis and predicting consequences (as applied to problem solutions), for comparing and contrasting (so that they would be comparing and contrasting with depth and understanding, rather than just listing a few superficial similarities and differences), and for determining the reliability of the sources of information used as they gathered information relevant to solving their problems. In the latter case, the students developed a checklist of questions that were important to ask about any source of information to make a well-founded judgment about its credibility and the accuracy of the information being obtained from the source.

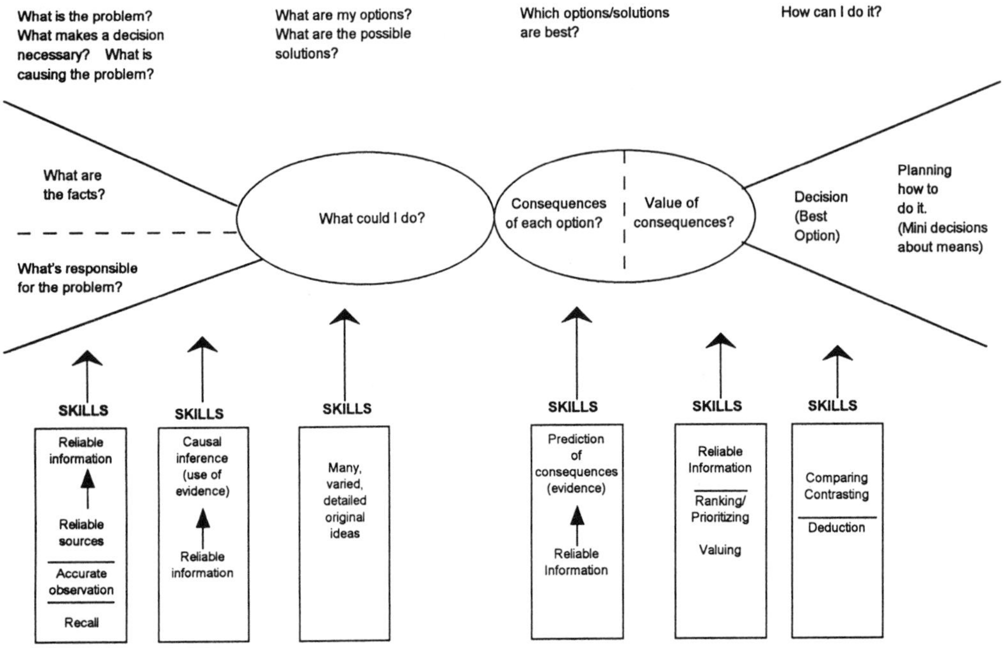

Figure 9.2. Thinking Skills Involved in the Decision-Making/Problem-Solving Process
SOURCE: Swartz & Parks, 1994, p. 8.

The relationships between these types of thinking can be illustrated by expanding the diagram in Figure 9.1 for the decision-making/problem-solving process into Figure 9.2. Figure 9.2, based on a diagram from *Infusing the Teaching of Critical and Creative Thinking Into Content Instruction* (Swartz & Parks, 1994), provides a conceptual framework for a comprehensive instructional program that aims at improving students' decision-making and problem-solving abilities by teaching the skills of critical and creative thinking that blend together when engaging in these complex thinking processes well. Figure 9.3 represents the instructional pattern in this enhanced version of problem-based learning.

Moving Through a Problem-Based Unit

"What can be done to make the noise level in the cafeteria more comfortable?" was the overarching problem Wilson's and Patricelli's students identified as they began their new problem-based unit. Although the way Wilson and Patricelli conducted their lesson differed from Hagevik's lesson in content, detail, and pacing, the structure they used was basically the same. In this chapter, I will interweave an analysis of the Wilson-Patricelli unit and the Hagevik-coordinated unit to develop a paradigm of an enhanced problem-based unit structured for both improved content learning and for the development of thinking skills.

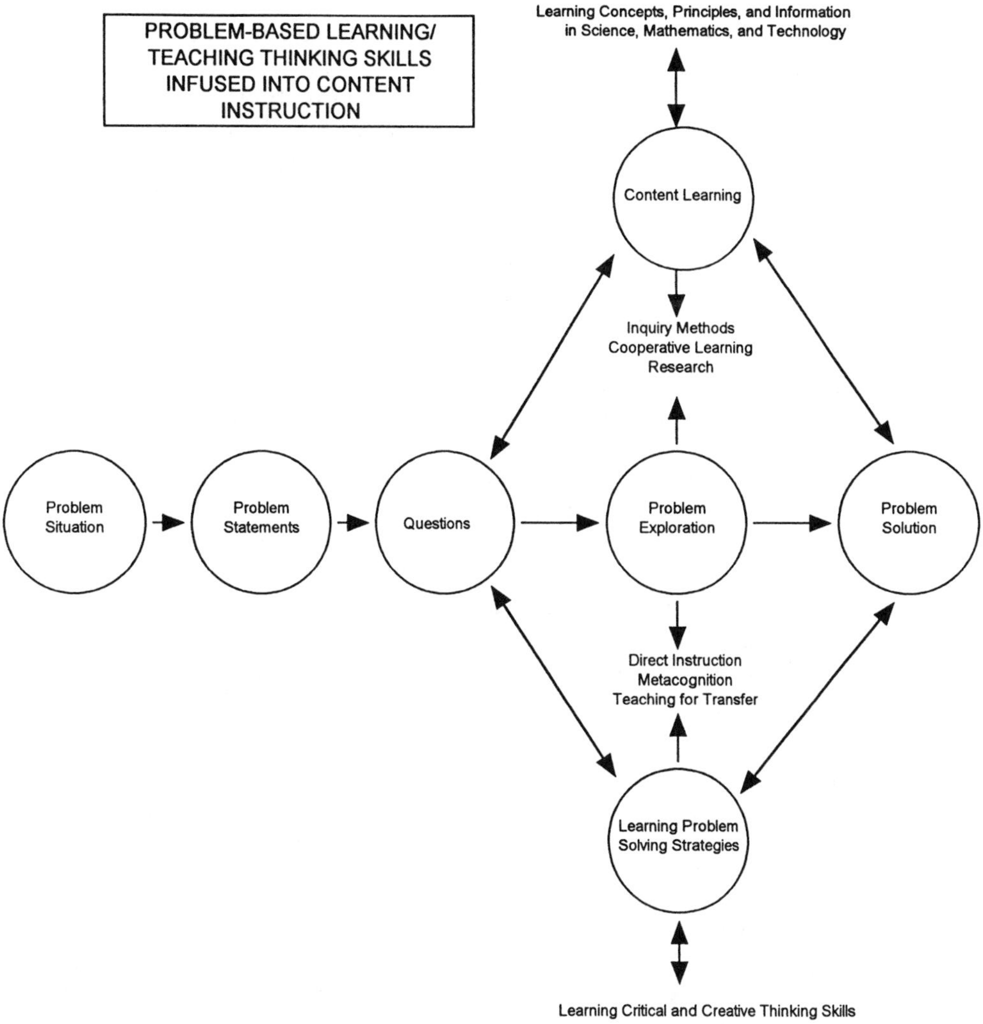

Figure 9.3. Problem-Based Learning/Teaching Thinking Skills Infused Into Content Instruction

The first engagement the students in Wilson's and Patricelli's classrooms had in grappling with what should be done about the noise level in the cafeteria involved them in generating questions that they felt were necessary to answer to come up with a viable solution. Some of the questions that the students generated through ordinary brainstorming were these:

How big is the cafeteria?	Is the whole school there at one time?
How high is the ceiling?	Is there a specific seating arrangement?
How loud is the burger maker?	What color is the interior of the cafeteria?

What type of floor?
Are the walls hollow?
Do they play music in the cafeteria?
What is the noise level?
Is there any structural damage?
Do students have to eat to stay in the cafeteria?
How does noise travel?
Do students pop their drink cartons?
Is the cafeteria air conditioned?
Do students make animal noises?

The students generated a total of 76 questions. They thought the answers to these questions would help them make a good recommendation about what to do to reduce the noise level. We should notice the appearance of some questions which will help students understand the mechanism of noise—how sound travels, how noise is measured, and so on—and some questions the answers to which will help students diagnose the cause(s) of the problem. Such a diagnosis will assist in determining an effective remedy.

Next, the teachers helped the students organize the questions into different categories. These categories served as a prelude to organizing the research students had to engage in as they searched for answers. The information was then used in undertaking a causal analysis of the problem and, eventually, in recommending a remedy. The question categories the class developed were these:

Complaints Noise Cafeteria Structure Students Food Served

The students worked in small collaborative learning groups. Each group developed plans for answering their questions. For example, some students conducted interviews to answer questions such as "Does the objectionable noise level happen every day?" In other cases (e.g., "How does noise travel?"), students consulted reference books, including their textbooks, whereas for other questions (e.g., "Where is the cafeteria located?"), they referred to an overall plan of the building.

Hagevik's unit on rocks, minerals, heat, and sound began the same way, although as might be expected in a middle school science unit rather than a high school physics-mathematics unit, the level of technical details that the students explored and grasped was appropriately different. First, students brainstormed questions. Among them were the following:

Can the cave be disguised?
Can we use any rocks in the cave to help us keep warm?
How can we keep warm?
Is anything growing in the cave that can be used to keep warm?

What are the rocks like (how big, heavy, and sturdy are they)?	How can we communicate with each other in the cave?
What can we eat?	How can we get light into the cave?
Will any rocks or the water in the cave help to make it brighter?	What will happen to the smoke?
	Do any rocks glow in the dark?
Can we burn anything in the cave?	How can we see at night?

Hagevik's group also helped the students categorize these questions. The categories were quite natural:

Heat in the Cave	Light in the Cave	Transmitting Sound in the Cave	Characteristics of Raw Materials in the Cave

Like Wilson's and Patricelli's students, Hagevik's class broke into smaller groups and the teachers helped the students develop plans for gathering information to answer their questions. For example, some referred to their science textbooks, one group of students purchased a rock and mineral book at the local bookstore, and one student found a videotape on caves and and stalactite and stalagmite formation so that the students could determine the characteristics of these typical cave structures. And, of course, Hagevik made available an elaborated version of the fictitious description of this particular cave (based on the features of a real cave in North Carolina).

Information the students discovered included the following:

- There was mica in the cave, and mica reflects light. It might be used to start a fire and for light.
- The calcite in the cave could be used for soap.
- The gypsum in the cave could be used to make plaster of paris; it could be mixed with water to make smooth places on which to sleep.

As in the Wilson-Patricelli unit, much of the information the students gathered during this initial stage of investigation was going to be quite useful to them as they went through the various problem-solving tasks they faced.

Instruction in Thinking Skills in the Unit

When direct instruction in thinking skills was used in these units, the teachers infused this instruction into the lessons. Students had to explicitly identify organized questioning strategies for the types of thinking emphasized and use graphic organizers to guide them through the thinking process. In addition, they were prompted by the teachers to reflect metacognitively about the way they were engaged in thinking so they could articulate the strategy they thought best to use and were able to use it again, when appropriate, in other contexts.

The types of thinking students were taught to do skillfully were, of course, the types of thinking already identified as important in diagnosing and solving a problem. The causal analysis Wilson's and Patricelli's students did of why it was so noisy in the cafeteria, for example, was a vehicle for direct instruction in which the students developed a strategy for use in the type of critical thinking needed to make well-founded judgments about causes. The comparison and contrast Hagevik's students did with the rocks found in the cave was a vehicle for direct instruction in an enhanced way to compare and contrast—emphasizing selecting important similarities and differences and drawing conclusions from these. And as students from each group gathered relevant information to determine which possible solution to the problem was best, this provided a context for developing a general strategy for judging that a source was reliable—a valuable critical thinking skill whatever the information is about. The following sections illustrate some examples of the way this type of instruction in critical thinking skills was woven into these units.

Teaching Thinking Skills in the Problem-Based Unit on Sound

The lesson that Wilson and Patricelli developed for giving a causal diagnosis of the problem was organized into three basic components.

Introduction of the Thinking Skill and Lesson Content

Students are introduced to the need to make careful judgments about causes, when the causes of an occurrence are unknown, through examples related to their own experience. They were guided to develop a series of important questions to ask in making these judgments—often questions that people don't ask when they make hasty or unsubstantiated claims about causes. Here is a causal diagnostic strategy that students typically develop for causal explanation:

Skillful Causal Explanation

1. What are possible causes of the event in question?
2. What could you find that would count for or against the likelihood of these possibilities?
3. What evidence do you already have, or have you gathered, that is relevant to determining what caused the event?
4. Which possibility is rendered most likely on the basis of the evidence?

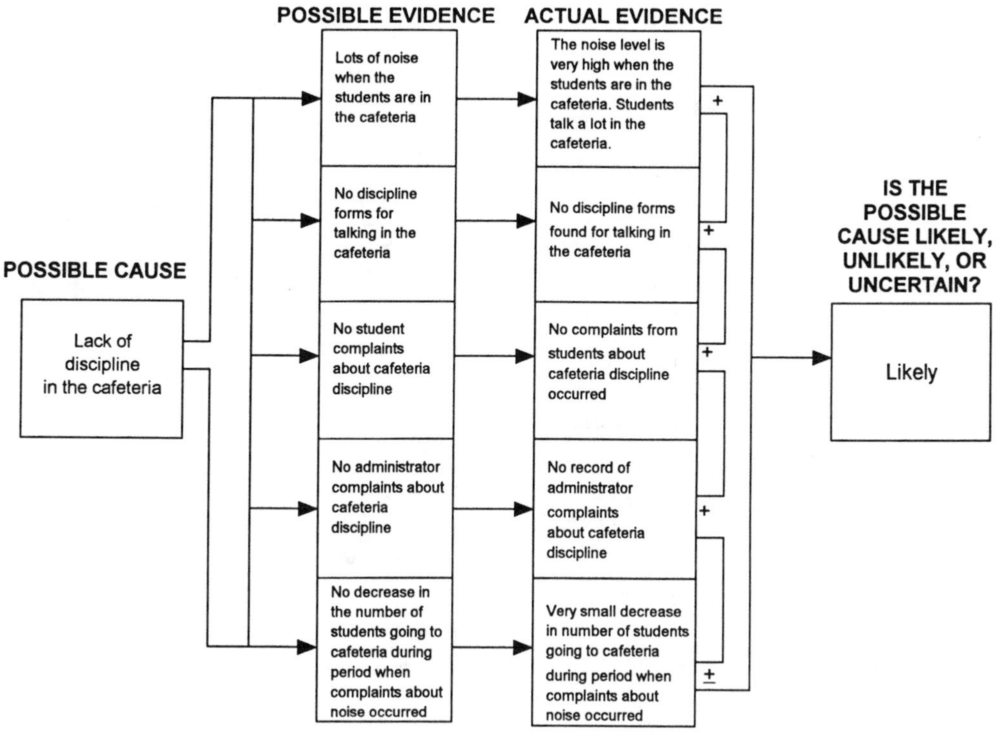

Figure 9.4. Evaluating Possible Causes: Why There Is Noise in the Cafeteria (Example 1)

In this case, the teachers used an example of misdiagnosing why a car would not start and asked students to come up with questions that had not been asked but that could have led to a better causal explanation. This is an important instructional strategy because it makes explicit a set of generic questions that effective thinkers ask when trying to make a well-founded judgment about the cause of something—and these questions came from the students.

Active Use of the Thinking Skill in Thinking About the Content

The second component of the lesson involved having the students actually use the strategy to develop a causal explanation of the noise in the cafeteria that they can defend with evidence or reasons. Asking these guiding questions is important as they go through this process explicitly and deliberately, but it is only part of what is needed to make a good judgment. Answering them and thereby developing a list of possible causes, a plan for obtaining evidence, a list

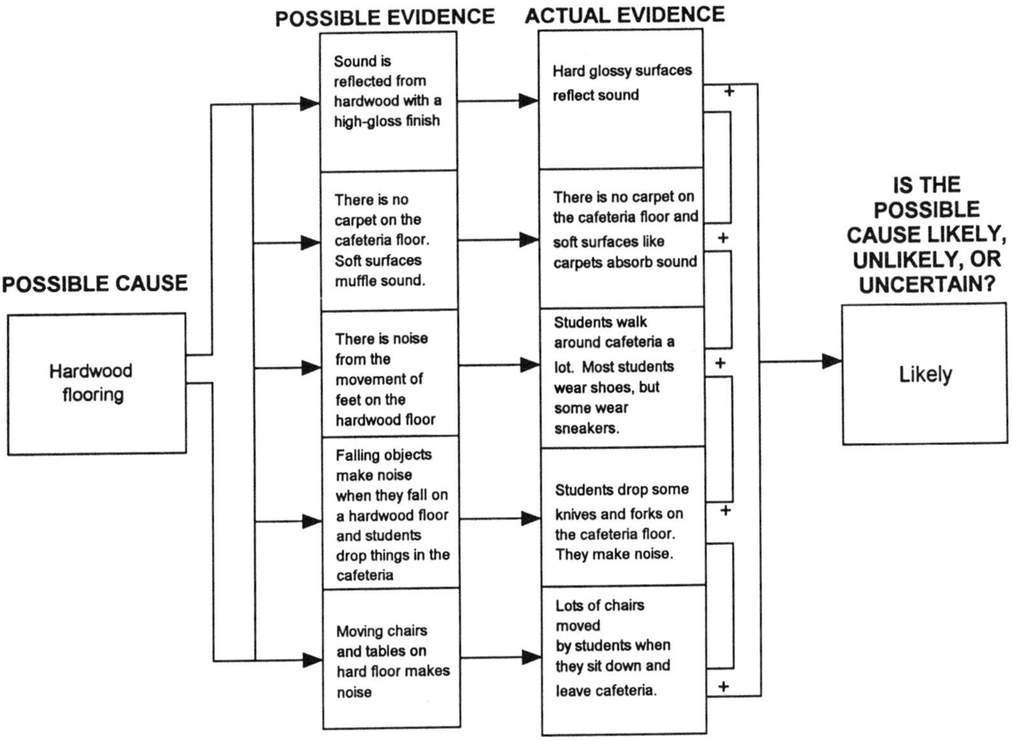

Figure 9.5. Evaluating Possible Causes: Why There Is Noise in the Cafeteria (Example 2)

of evidence obtained, and then a judgment of the likelihood of the possible cause based on the evidence are equally invaluable in bringing the process of well-founded causal explanation to fruition. Here Wilson and Patricelli followed recommendations of good practices in teaching thinking skills by using both collaborative learning techniques and a graphic organizer to guide their students' thinking. Figures 9.4 and 9.5 show two examples of the use of such an organizer from their class in which the students assessed the likelihood of some of the suggested possible causes of noise in the cafeteria.

Wilson and Patricelli were quick to help their students understand that a multiplicity of causal factors may blend together to account for the noise, so this result is put together with other student results to get a more comprehensive picture of the causal relationships. Both structural and people-related factors are causing the problem. This graphic organizer shown in Figure 9.6 helps record these results.

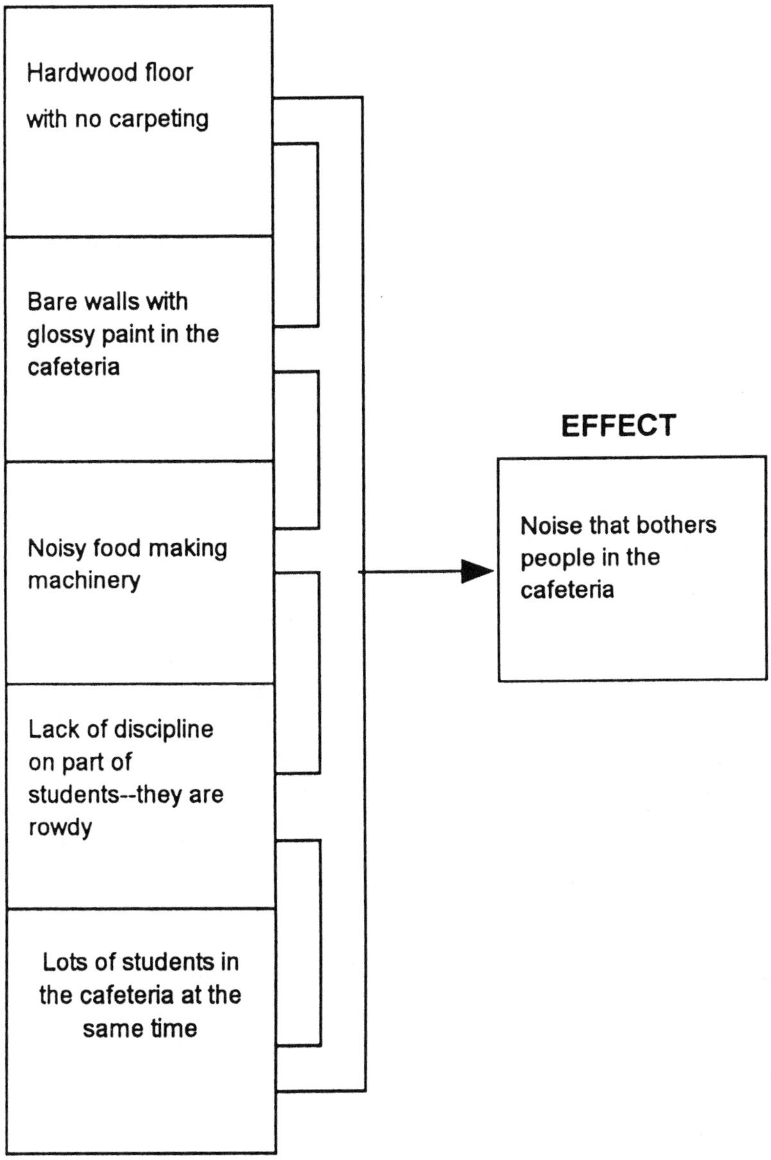

Figure 9.6. Multiple Causes: Why There Is Noise in the Cafeteria

Thinking About the Thinking That Just Occurred and Using the Same Thinking With Other Content

After the previous activity was completed, the teachers invited their students to engage in metacognitive reflection on the process in which they had just engaged. The students used a strategy developed earlier in the lesson to think through the best explanation. How can this strategy be articulated, and was it an effective one? Should it be modified? In this case, the students all endorsed this way of trying to figure out what caused something.

Soon, and again later throughout the school year, these teachers returned to some problems in which it was important to engage in careful causal thinking. When such problems were encountered, they asked students to apply the same strategy they used in this lesson and to once again think about whether it was effective in these new cases and, if not, to modify it. They also asked them to design their own graphics for helpful use in thinking through these questions.

Such lessons demonstrate the ability of teachers to help students take charge of their own thinking and to empower the learners to work on improving it. By integrating direct instruction in thinking skills and processes into a problem-based unit, these teachers have added a new dimension that dramatically enhanced the model as a vehicle for teaching of, for, and about science literacy.

To culminate this experience, Wilson and Patricelli helped students turn to problem-solving per se. They have defined a variety of problems connected to the major issue of noise reduction in the cafeteria. Because the students had already sorted through many of these related issues, they were able to tackle this major issue better informed than if they had voiced their opinions about what to do at the outset of the unit. Figure 9.7 is the problem-solving strategy that Wilson and Patricelli helped their students use as they think through the best way to bring about a reduction in the noise level so that eating in the cafeteria could be more comfortable. They used graphic organizers (Figures 9.8 and 9.9) to guide them through this stage in the process.

At this stage, a new set of issues emerged about the consequences of adopting one or another of the possible solutions: How costly will it be? How long will it take? And what will be the impact on the people who eat in the cafeteria? Students had a chance to discuss and defend their values when it came to which of these factors were more important. Although this class was split on whether a people solution or an acoustical redesign was the best approach, the potential for a combination of the two is something the students seriously considered.

Teaching Thinking Skills in the Middle School Problem-Based Unit on Heat, Light, Sound, and Minerals

In addition to the causal explanation strategy that Wilson and Patricelli introduced to their students, Hagevik introduced her students to an extended strategy for thinking carefully when they compare and contrast—a strategy

SKILLFUL PROBLEM SOLVING

1. Why is there a problem?

2. What is the problem?

3. What are possible solutions to the problem?

4. What would happen if you solved the problem in each of these ways?

5. What is the best solution to the problem?

Figure 9.7. Skillful Problem Solving: Guiding Questions
SOURCE: Swartz & Parks, 1994, p. 78.

especially helpful in problem-solving contexts. Instead of just listing similarities and differences, as many texts treat compare and contrast, she prompted her students to think in more depth about what they find when they identify similarities and differences. Textbook versions of compare and contrast usually lead to superficial and unprocessed exposure of what are often surface similarities and differences. Hagevik asked her students to elaborate the similarities and differences they find; to select the ones that are really important for their purposes; to determine whether there are patterns or major themes of similarity or difference that appear overall; and to advance conclusions, insights, or interpretations based on the similarities and differences that they determine. Figure 9.10 shows the "thinking map" for comparing and contrasting used in Hagevik's class. Figure 9.11 presents a graphic organizer on which her students recorded their thinking as they followed this strategy.

Like Wilson and Patricelli, Hagevik also helped her students develop and use the same overall strategy for problem solving by using the same explicit map (Figure 9.7) of important guiding questions after working with them on causal explanation, prediction, determining the reliability of sources of information, and the version of compare and contrast elaborated above. Just as with these critical thinking skills, her instruction in the development and use of the strategy for problem solving involved the students in reflecting on the science content they were learning about heat, light, sound, and minerals. Figures 9.12

SKILLFUL PROBLEM SOLVING

THE PROBLEM
How might I reduce the noise level in the cafeteria ?

POSSIBLE SOLUTIONS
How can I solve the problem?

Leave it the way it is More discipline--punish the people who are noisy Build a new cafeteria with modern acoustics Have open lunch Get new table-chair units with chairs attached Pass out ear plugs Put sound absorbers (blankets or egg boxes) on the walls.	Go off campus to eat. Cover the cafeteria floor with a carpet Don't have lunches. Have more lunch periods with fewer students Open up part of the cafeteria by taking a wall down Get new and more silent food machines Eat lunch in the school classrooms.

SOLUTION CONSIDERED
More discipline in the cafeteria

CONSEQUENCES What will happen if you adopt this solution?	PRO OR CON?	VALUE How important is the consequence? Why?
Cuts down the noise	Pro	**Very important.** Noise disturbs people. There would be no more complaints
Students won't like it	Con	**Somewhat important.** Students will get over it if it cuts down the noise and is fair.
Students will develop discipline	Pro	**Very important.** Discipline helps you in life and prevents anarchy.
Might infringe on civil liberties of students.	Con	**Somewhat important**. Liberty to talk is important but not if it hurts other people, and students can talk other times.
Students might band together and protest, and might not work.	Con	**Very important.** Students need a time to talk and visit with friends. A large student protest can be very disruptive in the school.
Won't cost much money.	Pro	**Important.** More Money for education.

NEW SOLUTION
How can the solution be changed to make it better?

Do everything we can to make better acoustics in the cafeteria and only discipline students for shouting or making an unnecessary racket. Discuss with students the need to talk in a normal way and let them discipline themselves

Figure 9.8. Skillful Problem Solving: Graphic Organizer (Example 1)

SKILLFUL PROBLEM SOLVING

THE PROBLEM

How might I reduce the noise level in the cafeteria **?**

POSSIBLE SOLUTIONS

How can I solve the problem?

- Leave it the way it is
- More discipline--punish the people who are noisy
- Build a new cafeteria with modern acoustics
- Have open lunch
- Get new table-chair units with chairs attached
- Pass out ear plugs
- Put sound absorbers (blankets or egg boxes) on the walls.
- Go off campus to eat.
- Cover the cafeteria floor with a carpet
- Don't have lunches.
- Have more lunch periods with fewer students
- Open up part of the cafeteria by taking a wall down
- Get new and more silent food machines
- Eat lunch in the school classrooms.

SOLUTION CONSIDERED

Carpet the floor and add sound absorbers to the walls

CONSEQUENCES What will happen if you adopt this solution?	**PRO OR CON?**	**VALUE** How important is the consequence? Why?
Absorbs the sound, cut down noise, and no more complaints	Pro	**Very important.** Noise disturbs people. People in the cafeteria would be happier
Carpets would get stained from spilled food	Con	**Somewhat important.** Stained carpets don't look or smell good. Could be cleaned.
Will cost quite a bit of money--thousands of dollars.	Con	**Important.** Need money for education. Maybe more quiet will lead to a better education.
Will cost money to clean the carpet.	Con	**Important**. Need money for education. Maybe more quiet will lead to a better education.
May not work because there is too much noise	Con	**Very important.** Noise disturbs people. That's what the complaints are about.
Will take time to do the work.	Con	**Somewhat important.** Will be inconvenient, but won't last a long time.
If egg boxes on walls. will not look good.	Con	**Somewhat Important.** Could paint the egg boxes.

NEW SOLUTION

How can the solution be changed to make it better?

Use only wall covering that looks good, like tiles or fabric, and ask the school committee for more money for school for this one year when the work has to be done. Combine with this a "no shouting" rule for the cafeteria.

Figure 9.9. Skillful Problem Solving: Graphic Organizer (Example 2)

OPEN COMPARE AND CONTRAST

1. How are they similar?

2. How are they different?

3. What similarities and differences seem significant?

4. What categories or patterns do you see in the significant similarities and differences?

5. What interpretation or conclusion is suggested by the significant similarities and differences?

Figure 9.10. Open Compare and Contrast: Thinking Map
SOURCE: Swartz & Parks, 1994, p. 102.

and 9.13 are two graphic organizers for problem solving used by her students as they considered one of the problems they were grappling with, making use of what they had learned to try to solve this particular problem.

Results

The teachers undertook this project to test the idea that students can learn at least the same science or mathematics content in a problem-based unit as they learn through standard textbook learning, if not more, using roughly the same time to cover the material. During the first year of these projects, their plan was to develop these units and do one run with them to work out the "bugs." Then, when the units are offered subsequently, the teachers plan to do a formal assessment of the results.

Although no formal assessment of the effectiveness of these units was undertaken during the first formative year, a large amount of informal information was collected by the teachers. In both cases described in this chapter, as well as in the other cases in which this approach was tried in these schools, these data led to revisions in the structure of the unit, as it would in any good formative evaluation. But the data also revealed enough to show initial positive results sufficient to warrant carrying this project further. All the teachers involved were

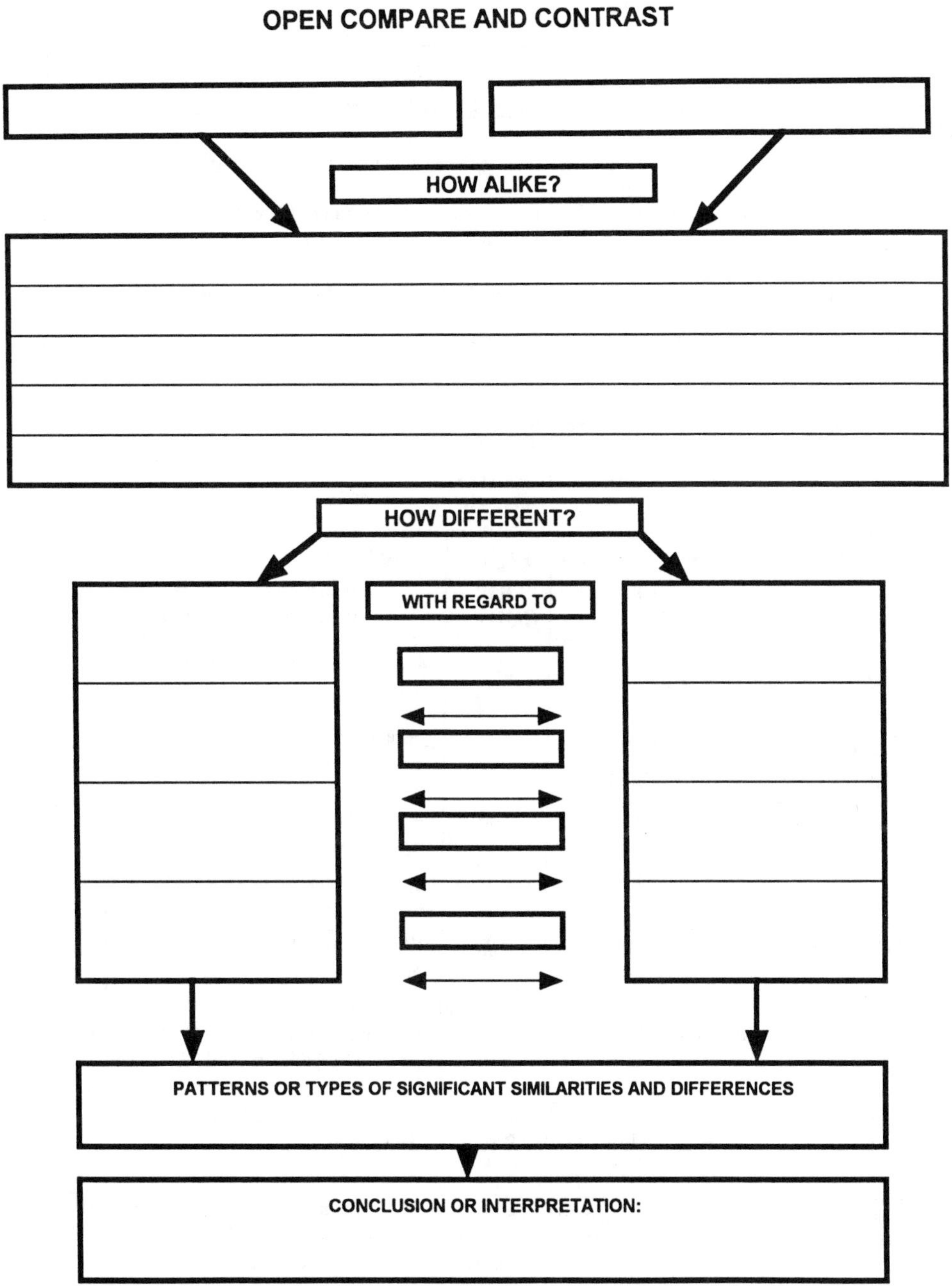

Figure 9.11. Open Compare and Contrast: Graphic Organizer
SOURCE: Swartz & Parks, 1994, p. 103.

SKILLFUL PROBLEM SOLVING

THE PROBLEM

How might I ___stay warm in the cave___?

POSSIBLE SOLUTIONS
How can I solve the problem?

Build a fire	Use soil as an insulator
Use leaves to make a blanket	Heat rocks in the sun or fire and keep them near us
Clean animal skins and use them as a coat or blanket	Reflect light and magnify it to produce heat
Get close to each other	Heat clothing in a fire

SOLUTION CONSIDERED

Use soil as an insulator

CONSEQUENCES What will happen if you adopt this solution?	PRO OR CON?	VALUE How important is the consequence? Why?
Must go outside cave to get soil	Con	**Important.** This could expose us to the British.
British may spot us when we are working outside the cave.	Con	**Very important.** We could be captured, disarmed, or killed.
Holes will be left in the ground.	Con	**Somewhat important**. The British might spot them; people could trip.
Could drop a trail of soil back to the cave.	Con	**Important.** This might lead the British back to cave. We could all be in danger
No heat will be generated by the soil.	Con	**Very important.** We need a source of heat.
Soil around the sleeping areas will keep in the heat.	Pro	**Very Important.** We need to keep warm as long through the night as possible.

NEW SOLUTION
How can the solution be changed to make it better?

We could try to get the soil at night, or get an insulator that doesn't expose us to danger as much, and we can only use soil when we have a source of heat. We would need to find a such a source.

Figure 9.12. Skillful Problem Solving: Graphic Organizer (How to Stay Warm in the Cave: Example 1)

SKILLFUL PROBLEM SOLVING

THE PROBLEM
How might I stay warm in the cave ?

POSSIBLE SOLUTIONS
How can I solve the problem?

Build a fire	Use soil as an insulator
Use leaves to make a blanket	Heat rocks in the sun or fire and keep them near us
Clean animal skins and use them as a coat or blanket	Reflect light and magnify it to produce heat
Get close to each other	Heat clothing in a fire

SOLUTION CONSIDERED
Heat rocks in the fire and bring them to areas where there are people

CONSEQUENCES What will happen if you adopt this solution?	**PRO OR CON?**	**VALUE** How important is the consequence? Why?
Dense or heavy rocks will stay hot for a while after they are heated	Pro	**Very Important.** We need to keep warm through the night.
We will get warmer.	Pro	**Very important.** We need warmth to survive.
We won't have to leave the cave.	Pro	**Important.** The cave keeps us hidden from the British.
Hot rocks become cool after a while unless they are insulated.	Con	**Important.** We need heat all night long.
Rocks can be very heavy to carry; some can't be carried	Con	**Very Important.** We need to move the rocks from the fire to our beds. We need heat where we sleep.

NEW SOLUTION
How can the solution be changed to make it better?

We should use only small rocks that can be carried and insulate them and us from heat loss.

Figure 9.13. Skillful Problem Solving: Graphic Organizer (How to Stay Warm in the Cave: Example 2)

satisfied that they had achieved an acceptable level of understanding of the concepts and principles through the use of the new format. In many cases, however, the teachers also reported results that went beyond what they believed they could achieve through regular classroom instruction on the same topics. For example, Hagevik reported that a group of male students who had not been doing well in science during the rest of the year became really interested in rocks and minerals as a result of this project. She was delighted when they went to the bookstore to buy a number of books on rocks and minerals—a topic that, as ordinarily taught, many students find dull and boring—and became the classroom experts on the rocks and minerals that were found in the cave.

Besides these content-related results, however, each teacher noted that the students also achieved an initial understanding of the thinking skills and processes that had been integrated into the units. In addition, teachers found that students began to change their habits of thought and their thinking dispositions to reflect the use of some of the key questioning strategies that had been taught.

Such reports are, of course, anecdotal and must be viewed against the backdrop of overall students' performance in a project such as this. All the teachers involved were quite pleased with what they saw happening—so much so that they have committed themselves to continuing to offer these topics through problem-based learning and to develop other units of this sort. They await, however, the results of more formal assessment of the project anticipated in the near future.

Summary

There is a good initial indication that problem-based learning in science provides the teacher with a powerful vehicle for teaching basic concepts and principles in science, for teaching the problem-solving and critical-thinking skills necessary to use these concepts and principles well, and for giving students practice in using both of these as they deal with authentic problems. It can be used as a framework for constructing a preprofessional science program as well as teaching for science literacy. In fact, problem-based learning is a powerful vehicle for use across the curriculum and in a variety of educational settings beyond the K-12 classroom.

This chapter has illustrated how problem-based learning works by describing a problem-based unit in high school physics and mathematics and a middle school science unit on heat, light, sound, and minerals. I hope that these descriptions will stimulate readers to try this approach in their own classrooms. Only through open and well-tried educational experimentation of this sort can we ascertain the range of application and effectiveness of new and interesting approaches such as problem-based learning.

Reference

Swartz, R., & Parks, S. (1994). *Infusing the teaching of critical and creative thinking into content instruction: A lesson design handbook for the elementary grades.* Pacific Grove, CA: Critical Thinking Press and Software.

10

Tools to Enhance Thinking and Learning

Sandra Parks

Using Tools to Improve Thinking and Learning

Using tools allows us to perform tasks more easily and efficiently, resulting in better accuracy, quality, and craftsmanship. With tools, we can access material that would be otherwise beyond reach. We use some tools to hold or to alter the material with which we work. Knowing how to use tools adds to our productivity and sense of mastery.

Cognitive processing tools perform similar functions in improving the quality of thinking and learning. Devices such as strategy maps summarize principles of efficient, effective learning and well-founded judgment and are used to guide thinking, learning, and information gathering. We use a variety of graphic and electronic tools to stimulate, organize, evaluate, and depict the results of our thinking. Using these devices allows us to manage our thought, promoting thoroughness in our consideration of issues, soundness and confidence in our judgments, and richness and elegance in expressions of our creativity.

This chapter describes how process tools help us access, organize, evaluate, and assimilate new facts and experiences and then transform that learning into new forms, applications, or products. It explores the curriculum implications of students' use of such tools as strategy maps, graphic organizers, computer technology, and simulations to improve student thinking and learning.

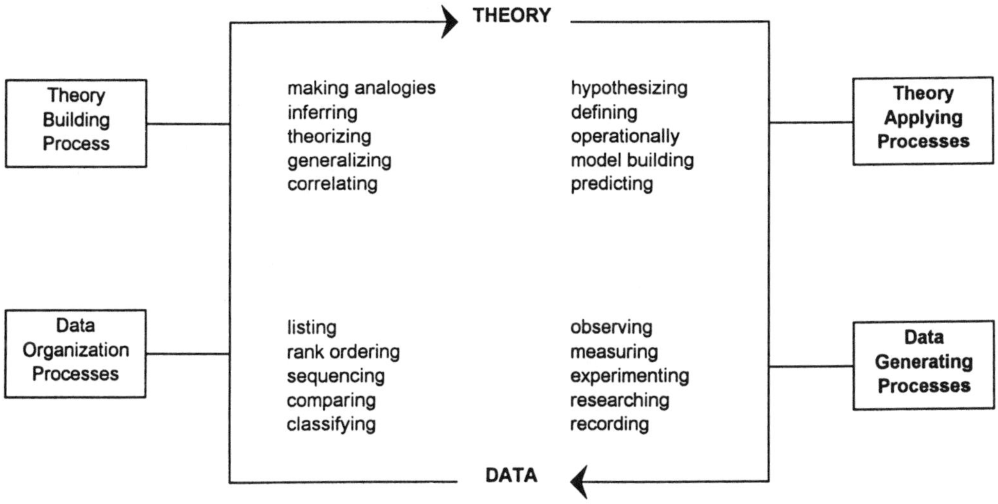

Figure 10.1. The Thinking Process
SOURCE: From J. Clarke's *Patterns of Thinking* (p. 20). Copyright 1990 by Allyn and Bacon. Reprinted with permission.

We can identify the function of cognitive tools by the role that they play in an information-processing model of learning. Costa (1991) organized thinking skills and processes according to recursive, nonlinear phases in a learning cycle—turning facts and experience into concepts, principles, or theories that then are evaluated, expanded, and transformed into action or new knowledge. Figure 10.1 depicts the different cognitive processes that occur at various phases of the learning process. The left side of the cycle depicts thinking tasks that serve an input function—gathering and organizing data or stimuli to make sense of them. The thinking tasks in the center are involved in mental processing—reformulating and evaluating information to incorporate it into present belief systems, theories, or behavior. The thinking tasks on the right side of the diagram involve expanding, transforming, or operationalizing what we have learned.

The cognitive tools explored in this chapter often serve more than one of the functions of inputting, processing, and outputting information. Knowing how to use a variety of devices commonly employed in instruction, business, and personal decision making and exploring how these cognitive tools facilitate their thinking and learning, teachers and students can decide which tools they will use at various stages in processing and using information.

Thinking and learning tools provides cognitive scaffolding to allow teachers and learners to clarify both the processes and the products of learning. Some instructional time be spent showing students how to use devices that support their thinking and learning. After students become proficient in using these tools, they do so naturally without further prompting. Students may modify these devices to fit individual styles, purposes, and interests. The goal of such instruction is self-initiated, efficient thinking and learning in which learners are proactive in conducting and managing their own mental tasks.

If curriculum significantly addresses improving thinking and learning processes, teachers and students must be familiar with different cognitive tools and understand how these tools help guide, picture, and stimulate thought. Classroom instruction should include explaining and using a variety of these tools in content and personal application. Curriculum planning involves deciding how and when to teach students to use cognitive tools in content learning and how to organize classroom space and time to employ them effectively.

Strategy Maps as Thinking-Learning Tools

Considerable cognitive research in the 1970s and 1980s involved clarifying thinking and learning processes, making explicit the mental operations that are commonly implicit in classroom instruction. Drawing on educational psychology and cognitive science, learning specialists developed cognitive strategy maps, metacognitive devices that make learning easier, more efficient, and more effective. In the 1990s, information literacy specialists developed strategy maps of key questions to ask when seeking, organizing, and evaluating information in a particular situation, application, or issue. Thinking strategy maps prompt users to consider the questions that a thoughtful person asks and answers when making well-founded judgments. Such devices prompt users to think about and research aspects of an issue that may otherwise be overlooked.

Learning Strategy Maps

During the 1970s, instruction emphasized using instructional strategies that make the teaching-learning process explicit. Curriculum specialists such as Madeline Hunter and Hilda Taba left a legacy of instructional strategy maps for teaching various content objectives. Teachers learned that if the teaching of concepts or processes was proceduralized for clarity, students learned more efficiently and effectively.

For any instructional technique that teachers use, students engage in a similar metacognitive pattern to comprehend what is being taught. In the example in Figure 10.2, students are taught a strategy map for learning how to do a new operation. Based on Hunter's (1983) expository teaching model, the lesson involves helping students understand what the teacher will do when explaining a new process. By understanding how the teacher will conduct the lesson, learners understand their part in the teaching-learning transaction. Students can follow the steps in the instruction process and understand how to self-correct when losing the train of thought in a demonstration or explanation. The learners can then return to that point in instruction in which conceptualization went awry and recover understanding the operation.

Using a modification of Taba's concept development model as a review tool (see Eggen, Kauchek, & Harder, 1979), students can self-assess how well they understand a concept. If students can answer six basic questions about a concept, they can be confident of their own conceptualizations. The money example in Figure 10.3 shows how concept development yields clear definitions. Lack of clarity in answering any of these questions indicates how omissions or incomplete understanding should be corrected.

HOW DO I LEARN TO DO IT WELL?

When Have I Learned To Do Something Like This Before?
Why Important? To tie this explanation to something I already know; to save time; to reduce anxiety or confusion.
What To Ask? Please remind me again of the process or terms; give me another example.

↓

What I Am Learning?
Why Important? To be sure about what I expect to learn; to
What To Ask? Please clarify unfamiliar terms or restate what we

↓

How Is It Done?
Why Important? If I misunderstand the steps, the order of the steps, or why I do them, then I won't use this
What to ask? To clarify terms or repeat the operation: to explain it in other words.

↓

Can I Do It Correctly?
Why Important? To prevent Practicing doing this operation incorrectly.
What to Ask? Please check my work with me to see where I started making mistakes; to listen to my description to hear where I began making an error.

↓

Can I Do It Fast And Well?
Why Important? To be sure that I can do this operation quickly and accurately; for personal confidence.
What To Ask? Please give me extra practice or show me shortcuts or ways to check the operation.

↓

Do I know When To Use It Again?
Why Important? To remember better and to be prepared the next time I use it; to reduce anxiety.
What To Ask? Please suggest other examples in school or life situations.

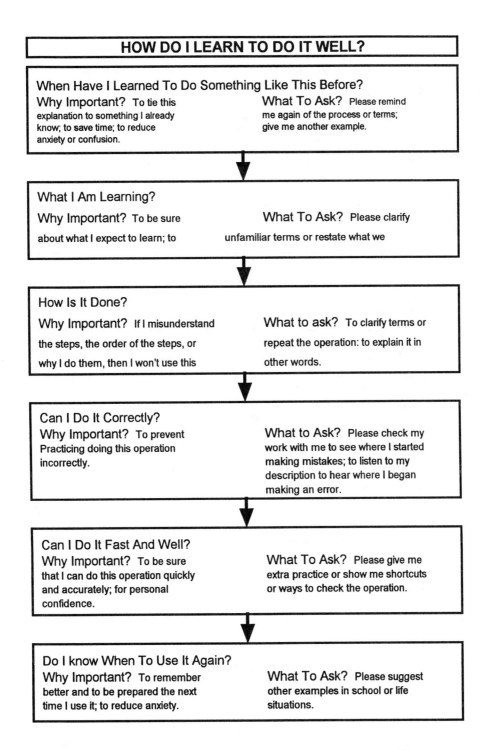

Figure 10.2. Learning Strategy Map: How Do I Learn to Do It Well?
SOURCE: Parks & Black, 1990. Used with permission.

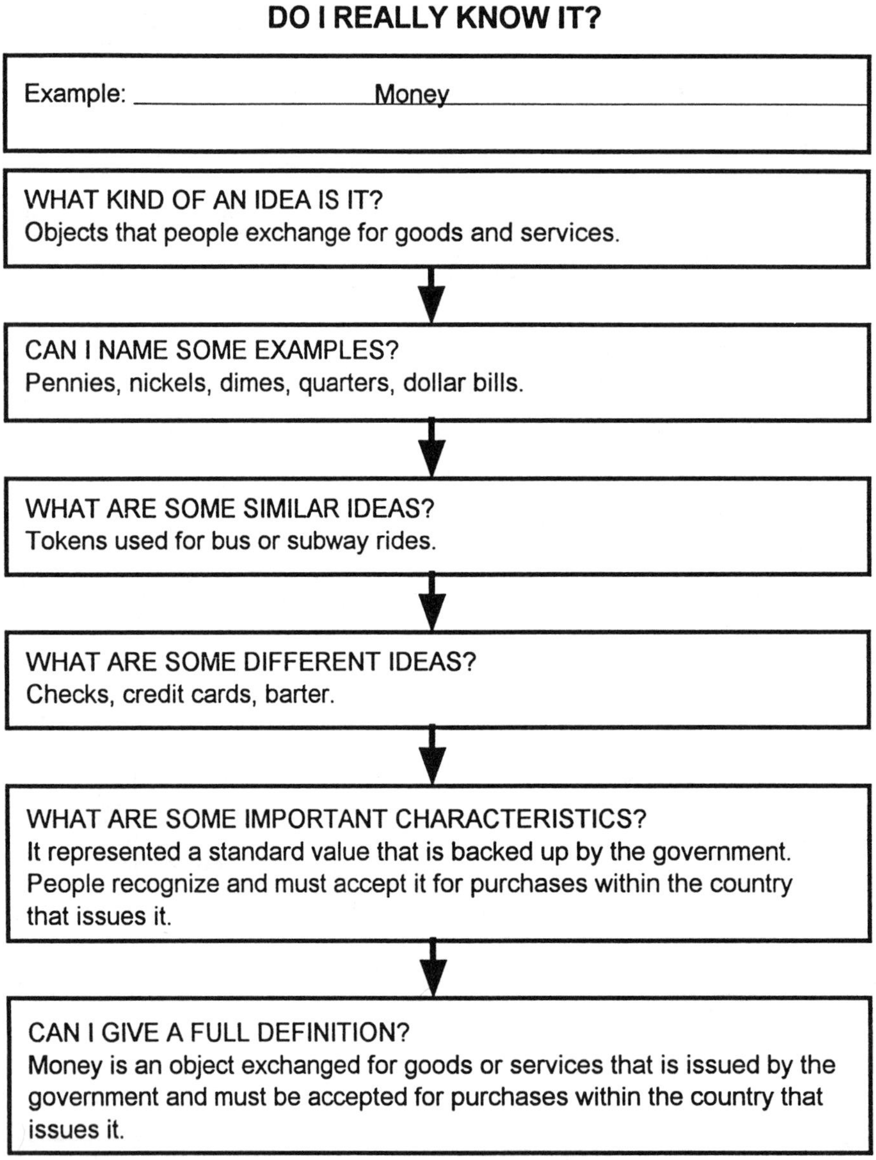
DO I REALLY KNOW IT?
Example: Money
WHAT KIND OF AN IDEA IS IT?
Objects that people exchange for goods and services.
CAN I NAME SOME EXAMPLES?
Pennies, nickels, dimes, quarters, dollar bills.
WHAT ARE SOME SIMILAR IDEAS?
Tokens used for bus or subway rides.
WHAT ARE SOME DIFFERENT IDEAS?
Checks, credit cards, barter.
WHAT ARE SOME IMPORTANT CHARACTERISTICS?
It represented a standard value that is backed up by the government. People recognize and must accept it for purchases within the country that issues it.
CAN I GIVE A FULL DEFINITION?
Money is an object exchanged for goods or services that is issued by the government and must be accepted for purchases within the country that issues it.

Figure 10.3. Concept Development: Do I Really Know It?
SOURCE: Parks & Black, 1990. Used with permission.

To promote deep understanding of concepts, Perkins, Goodrich, Tishman, and Mirman-Owen (1994) developed the Understanding Through Design Strategy for analyzing "designs" (objects, concepts, and events). Students learn to identify the purpose of a design (key purposes, varied purposes, creative purposes, and hidden purposes), its features and the reasons for them, the pros and cons of how well the design works, and how the design can be improved. As students apply this strategy to the circulatory system, a poem, a ruler, or the preamble to the Constitution, their evaluation of key attributes of a thing or idea yields thorough comprehension, clear retention, and creative thinking about important concepts.

Information Use Strategy Maps

The information explosion, involving new computer technology such as videodiscs, CD-ROMs, and the Internet, has made information literacy a timely curriculum initiative. These cross-disciplinary curriculum goals prompt learners to reflect about the type, quality, and availability of information, how to retrieve and evaluate it, and how to express or depict it for more effective understanding and decision making. Figure 10.4 reminds information users of key questions to ask to define the type of information that is needed; to select a search strategy; to locate resources and retrieve the needed data; to access the accuracy and quality of information; to interpret, evaluate, and communicate that information; and to draw well-founded judgments or produce creative products based on it.

The basic shift in the teaching-learning transaction when using strategy maps significantly involves students becoming proactive in their own learning. Students learn the procedures of the instructional strategy that the teacher is using to explain concepts and procedures. Then students can monitor metacognitively how well they are understanding what is being explained and know the point in the process at which clarification is needed.

Thinking Strategy Maps

"Teaching thinking" commonly means teaching a thinking skill or process directly, either by explaining the procedure didactically or by eliciting it inductively. For example, in de Bono's CoRT program (1987), teachers explain the "PMI scanning tool," a strategy map in which students brainstorm all the *P*lus (good points), *M*inus (negative points), and *I*nteresting aspects of a decision. Students then use the abbreviation PMI to prompt themselves to consider these factors when exploring decisions, either in content lessons or in personal application.

Students may also learn thinking strategy maps inductively. In the infusion program (Swartz & Parks, 1994), teachers use a strategy map for decision making to organize students' comments about their own decision making. Although the thinking strategy may be expressed in students' own words, the decision-making process will contain the key questions on the strategy map.

Whether shown didactically or derived inductively, thinking strategy maps are used for the same purposes: to clarify the processes of clear, systematic, effective thinking; to provide a schema that can be easily remembered; and to show how the strategy can be used in a variety of contexts. Students understand and use a common language to describe and express their thinking and have a

HOW DO I FIND AND USE THE INFORMATION WELL?

WHAT INFORMATION DO I NEED?
WHAT KIND? Statistics, facts, observations, reports, interpretations, depictions, creative works, explanations?
WHAT FORM? Text, tables, lists, maps, diagrams, outlines, pictures interview, speeches, diaries?
WHAT MEDIUM? Print, film, videotape, video disk, photograph, microfiche?

↓

HOW DO I FIND IT?
WHAT RESOURCES SHOW WHERE INFORMATION LIKE THIS IS LOCATED? *Books In Print, Reader's Guide,* Internet Gopher, etc.
WHAT SEARCH PLAN WILL OFFER ADEQUATE INFORMATION EFFICIENTLY? Steps in search and retrieval?

↓

WHERE IS THIS INFORMATION LOCATED?
TYPE OF SOURCE? Public libraries specialized libraries, research or government agencies, computer file, internet, CD rom?
SPECIFIC SOURCE? Title, Author, publication, date, file name, volume, e-mail listing, publisher's address, telephone number?

↓

HOW DO I OBTAIN IT?
POLICIES? Authorization for access and use, limitations on volume and application, restrictions on photo-copying, royalties, access fees?
HOW TRANSMITTED? Print material, computer disk, fax, e-mail? Time necessary? How converted? Technological compatibility?

↓

HOW RELIABLE IS THIS INFORMATION?
PRIMARY OR SECONDARY?
RELIABILITY OF OBSERVATION REPORT. Observer? Procedures? Corroborated? Report documented?
REGARDED IN THIS FIELD?
FITS KEY FACTORS IN THIS USE? Timeliness, comparable definitions, compatible procedures

↓

HOW CAN I CONVEY WHAT I LEARN FROM THIS INFORMATION?
TYPE OF PRODUCT? Text, display, performance, computer file?
CRITERIA FOR REPORTING? Documentation, standards for this type of product, citation, format, user-friendliness.
AUDIENCE? Reader, listeners, size and background of audience?

Figure 10.4. Information Use Strategy Map
SOURCE: Parks (forthcoming).

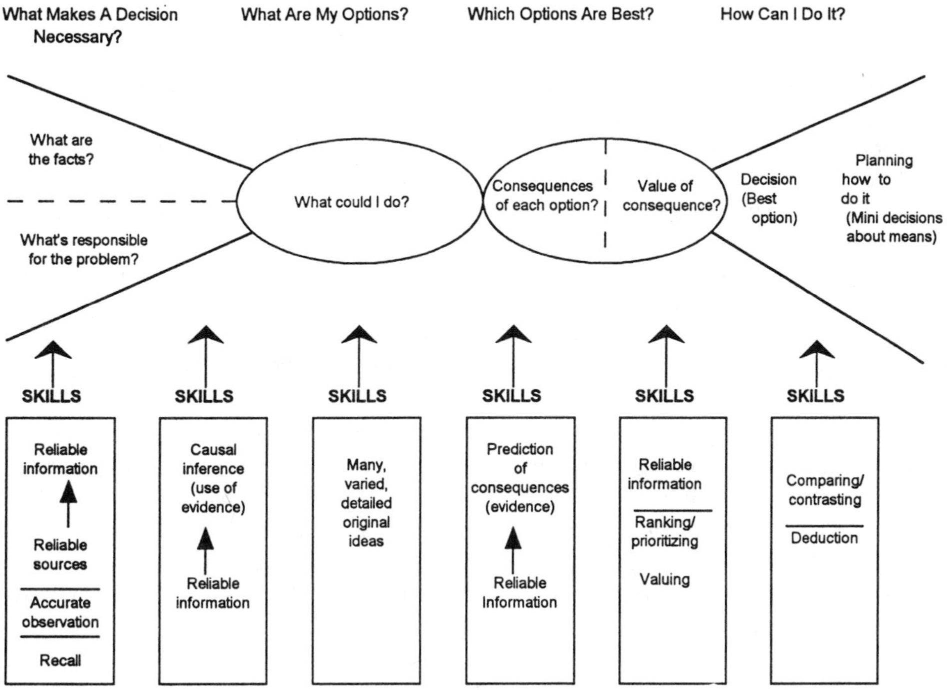

Figure 10.5. Thinking Skills Involved in the Decision-Making Process
SOURCE: Swartz & Perkins, 1990. Used with permission.

metacognitive framework for executing and monitoring their thinking (see Figure 10.5).

Graphic Organizers as Thinking and Learning Tools

In the previous examples, strategy maps have been supplemented by graphic organizers. Diagrams depict how information is related, "picturing" issues so that users can make interpretations or judgments. Using graphic organizers, teachers and students can access, organize, and display complex information involved in evaluating issues, solving problems, and making decisions. Graphic organizers may also be used to guide or stimulate thinking, to demonstrate or review what has been learned, and to plan projects.

Graphics That Hold and Organize Information

Matrices are commonly used in textbooks, newspapers, and periodicals to organize complex information. The matrix on alternative energy sources (Figure 10.6) serves as a "data retrieval chart," a graphic organizer that Taba (see Eggen et al., 1979) used to guide students' research and observations for conducting inductive reasoning. The matrix in Figure 10.6 contains information involved when considering what energy sources should be developed and used. Students are not given this information but instead use the matrix to organize their research. The empty cells of the diagram remind students of the types of data needed to make informed judgment.

Students list their options (various energy sources) down the left side of the diagram. They label each column with a type of consequence that should be considered in deciding energy use (its availability, its impact on the environment, its cost to use and produce, etc.). After each student group has reported its findings about an energy source, its information is added to this matrix, a huge bulletin board to organize and display the class's combined research on sources of energy.

Having organized this mass of information, students must then interpret it. Individually, in small groups, or as a whole class, students then summarize information in each row, creating what Taba called a *generalization* about a particular form of energy (see Eggen et al., 1979). For example, the student group responsible for gathering the data on solar energy prepares a summary statement that synthesizes the important information that its research uncovered about solar energy.

Then students summarize the information in each column to state a generalization that addresses the next important question: "What kinds of consequences are more important than others?" This summary statement addresses which factors in considering energy use warrant greater weight than others. Finally, by reflecting on the summary statements for the rows and the columns, students prepare a recommendation about what energy sources should be used.

Graphics That Guide Thinking

The matrix serves as an information holder to organize complex information so that users can make judgments about it. This matrix, however, is more than a chart of rows and columns to hold data, such as a bus schedule or television timetable. This specialized matrix is also designed to guide students' decision making. It contains information exchanged in students' deliberations as they follow the decision-making strategy depicted in Figure 10.6.

The decision-making graphic organizer in Figure 10.7 depicts students' research on President Truman's decision regarding how to end World War II. Truman's options, the consequences of each option, information to evaluate the likelihood of the consequences, and consideration of the value of the consequences are summarized on the diagram. Students then evaluate each option to arrive at a judgment regarding the best action to end the war.

SAMPLE STUDENT RESPONSES * ALTERNATIVE ENERGY				
DECISION MAKING MATRIX				
OPTION	RELEVANT CONSEQUENCES			
	EASE OF PRODUCTION	ENVIRONMENT	COST	AVAILABILITY
SOLAR Active Passive Photovoltaic	Easy, if location, latitude and weather conditions are favorable. Little maintenance. Limited service for repairs. Photovoltaic not cost effective until improved technology makes it more efficient?	No undesirable air or water pollution. Unsightly equipment or circular fields of mirrors. Loss of trees. Environmental impact of manufacturing materials and equipment or disposing of batteries?	Start up is costly (could be reduced by mass manufacture). Low maintenance and repair? Operation costs are minimal. Research and development costly?	Limited by location, latitude and weather. Seasonal in some areas. Distributing and storing resulting electricity is limited. Renewable.
NUCLEAR	Complex, requiring sophisticated instruments, specialized technicians, and unusual safety measures. Waste disposal is risky and requires long-term safeguards.	Radiation danger. Mining erosion and toxic tailings are produced to secure uranium. Storage of waste may result in radiation contamination. Production structures are huge.	Protective measures in operation and start-up costs are high. Licensing, certifying, and inspecting plants are expensive. Maintenance costs?	Uranium is scarce Breeder reactors are controversial and limited.
PETRO-CHEMICAL	Complex, but commonly practiced.	Oil spills may result. Depletion of the oil supply. Hydrocarbons pollute the air, damage the ozone layer, and create acid rain. Processing pollutes air.	Exploration, research, distribution and cleanup costs are high. Importing is costly; depends on international pricing. Valuable for uses other than energy.	Limited regional supplies. Non-renewable.
COAL	Complex, but commonly practiced	Strip and shaft mining scars the land. Use creates a gray film on surfaces. Particulate emissions pollute the air. Acid rain pollutes air and water.	Research and development of soft coal use is costly. Labor, transportation, and conversion are costly.	Diminishing supply. Underutilize soft coal.

Figure 10.6. Decision-Making Matrix Graphic Organizer: Sample Student Responses
SOURCE: Swartz & Parks, 1994. Used with permission.

SKILLFUL DECISION MAKING

OPTIONS

Demonstrate the bomb on or near the Japanese homeland, but not in a populated area.	Increase conventional bombing
Surrender	Incite Japanese people against their government
Capture the Emperor	Use chemical weapons
Embargo/Blockade	Invade Japan
	Drop A-bomb on a populated military target
	Cease fire

OPTION CONSIDERED
INVADE JAPAN

CONSEQUENCES What will happen if I	**SUPPORT** Why do I think each	**VALUE** How important is the
— Heavy US casualties	Japanese military officers claim preparedness for an invasion. Iwo Jima and Okinawa reports indicate heavy US and Japanese casualties. US lost 300,000 men breaking through the perimeter islands. Kamikaze attacks kill 13,000 US men in 2 days off Okinawa. Stimson	**Very Important** Loss of life is the most important consideration.
— War Prolonged	Invasion scheduled for November, 1945. Fierce fighting on Iwo Jima and Okinawa shows slow gains.	**Very Important** Prolonged war means more loss of life and material costs.
— High economic costs and loss of equipment	Iwo Jima and Okinawa reports indicate fierce fighting destroying tanks and losses of 15 ships and damage to 200 others.	**Very Important** Such losses affect ability to wage war and US economy
— Worsen morale and lose public support	Brutality of Pacific fighting was abhorrent to public. Letters to newspapers and officials show opposition.	**Important** Public support needed for congressional funding.
+ War contractors do well	Iwo Jima and Okinawa reports indicate heavy losses of tanks and ships. Invading the mainland will result in more fierce fighting and losses. Prolonged war requires more equipment.	**Not important** They are a special interest group. War affects whole country
— Heavy Japanese casualties	Cultural disposition to "fight-to-death....' Heavy Japanese losses on Iwo Jima and Okinawa.	**Very Important** Loss of life is the most important factor.
— Destroy Japanese cultural and economic resources	Heavy bombing had already destroyed cities and industrial plants and created fire damage. Invasion in Europe lead to great destruction.	**Important** Industries can be rebuilt but shrines may be lost forever
— Invasion Fails	Military reports indicate massive destruction of cities and dwindling food and resources. Fierce fighting on Iwo Jima and Okinawa shows Japanese determination	**Very Important** Successful end to war requires that invasion succeeds.
— Soviet Union invades Japan	At Potsdam the Soviets said that they would invade Japan by August 8, 1945	**Important** Soviet presence in Japan will affect US influence in Pacific
— Truman loses election	Letters to newspapers and officials show opposition to the war. Election is three years away.	**Important** Truman's policies are sound.

Figure 10.7. Decision-Making Graphic Organizer: Student Example
SOURCE: Swartz & Parks (forthcoming). Used with permission.

As in the energy example, the graphic organizer "pictures" the decision-making process. The graphic organizer displays evidence for or against the likelihood of various consequences and the relative significance of them. Comparing graphics for several options, students can "see" easily which options have significant numbers of important positive or negative consequences.

Graphic organizers can be used to depict the questions that thoughtful people ask and answer in skillful critical thinking: assessing the reliability of the sources of information, evaluating reasons given for conclusions, reasoning by analogy, using causal explanation and prediction, evaluating, making generalizations, and using conditional and categorical reasoning (Swartz & Parks, 1994). In each case, the graphic organizer summarizes the information required in making such judgments and depicts the steps in the evaluation process by appropriate symbols and design elements (arrows, circles, boxes, etc.).

To assess the reliability of an observation report, students list questions that they would want satisfied to decide whether the account is accurate. From their list of questions, they generate a strategy map of the factors that they would take into account when evaluating the reliability of any observation report. In the example shown in Figure 10.8, students generate questions about Percival Lowell's turn-of-the-century observations of Mars, in which he reported seeing lines on Mars that he described as canals.

Using arrows, lines, and color, students create a strategy map by "lining up" their questions with categories of questions represented on their list. Questions generally fall in four main categories: questions about the observer (capacity, expertise, background, objectivity, etc.), the observation itself (conditions, procedures, equipment, etc.), the nature of the report (type and reputation of the publication, audience, use of pictures, tables, etc.), and whether other observers corroborate the findings.

Once the types of questions have been established and criteria for reliability clarified, students apply the strategy to evaluate the observation to decide whether the observation is reliable enough to accept as accurate. In the example shown in Figure 10.9, students decide that the technology available to Lowell and his predisposition to believe that there were canals on Mars biased his observation and outweighed his credentials and other scientific achievements.

Graphics That Show Relationships

Graphic organizers featured in textbooks or magazines generally show how information is related. Common graphics, such as matrices, flowcharts, Venn diagrams, branching diagrams, and concept maps, depict analysis: sequence, rank, classification, subdivision, analogy, part-whole relationships, or attribution.

Concept maps, also called "bubble maps" or "web diagrams," can be used to show a variety of relationships (attribution, classification, part-whole relationships, etc.). They can stimulate creative thinking and are versatile for numerous instructional or personal uses. In the example in Figure 10.10, the concept map shows the activities in a course on design technology for children.

SAMPLE STUDENT RESPONSES · THE CANALS OF MARS

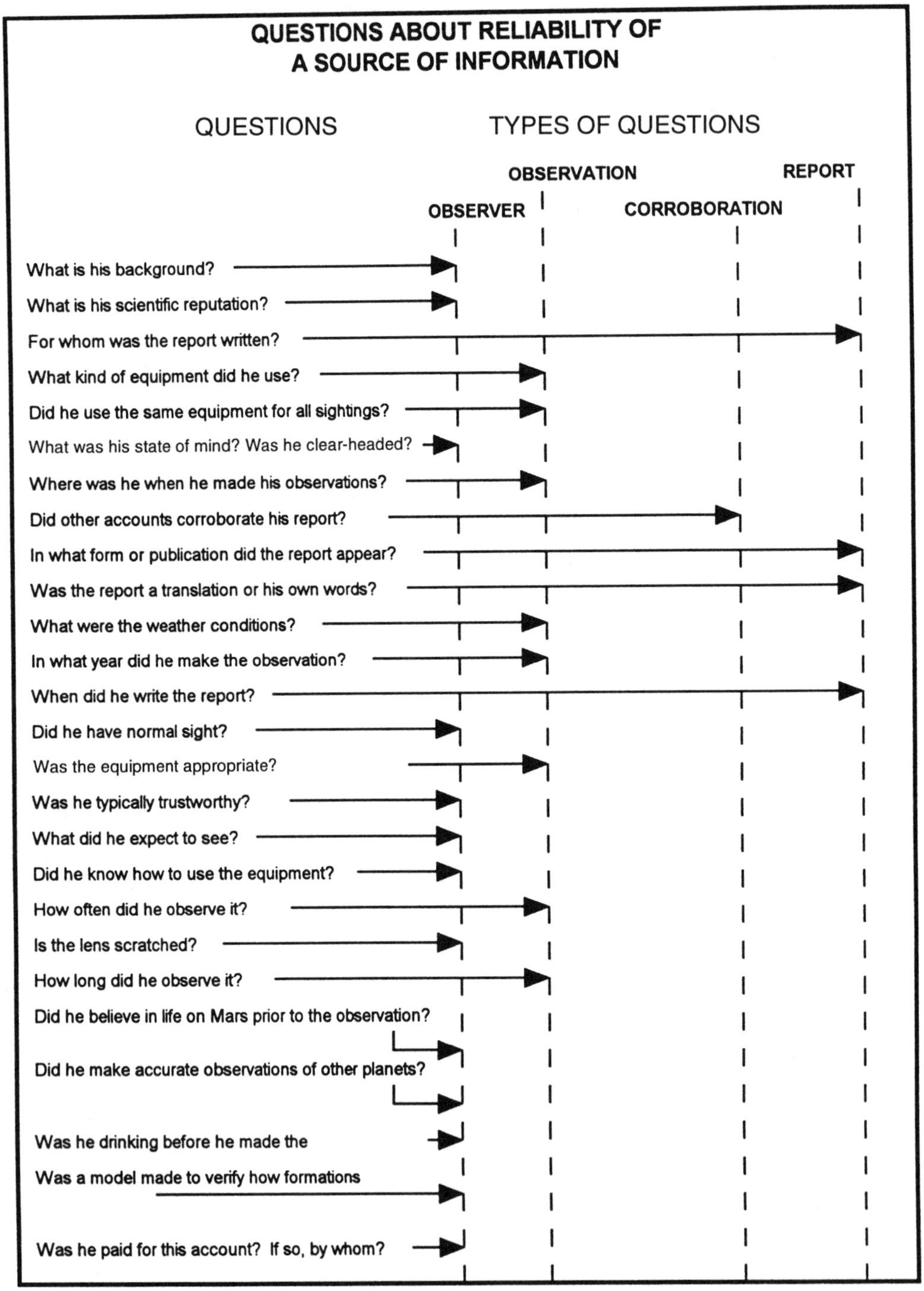

Figure 10.8. Graphic Organizer: Strategy Map to Assess Reliability
SOURCE: Swartz & Parks, 1994. Used with permission.

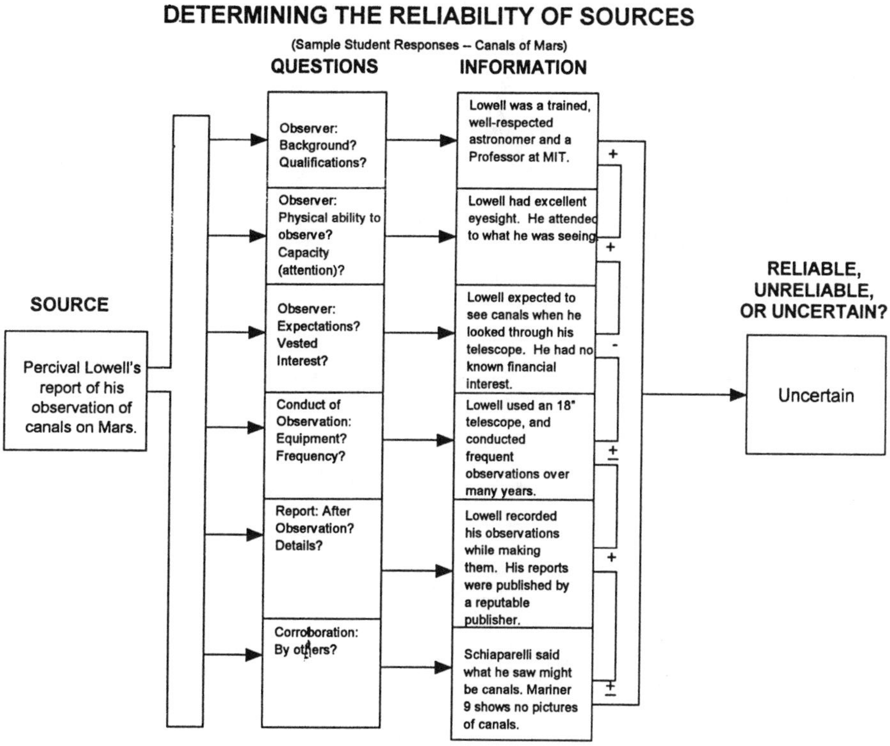

Figure 10.9. Graphic Organizer: Strategy Map to Determine Reliability of Sources
SOURCE: Swartz & Parks, 1994. Used with permission.

This concept map may be the teacher's planning tool to design the course, an advanced organizer for students (showing what they will learn in the course), or a review tool to summarize instruction when the unit is completed.

The second concept map, depicted in Figure 10.11, shows how the topics in the unit address interdisciplinary objectives. Although this concept map is clearly the teacher's planning tool, students similarly use concept maps in planning projects. The teacher may show this plan to the class to illustrate how the various subjects are "webbed" around the topic and to track the implementation of the unit.

The third concept map (Figure 10.12) shows simple tools that students use in the course. The goal in using this concept map is improving students' conceptualization of content. In this case, the concept map depicts classification, illustrating different types of simple machines featured in the course. Students soon learn that although diagrams may have the same basic design, the same graphic form may serve different purposes. Learning to "read" graphics be-

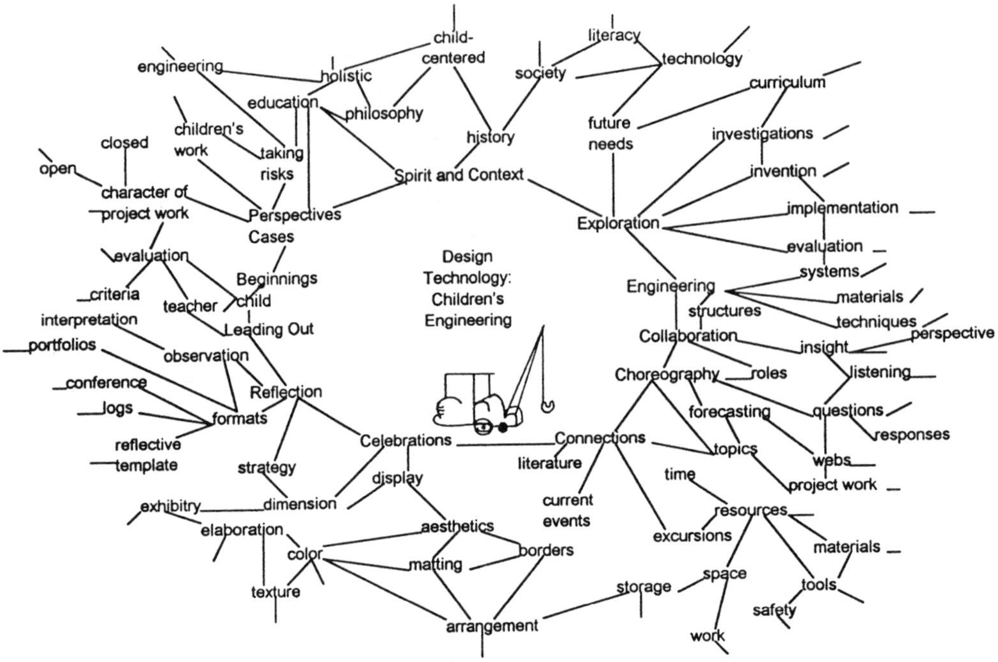

Figure 10.10. Concept Map for Course on Design Technology for Children
SOURCE: Dunn & Larson, 1990. Used with permission.

comes an instructional outcome, a valuable skill in an increasingly technological society.

Graphics That Stimulate Thinking

The fourth concept map from the design technology unit (see Figure 10.13) is used to stimulate students' inquiry about creatures they find on the playground. Using the graphic organizer promotes associative thinking in which one question quickly generates another. The graphic organizer serves as both a stimulus and a display for questions to raise when investigating this topic.

Using graphic organizers to generate ideas can take several forms: graphics to guide a creative thinking process, graphics to analyze a creative product, and mind mapping. The exercise shown in Figure 10.14 involves generating possibilities for what could be done with a pile of dirt at a construction site. To prompt fluency, students brainstorm possible uses, writing their suggestions in the second box. They then categorize their ideas and are prompted by each category heading to think of new uses of that type, adding new suggestions to the "possibilities" box as shown by the arrow. They then check whether their ideas are unusual ones, prompting themselves to find original possibilities.

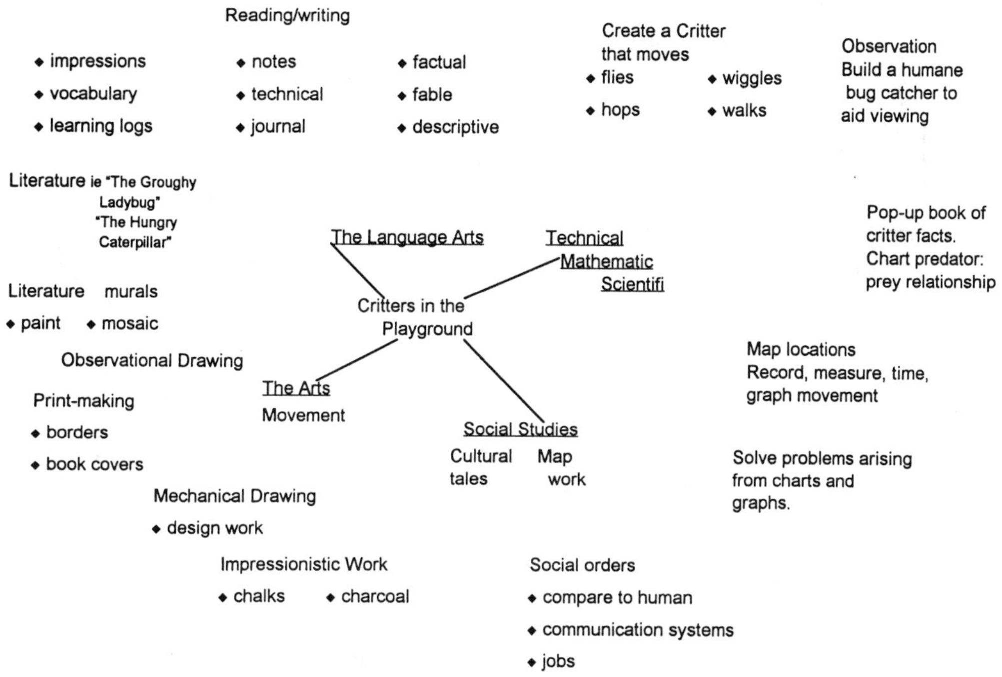

Figure 10.11. Concept Map for Planning Interdisciplinary Objectives
SOURCE: Dunn & Larson, 1990. Used with permission.

Students then use a second diagram, shown in Figure 10.15, to generate additional possibilities. Forcing a connection between categories that normally do not go together generates new ideas. For example, by combining "to use it for fun" with "move it elsewhere," students come up with "take it to the playground and make a hill with tunnels for kids to play in." Using the matrix prompts students to think about ideas to fill the blank boxes. The connection among existing ideas generates new ones. By linking different types of ideas, students come up with new solutions to the problem of using the dirt. Even working alone, a student can use a matrix as a framework in order to combine some of the interesting features of ideas that have already been generated to create new possibilities.

A graphic organizer can also be used to analyze or create a metaphor. Class discussion recorded on this graphic organizer shows how metaphors serve as idea bridges to convey other characteristics or images with playfulness and richness. Consider the cat metaphor in Carl Sandburg's poem "Fog." Using the diagram shown in Figure 10.16, students name a characteristic of a cat that is also true of fog, such as *silence*. Students brainstorm words for silence, associated with either a cat or fog, and write these details or descriptors in the boxes on each side of the diagram.

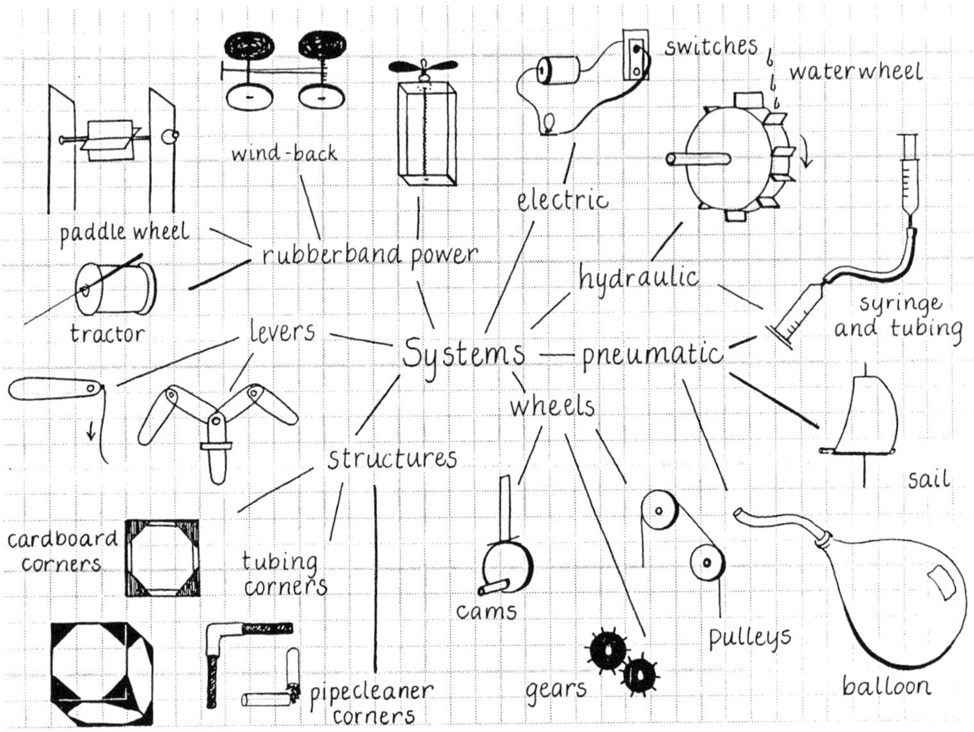

Figure 10.12. Concept Map for Students' Conceptualization of Content: Tools
SOURCE: Dunn & Larson, 1990. Used with permission.

How does the graphic organizer help stimulate connections, details, and insights that students may otherwise overlook? As students discuss the characteristics and details on one side of the diagram, the boxes on the other side have yet to be filled. Searching for more descriptors, they are prompted to suggest additional connotations or examples. Students uncover not just concrete details but also multiple characteristics, dimensions, and implications that connect the two ideas.

Words suggested for one characteristic may also describe another. *Soft* may suggest the silence, as well as the texture, of a cat. The graphic organizer summarizes a whole collection of characteristics and details about one thing that may also have meaning about the other. When students are asked what the image of a cat tells the reader about fog, they now realize that an array of attributes and details are conveyed by the metaphor.

In this case, the graphic organizer not only holds ideas but also stimulates users' responses. This technique is particularly valuable for language-limited students because the graphic organizer becomes a visual record of descriptors from which students can then select words to create new poems or prose.

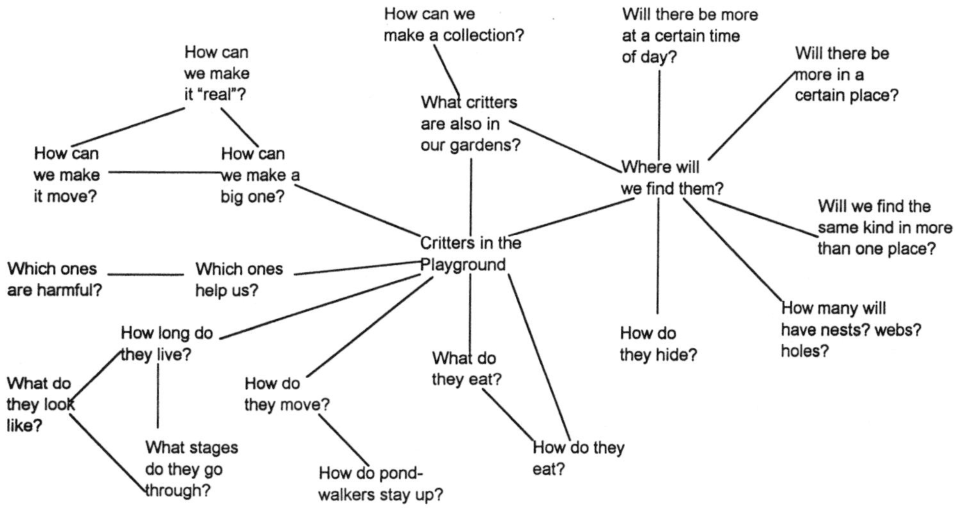

Figure 10.13. Concept Map to Stimulate Thinking: Playground Creatures
SOURCE: Dunn & Larson, 1990. Used with permission.

One of the most common techniques for using graphics to stimulate thinking is mind mapping. Its use of whole-brain learning and its many applications as a memory, study, or planning aid make mind mapping a valuable tool for thinking and learning. In *Mapping Inner Space,* Margoulos (1994) created this mind map of the technique (Figure 10.17). It depicts her observation that mind mapping stimulates creativity and is fast, fun, and memorable.

Mind maps feature pictures, color, codes (numbers or arrows), or a central image. The print can be varied (upper or lower case, different fonts or styles, and color) to show different features. Mind mapping can be used not only to show to others the product of thought but also as a device to generate ideas.

Graphic Organizers for Assessment

Portfolio and performance assessment increasingly includes graphic organizers for teachers' evaluation and students' self-assessment. Graphics allow students to self-assess what they knew, what they have learned, and what questions remain unanswered about concepts in an instructional unit. Using graphics to show what they know is particularly important for language-limited students whose knowledge and level of understanding may not be expressed well in writing.

BRAINSTORMING IN ORDER TO GENERATE POSSIBILITIES

PURPOSE What are these possibilities for?
The use of a pile of dirt left after a foundation hole is dug at a building site.

POSSIBILITIES

Spread it all over the rest of the site. Sell it to someone who needs fill. Package it as potting soil for plants. Extract the worms and sell them. Use it in school to study life in the soil. Use it as a winter sledding run. Bag it and use it on river banks to prevent flooding. Dump it in a vacant lot. Extract the rocks for a rock garden. Bury a treasure in it for a treasure hunt. Hollow it and use as a club house. Use it for a sod roof. Use it for mud packs for facials. Make terraria with it. Put it in flower pots and plant bulbs in the pots.	Use it as a hill for a bicycle run. Use it as a mud slide. Mix it with water to make mud balls. Mix it with compost to make rich topsoil. Mix it with rocks to put dirt on a road. Grow Grass on it. Make it into a fenced goat hill. Make it into a huge ant hill. Plant trees on it for a shady knoll. Bury trash in it. Store apples in it. Use it for a meteoric display in the atmosphere. Mix it with water and clay to make bricks. Make a hill with tunnels for children in the playground. Make a traveling mud-wrestling show.

Moving elsewhere	Extracting Things	Used for fun	Used for learning	Mixed with something
Spread over site. Fill hole elsewhere. Bags for flooding	Sell worms. Study living things. Potting soil. Rocks for garden.	Winter sled run. Bicycle run. Winter ski run. Mud slide. Mud balls.	Study living things. Test impact of acid rain.	Water for mud balls. Compost for top soil. Rocks for dirt for road.
Habitat	**Putting things in**	**Health & Beauty**	**Decoration**	**Building**
Grow grass Goat hill Ant Hill Plant Trees	Bury trash Store apples Bury treasure	Minerals for health Mud pack for facials	Make terraria Put in pots and plant bulbs	Hollow for club house Sod roof

UNUSUAL POSSIBILITIES

Extract and sell worms Hollow it for a club house Use it for mud packs for facials. Bury a treasure for a treasure hunt. Extract rocks for a rock garden Make it into a fenced goat hill.	Send it up in the space shuttle and eject it into the atmosphere for a meteoric display. Mix it with water and clay and make bricks for building Take it to the playground and make a hill with tunnels for children to play in. Put it in the back of a truck, mix it with water, and have a traveling mud-wrestling show.

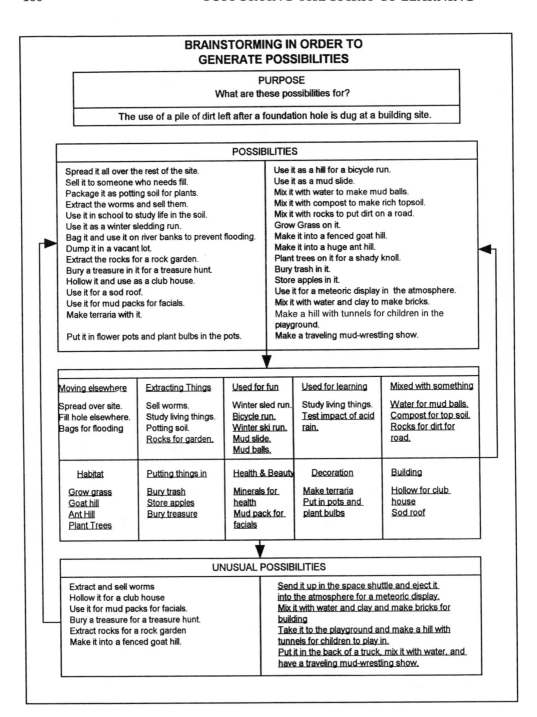

Figure 10.14. Graphic Organizer to Generate Ideas
SOURCE: Swartz & Parks, 1994. Used with permission.

MATRIX FOR GENERATING ORIGINAL POSSIBILITIES

Interesting Features Of Possibilities Already Generated	Interesting Features Of Possibilities Already Generated			
	Move It Elsewhere	**Use it For Fun**	**Use It In Building**	**Mix With Something**
Move It Elsewhere		Take it up in the space shuttle and eject it into the atmosphere for a great meteoric display visible from Earth.	Use it to build a ramp that cement trucks can drive on to pour cement into a form for a new, high, prison wall.	Mix it with fertilizer and move it to a place on the property where it can be used to start a garden.
Use It For Fun	Take it to the play-ground and make a hill with tunnels for children to play in.		Build a dirt model of the castle at Disney World	Mix it with water, put it in the back of a truck, and make it into a traveling mud-wrestling show.
Use It In Building	Move it to a river that has to be dammed up and use it to build a dam. Add large rocks to hold it in place.	Hollow it out and make it into a haunted house that people can visit on Halloween.		Mix it with grass seed and use it t o make the sod roof of your new house.
Mix with Something	Move it to a road construction site, mix it with more dirt from other building sites, and use it to build up the road bed.	Mix it with water, put it in an empty swim-ming pool, and use it for mud wrestling	Mix it with water and clay; make bricks, dry them, and use them in building.	

Figure 10.15. Matrix for Generating Original Possibilities: Sample Student Responses
SOURCE: Swartz & Parks, 1994. Used with permission.

Standardized graphic organizers can serve as learning frames for students to show their learning. Hyerle (n.d.) developed a portfolio of Thinking Maps™ for various instructional and evaluation tasks. Using this tool, students can complete the Thinking Map™ as an artifact for their portfolios for self-assessment of their learning or as a prewriting or planning record of writing assignments or projects (see Figure 10.18).

As the example in Figure 10.19 shows, an eighth-grade teacher used Thinking Maps™ to explore students' prior knowledge and then assessed effectiveness of instruction when teaching the causes and effects of the Civil War. These diagrams help both teachers and students identify students' knowledge and thinking before, during, and after instruction, as well as record improved performance through time.

In *Patterns of Thinking*, Clark (1990) illustrated the usefulness of concept maps in teachers' planning and decision making. One technique involved using student-generated pre- and postinstruction concept maps. These diagrams indicate student preparedness before beginning an instructional unit and the learning that has resulted from instruction. Whether drawn individually or compiled as a class, graphics provide important information on students' progress.

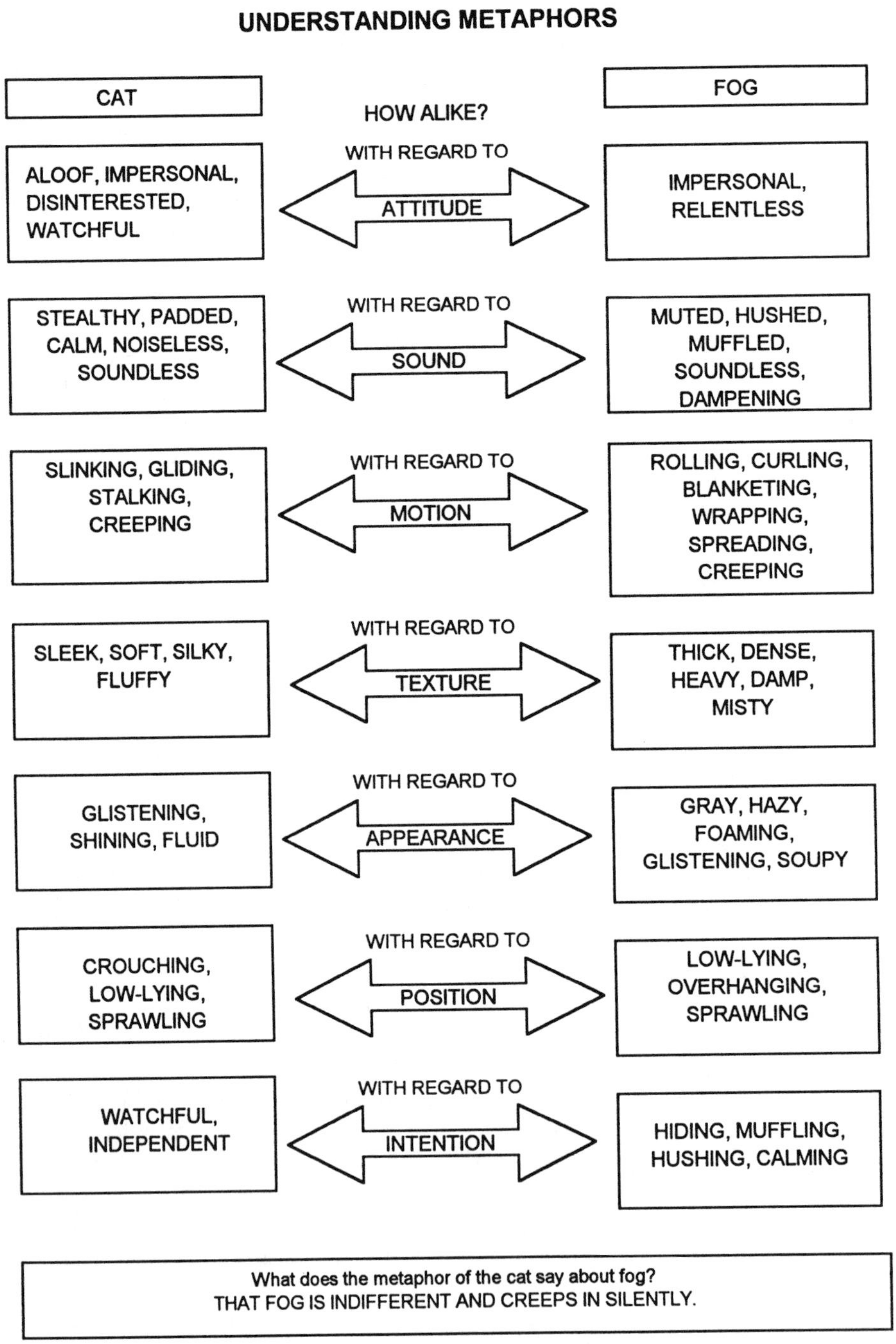

Figure 10.16. Graphic Organizer for Understanding Metaphors
SOURCE: Parks & Black, 1990. Used with permission.

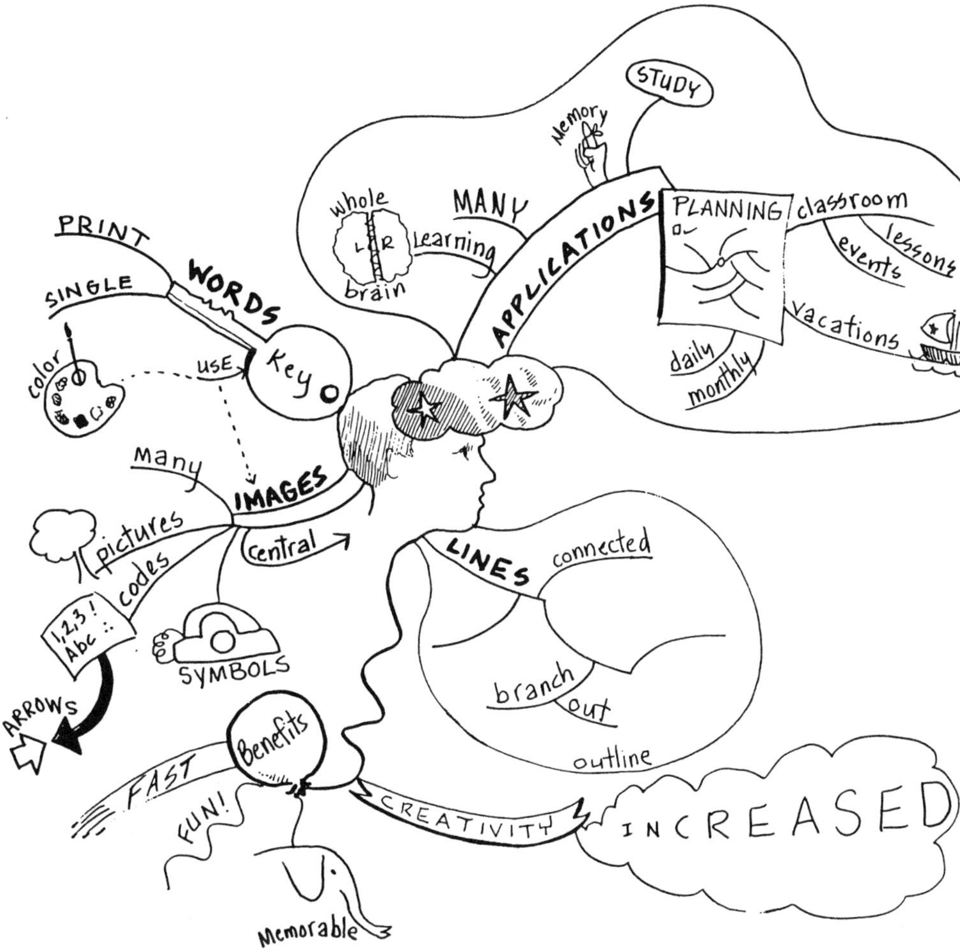

Figure 10.17. Mind Mapping to Stimulate Thinking
SOURCE: Margulies, 1994, p. 35. Used with permission.

The sample pre- and postinstruction concept maps shown in Figures 10.20 and 10.21 illustrate dramatic gains in primary students' understanding of colonial America. A class concept map summarizes their individual diagrams, showing that their previous knowledge of colonial America involved many misconceptions and some understanding of what was *not* true of that period. Their teacher now knows what background information is needed, which concepts should be emphasized or minimized, and what resources must be used to fill in the gaps in students' prior knowledge.

The postinstruction graphic shows not only the factual information that students have gained but also their understanding of the relationships between facts.

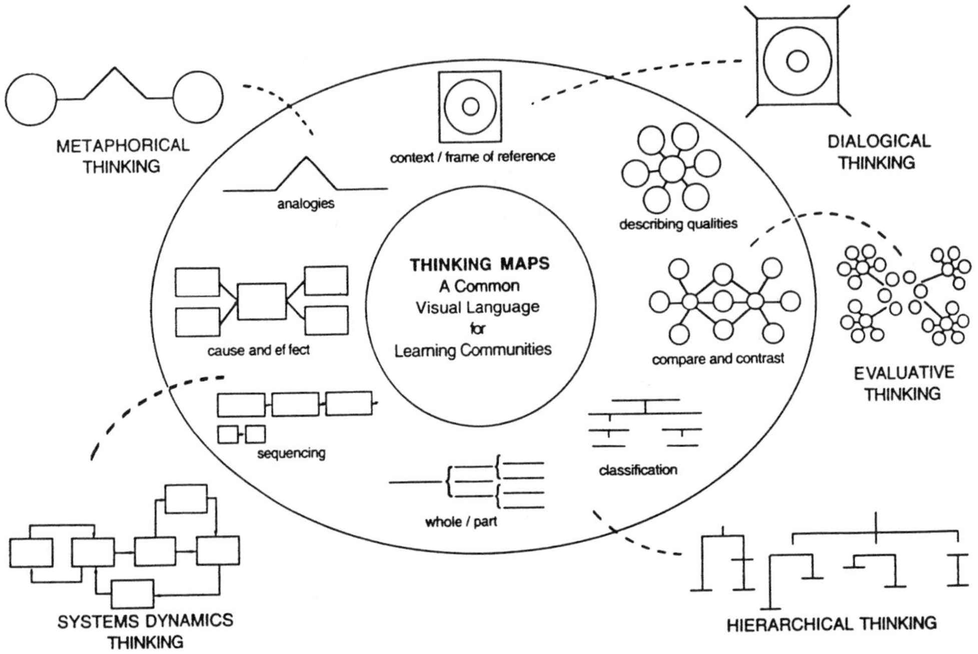

Figure 10.18. Example of Thinking Map™
SOURCE: *Thinking Maps* (p. 14), by D. Hyerle, n.d., Cary, NC: Innovative Sciences, Inc. Used with permission.

Show what you know about the causes and effects of the Civil War, using the Multiflow map. Add to the map as much as you can.

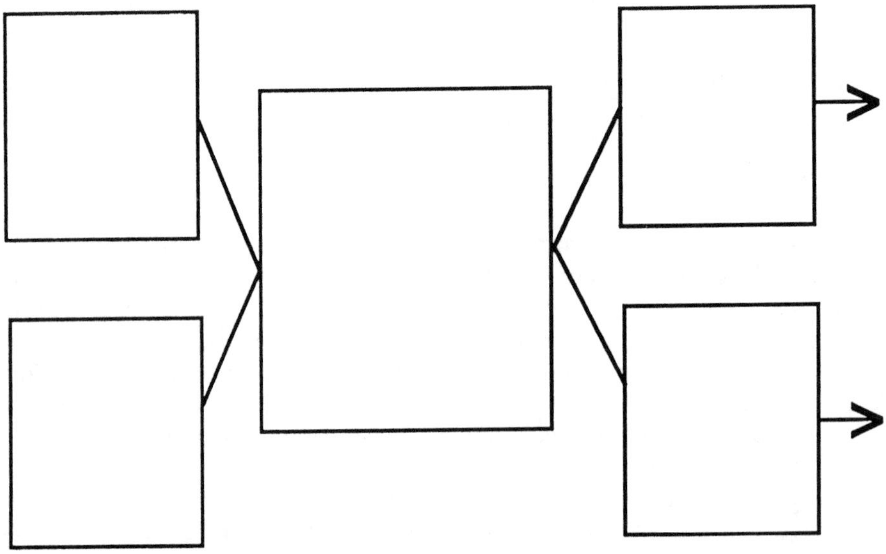

Figure 10.19a. Using Thinking Maps™ in Assessment: Eighth-Grade Example
SOURCE: *Thinking Maps* (p. 14), by D. Hyerle, n.d., Cary, NC: Innovative Sciences, Inc. Used with permission.

Students can recognize easily how much they have learned, individually and collectively. Students can use information from individual and class concept maps to evaluate the extent to which their learning included concepts identified by the group. Both teachers and students can then decide whether additional review or supplemental instruction is advisable before beginning another unit.

Using graphic organizers allows teachers and students to depict learning quickly and easily, appealing to the cognitive styles of holistic, visual learners. Although graphics are well suited to show gains in learning factual information, the types of inferences that can be drawn from using graphics in assessment warrant further investigation. Rubrics for scoring for individual products and guidelines for interpreting graphics should be clarified and carefully reviewed before making quantitative judgments. As one indicator of individual and class growth for broad interpretation of students' learning, however, using concept maps provides helpful information.

Computer Software and Technology Tools

Computer technology offers access to an array of information resources, promotes interactivity between people, and allows users to manipulate images and information on a scale unprecedented in human thought. CD-ROMs hold enormous databases that make information available in word processing form that can be reorganized.

Computer Software

Teachers are only beginning to understand the richness of using interactive software that allows users to engage in inductive thinking in situations that cannot be modeled with concrete objects. For example, the software Gertrude's Puzzle (Learning Company, 1983) simulates using attribute blocks and Venn diagrams to show characteristics. Students are not told the attributes of various

Now that you have completed this unit, present your viewpoint of the causes and effects of the Civil War.

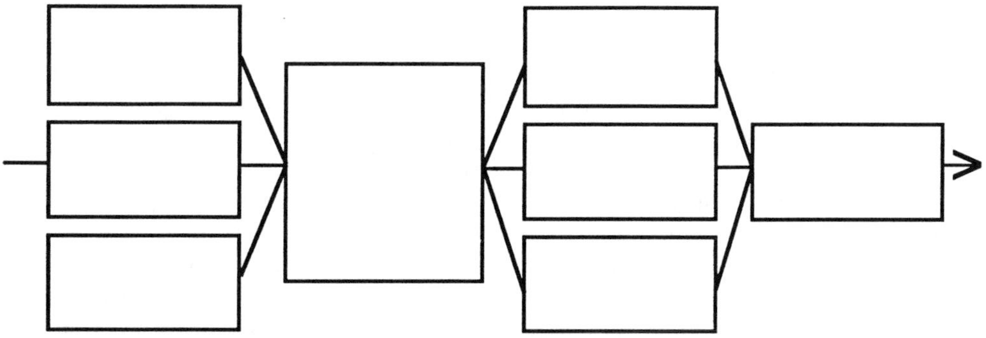

Figure 10.19b. Using Thinking Maps™ in Assessment: Eighth-Grade Example
SOURCE: *Thinking Maps* (p. 14), by D. Hyerle, n.d., Cary, NC: Innovative Sciences, Inc. Used with permission.

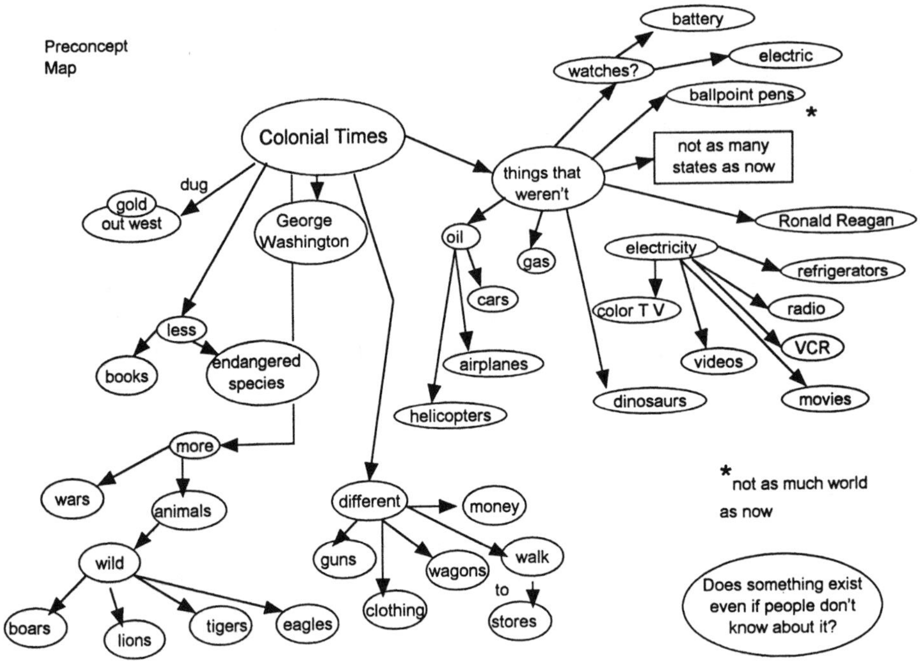

Figure 10.20. Preinstruction Concept Map
SOURCE: From J. Clarke's *Patterns of Thinking*. Copyright 1990 by Allyn and Bacon. Reprinted by permission.

sets, however, and must inductively infer the characteristics of a set by observing whether their placement of the figures remains in the circle or falls out, an activity that one cannot carry out placing the actual blocks on a flat surface. Thus the concept attainment is superimposed to a classification task.

One of the key benefits of using computer software to stimulate ideas is demonstrated in MindLink (Mauzy, 1995). This software is designed to guide users through the synectics process even if users have not been trained in creative thinking. One principle of synectics is that people have an enormous bank of background information that can be applied to a specific problem, if accessed analogically.

MindLink prompts the user to generate new ideas in much the same way that think tanks work. The software is programmed to prompt metaphoric thinking as the user applies both the synectics process and the user's own background information to a particular problem (Figure 10.22). As an individual interacts with the software, he or she is guided to think about new perspectives, different speculation, and more ideas than that same individual working alone or in a group is likely to uncover.

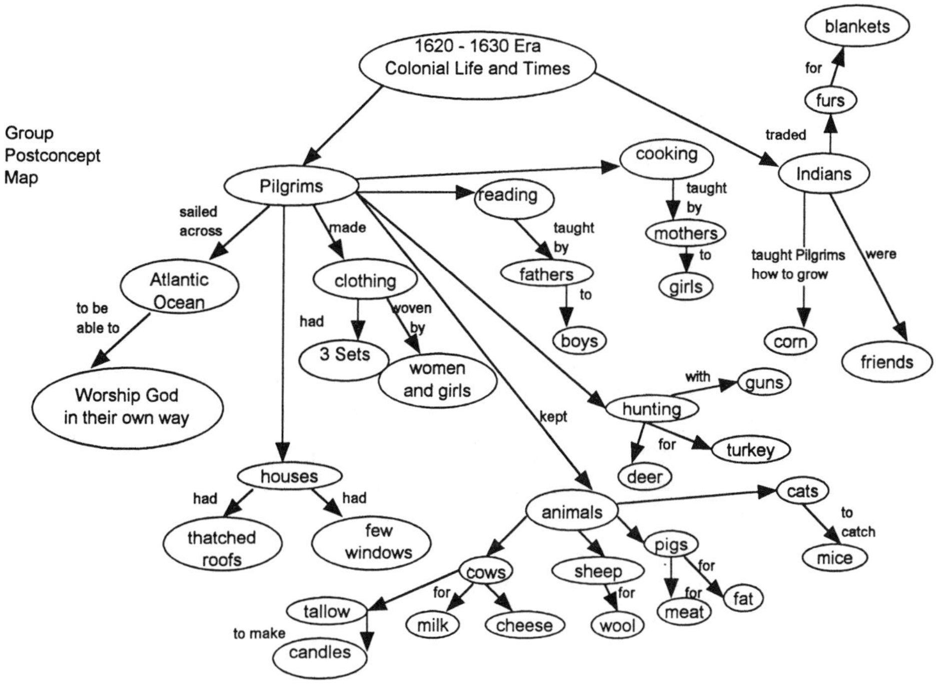

Figure 10.21. Postinstruction Concept Map

SOURCE: From J. Clarke's *Patterns of Thinking*. Copyright 1990 by Allyn and Bacon. Reprinted by permission.

At certain points in the process, the software also guides the user on a creative "bird walk," an imagery experience seemingly unrelated to the problem. This cognitive side trip diverts the user from the content of the specific problem and prompts analogical connections that the user would perhaps not access by staying focused on the same issue.

Because using graphic organizers allows users to depict ideas quickly and easily, computer software that helps "download" ideas onto diagrams becomes an aid to creative thinking and planning. Some graphics software, such as Inspiration software (1994), is programmed to reproduce standard design elements of graphic organizers (flowchart symbols, arrows, boxes, ovals, icons, clip art, etc.) so that users can "doodle" with a computer. Because some spacing and size features are standardized, users can "draw out" their thought almost as quickly on the computer as they could sketch it on paper, producing a first-draft diagram of surprisingly good craftsmanship. Helping students use computer drawing to depict their thinking and learning improves students' motivation to show what they know and models the "thinking-with-a-computer" skills that are becoming increasingly common in the workplace.

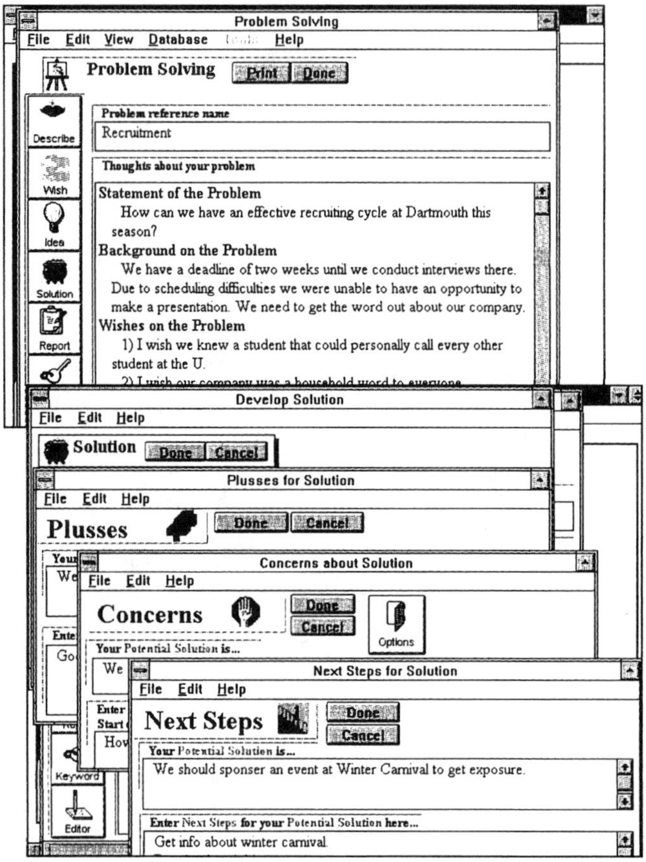

Figure 10.22. MindLink Software for Problem Solving
SOURCE: Mauzy (1995). Copyright © 1995 MindLink Software Corporation. Used with permission.

Video technology can provide the context for students to develop problem-solving skills contextualized in real-world problems. The Learning Technology Center at Vanderbilt University has developed a series of videodiscs that present complex but authentic problems in which students must generate and solve many subproblems to resolve the larger issue. One videodisc, *The Adventurers of Jasper Woodbury: Episode One* (Learning Technology Center, n.d.), presents a situation in which Jasper must decide what to do to get his boat home late in the afternoon, realizing that his boat has no lights. Based on a principle of embedded data design, the videodisc provides relevant and irrelevant data (time of sunset, a river map, weather conditions, etc.) that middle school students use to define and solve Jasper's problem. The design features of this videodisc (embedded data, a videodisc format with its random access capability, and a context in which students must define problems and use mathematics operations and problem-solving skills) provide a rich source of data not commonly available in middle school mathematics classes and offer an authentic, cooperative problem-solving experience for students.

New computer technology presents an increasing array of electronic tools for classroom use. Fiber optics turn computers into television receivers for visual, as well as verbal, information. Virtual reality and computer modeling allow users to manipulate objects, texts, or data that would otherwise be unaccessible, impractically expensive, or unsafe for student use.

Implementing a Curriculum That Incorporates Tools for Thinking and Learning

To use thinking and learning tools meaningfully, both teachers and learners must be familiar with these techniques and appropriate contexts for using them within the curriculum and in personal application. Some staff development and classroom time must be set aside to acquaint teachers and students with these devices and to build capacity in using them. Surveying available resources for graphic organizers, software, databases, and telecommunication networks must become one facet of each teacher's personal and professional development and each student's learning repertoire.

Curriculum development in the next decade may feature strategy maps and graphic organizers for the more specialized processes described in the new reform standards. Science process objectives, such as objectives described in Benchmarks, problem-based learning strategies across disciplines, and inquiry and evaluation processes emphasized in the new social studies standards can be clarified and translated into strategy maps, graphic organizers, and computer software that can make implementing the type of instruction recommended by those guidelines more effective, more commonly practiced, and more significant for students.

Assessment procedures will increasingly involve students' use of these devices. If cognitive tools are used in instruction, it follows that they should also be featured in evaluating students' learning. The design and conditions of assessment (location, time interval, materials, and equipment) must be modified to incorporate these tools.

Writing assessment increasingly involves using graphic organizers. Students frequently submit prewriting material so that the teacher can understand the process, as well as the product, of students' composition. Although teachers must guard against assessing artificial standardization of the tool (such as "proper" or "improper" use of a student-generated graphic organizer), teachers can make assessment tasks more flexible, incorporating these tools into portfolio and performance assessment.

Text materials should increasingly incorporate these tools into text formats and supplemental material. Ten years ago, few text publishers used graphic organizers extensively; today, most textbooks feature them liberally. In the future, text publishers may reference government databases, videodiscs, and CD-ROMs to supplement text material. Teachers, school districts, universities,

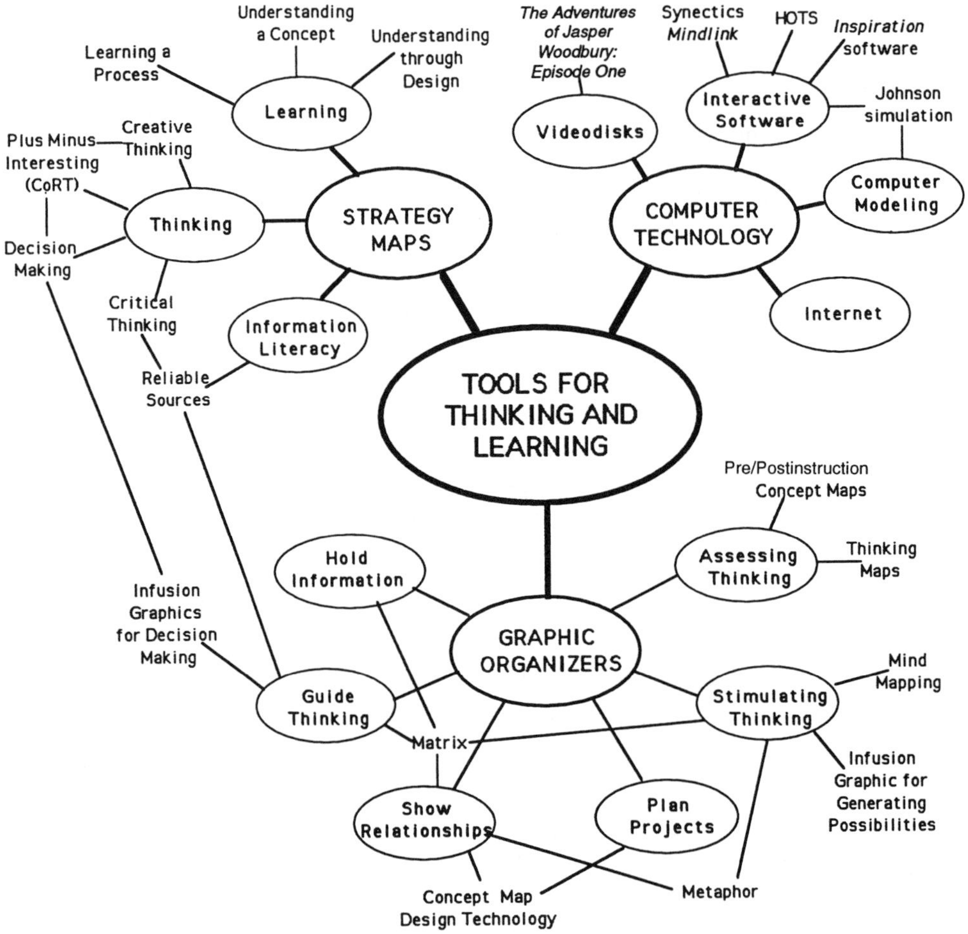

Figure 10.23. Concept Map for This Chapter

and publishers may form consortia to make databases or World Wide Web access available to all teachers.

In the increasingly multicultural classrooms of the 21st century, equality of opportunity will mean more than removing legal, political, and economic barriers to allow all students access to challenging instruction. It will also involve removing the programmatic and instructional barriers that limit some learners because of differences in learning style, language development, and background. Thinking and learning tools are currently used to "level the playing field" in schools that are detracking instruction.

All students, particularly learners who are at risk, should know how to use cognitive and electronic tools. The difference in opportunity between students who have such tools and know how to use them and those who do not may widen the performance gap between privileged and less privileged schools and learners. Poor academic performance should not be a detriment to accessing these tools nor a predictor of students' capacity to use them. These devices help teachers provide information for students whose academic knowledge is limited. Using these cognitive tools stimulates and clarifies thinking and learning skills and accelerates the pace of learning for students who most need those benefits. A concept map for this chapter is shown in Figure 10.23.

Thinking and learning tools are becoming increasingly common in teachers' instructional methods and repertoires, in texts and supplemental materials, and in students' own learning habits. Continuing to develop such devices, using them in significant ways, recognizing both limitations and the potential of these tools, including them in assessment, and making them available to all learners are the tasks that curriculum specialists and classroom teachers will undertake when schools of the future consider process as content.

References

Clarke, J. (1990). *Patterns of thinking.* Needham Heights, MA: Allyn & Bacon.

Costa, A. (Ed.). (1991). *Developing minds: A resource book for teaching thinking.* Alexandria, VA: Association for Supervision and Curriculum Development.

de Bono, E. (1987). *CoRT thinking program.* London: Pergamon.

Dunn, S., & Larson, R. (1990). *Design technology: Children's engineering.* Bristol, PA: Falmer.

Eggen, P. D., Kauchek, D. P., & Harder, R. J. (1979). *Strategies for teachers: Information processing models in the classroom.* Englewood Cliffs, NJ: Prentice Hall.

Hunter, M. (1983). *Mastery teaching, improved instruction.* El Segundo, CA: TIP.

Hyerle, D. (n.d.). *Thinking maps.* Cary, NC: Innovative Sciences.

Inspiration [Computer software]. (1994). Portland, OR: Inspiration Software.

Learning Company. (1983). Gertrude's puzzles [Computer software]. Palo Alto, CA: Author.

Learning Technology Center. (n.d.). The adventures of Jasper Woodbury: Episode one [Computer software]. Nashville, TN: Vanderbilt University.

Margulies, N. (1991). *Mapping inner space: Learning and teaching mind mapping.* Tucson, AZ: Zephyr.

Mauzy, J. (1995). MindLink [Computer software]. Cambridge, MA: Synectics.

Parks, S. (forthcoming). *Drawing out thought: Improving thinking to improve understanding.*

Parks, S., & Black, H. (1990). *Organizing thinking II.* Pacific Grove, CA: Critical Thinking Press and Software.

Perkins, D., Goodrich, H. Tishman, S., & Mirman-Owen, J. M. (1994). *Thinking connections: Learning to think and thinking to learn.* Menlo Park, CA: Addison-Wesley.

Swartz, R., & Parks, S. (1994). *Infusing the teaching of critical and creative thinking into content instruction: A lesson design handbook for the elementary grades.* Pacific Grove, CA: Critical Thinking Press and Software.

Swartz, R., & Parks, S. (forthcoming). *Infusing the teaching of critical and creative thinking into content instruction: A lesson design handbook for secondary social studies.* Pacific Grove, CA: Critical Thinking Press and Software.

Swartz, R., & Perkins, D. (1990). *Teaching thinking: Issues and approaches.* Pacific Grove, CA: Critical Thinking Press and Software.

11

Processes for Diverse Voices

Rosemarie M. Liebmann
Anthony Colella

> Life is created from the difference, not the sameness.
>
> *Carol Frenier*

In Western culture, it has not been acceptable for men and women in high-ranking bureaucratic positions to share deep feelings, be overtly compassionate, and/or demonstrate an ability to nurture others. The great social changes of our times demand that all of us become more sensitive to the network in which we live and to value the wonder, beauty, and benefits of its diversity.

This all-inclusive network comprises not only human beings but also plants, animals, and all other natural resources. We are beginning to witness the effects of humans' unwillingness and reluctance to recognize and be concerned with our connectedness to the planet on which we exist. We seem to have forgotten that it is part of who we are. Cohen (cited in Waldrop, 1992) states,

> There is basically no duality between man and nature. We are part of nature ourselves. We're in the middle of it. There's no division between doers and done-to because we are all part of this interlocking network. If we, as humans, try to take action in our favor without knowing how the overall system will adapt we set into motion a train of events that will likely come back in a different pattern for us to adjust to, like global climate change.
>
> As we begin to see the world as a complex system, we begin to understand that we're part of an ever-changing, interlocking, nonlinear, kaleidoscopic world. (p. 333)

The urgent need to live in balance with the earth ultimately depends not only on our intellectual understanding of ecology but also on an experience of the natural world as sacred. Technology and mass media have created a shrinking world in which natural boundaries become permeable. Global ecological challenges demand global cooperation. Trying to control nature will not work. Humanity needs to shift from a paradigm of "power over" to one of love that allows for deep knowing, understanding, and "living with."

Our success depends on our ability to achieve a collective consciousness, and, paradoxically, such action depends on heightened expression and acceptance of regional and ethnic uniqueness. Educators need to help the diverse, passionate, and struggling choir of humanity create a higher order of harmony, to find its collective song: east and west, north and south; past, present, and future. Survival of this planet is directly related to the ability of humans to address the strengths to be found in the multiplicity of the world's occupants. Required is "a worldview that delights in diversity and sees differences as complementary, equally valuable, beneficial to the whole, allows differences to be embraced and celebrated" (Shepherd, 1993, p. 246).

There has been much talk about multiculturalism, feminism, racism, and Eastern and Western philosophies but little recognition of different perspectives in the curriculum. According to Blanchard (1995), "While the gospel of 'valuing diversity' is preached in seminars and meeting rooms throughout American business, government, education, and religious institutions, the rhetoric does not always match the reality." Blanchard clarifies what we address in this chapter by elaborating on the concept of diversity. He states,

> Being "different" is much more than a matter of race and gender. Diversity in its fullest sense involves a broad range of human uniqueness—personality, work-style, perception and attitudes, values and lifestyle, work ethic, world view, communication style, and much more. Valuing diversity means appreciating and encouraging people to be who they really are, helping them develop to their full potential, and utilizing their special talents, skills, ideas, and creativity.

Much is being written today concerning the importance of diversity in American organizations. As we considered this research in light of educational organizations, we began to envision a shift from the traditional industrial model school, with its labels, to a learning organization that celebrates differences. In so doing, we come to understand that acceptance of diversity *is* process—process that results in nurturing each learner to maximize his or her fullest potential—to embrace the whole of who they are. Truthfully recognizing what we have said here, *each learner*, we felt it necessary to focus on the exceptional learner as a separate entity because that is what should *not* be—*learner* must include even those who are different. This chapter reflects on what has been and what might be, the importance of including all students, and, finally, the processes needed to provide students with the attitudes, skills, and dispositions necessary to embrace and celebrate diversity throughout their lives.

Industrial Model Schools

Schools can be places in which some students must clone themselves into accepted ways of thinking, learning, and acting. Successful programs and teachers, however, have always shared one trait in common. They are able to connect with learners at a feeling level—namely, love, trust, authenticity, and nourishment of the human spirit. Learning in these classrooms becomes an arena for self-discovery. Trust and a willingness to risk are evident, as is a search for personal and spiritual freedom. The teachers and students look to the self, not the system, for solutions to problems. In looking to the self for solutions to problems, the role of the school in society must be questioned. The basic question remains, "Why do schools exist, and in what ways do they facilitate the growth of the person in the process of becoming 'whole'?" As new models for schooling emerge in the 21st century, new partnerships with teachers, learners, and the community will also develop. There is no need to repeat or paraphrase the old paradigm but rather to accept the challenge of creating new pathways that recognize the strength of diversity and the power of the human mind.

Historically, schools have encouraged students and teachers to leave part of their selves outside. This is the same observation that Barrantine (1993) made about society: "Society has encouraged workers to 'leave their selves at the door' " (p. 11). Yet for authentic and meaningful learning to occur, we must bring all our selves to the classroom. The *all* of our selves refers to our unique human spirit. It has been asserted that spiritual poverty is a hunger of the soul that can be as devastating as physical hunger. In the words of Shipka (1993), "Fear, anxiety, a sense of isolation, apathy, and despair are the results of spiritual poverty, and their effects on us are similar to the disease, starvation, and death in the refugee camps" (p. 97). Spiritual poverty robs us of our creativity, sense of meaning, and joy in our work.

We need to connect at a deeper level, to have authentic relationships and clear communications. Frequently, we hear such words as *networking, team building,* and *community.* Because schools are based in communities and are themselves learning communities, members experience strong bonds with friends, family, and coworkers. These learning communities require authentic listening, authentic dialogue, and authentic being.

Effective schools may also be described as *functional,* and ineffective schools may be described as *dysfunctional* in the same way families are described as functional and dysfunctional. To more fully understand this concept, it is necessary to identify the characteristics of a functional family and to determine the extent to which these same characteristics may be found in functional schools. A functional school provides children with the intellectual, emotional, and psychological skills needed to survive in the world. Intellectual skills refer to the thinking process, that is, allowing children to gain access to independent problem-solving skills and consequently permitting them to become more resourceful. Emotional skills refer to feelings, that is, helping children understand that feelings are neither right nor wrong. They are just feelings, and children's acceptance of their own feelings is of prime importance in the development of self-worth. Psychological skills refer to actions. A functional family allows children to assume responsibility for their actions. Simply stated, intellectual, emotional, and psychological skills provided by the functional family offer a framework for thinking, feeling, and acting in life. In the same sense, a functional school becomes an effective school when it provides resources for the development of these life skills. As teachers and learners become authentic and, in this process, *whole,* they experience thinking, feeling, and acting as connected.

Exceptional Children

> Most people look to elders as teachers. They are. But we also look at the children, look at them as teachers.
>
> *Vickie Downey*

In accepting diversity, we are advocating a new look at special education. Many parents are skeptical about the concept of inclusion. Yet exceptional children teach us that they also have wonderful gifts to offer (DeMartino, 1995). When given the opportunity, they contribute productively to society—they challenge customary thinking and allow us to see through a different set of eyes. They remind us that a wisdom far greater than ours works Her wonders in mysterious ways. These children bring out the best in who we are. They are active members of a Renaissance Community. The movies *Rain Man, Forrest Gump,* and *Awakenings* have reminded us that all too often society has underestimated the potential of the exceptional population.

Biklen, Ferguson, and Ford (1989) developed the metaphor of special education as a repair shop. Disabled students with problems (an object that is broken) are brought to the resource rooms for pull-out programs and often private institutions to be repaired. "The metaphor ends here because unlike the object that usually can be repaired, the vast majority of disabled students usually remain in special education (the repair shop) and never lose the 'special' label" (DeMartino, 1995, p. 79). Yet students who are participating members of their home school lead more integrated lives and are taught to celebrate their differences by functioning in the same space. As Davis (cited in DeMartino, 1995) suggests, "a new human services paradigm . . . for an even larger and more diversified population of children and youth than are presently being served" (p. 56) will be required if the future of education and the future of business are to be protected. Teachers express the feeling that the most creative, thoughtful students have been labeled and are stored in little classrooms apart from the rest of the population.

Although we, as humans, are responsible for ourselves, we are also responsible for each other. Individuals who are exceptional require process education perhaps more so than the norm (see Chapter 1 of this volume). It is believed that process education can help their minds make the connections and see the patterns that are elusive to them under a content-driven curriculum. Interaction with their peers enables them to experience how others make meaning out of information.

Davern and Schnorr (1991) have stated that integration of special education students in the regular classroom benefits all students. Special education students benefit with general knowledge development, language development, and social skills development that result in the building of friendships and the transition into democratic society. Nondisabled students learn to accept other students as neighbors, coworkers, and friends. According to research by Galant and Hanline (1993), parents agree that inclusion "offers opportunities to learn about individual differences and therefore has positive effects on young children, their families and their communities" (p. 294).

These special individuals bring back to us the wonders of the world in which we live. They put the colors back into our hurried lives. They stop to take the time to see the richness in our world and don't ask "why not." These students accept the world and others for what and who they are. They have no desire to change us. They simply yearn for relationships (DeMartino, 1995).

In accepting all students as active and productive members of the learning community, we begin to foster the skills recommended by Brock (Secretary's Commission on Achieving Necessary Skills [SCANS], 1991) that today's students will need to be effective workers tomorrow:

> Students must be trained to work in teams and to be creative problem solvers so that they not only will make a living but will also live full lives raising their families as respected members of their communities making optimum use of their leisure time. (p. 3)

Diversity *Is* Process

Traditionally, teachers have been seen as wise sages, possessing and dispensing truth and wisdom and having the capacity to answer all students' questions. With the rapidly increasing rate of knowledge, however, teachers are no longer able to be these fountains of enlightenment. This is compounded by the recognition that teachers have much to learn from those who are different. The role of educators is shifting to enhancing creativity, providing learners with greater freedom, setting the stage for accepting responsibility for decisions and learning, and creating an environment conducive to intellectual and spiritual growth.

As the role of teachers continues to evolve in society, new insights are gained with respect to the learning-teaching process. Teachers' personal educational philosophies and visions of education change, allowing attitudes, beliefs, assumptions, and values to be challenged and modified. This process should be viewed as social in nature, involving a significant degree of human interaction and leading teachers to a greater understanding of self while arriving at new knowledge. The entire educational process is characterized by a dynamic, fluid relationship between learners and the environment. Thus, teaching and learning may be viewed as highly interactive in nature, with primary emphasis placed on the varied aspects of the learning process and secondary emphasis on acquisition of facts. It is of great importance to create a learning environment that encourages individuals to learn *how* to learn, thereby placing the focus on the processing of information while aiding learners in developing an awareness of their unique styles employed to arrive at new truths and understandings.

To become introspective and learn how to learn, learners need to value their own styles of learning. In this regard, the interactive teaching-learning process provides a means for the development of self-acceptance. As facilitators of learning, teachers need to first investigate the extent to which they value diversity and are prepared to foster the development of self-acceptance in all learners. This learning environment must be free of constraints and obstacles that block open communication between and among individuals. More specifically, factors that inhibit human interaction and block the free flow of ideas must be eliminated. It is, therefore, extremely important for teachers to assess their own assumptions regarding the nature of learning and the learning process. This self-analysis leads to a greater understanding of the interchangeable roles of teachers and learners.

An additional significant aspect of the educational process includes the role the learners play in developing an understanding of their own behaviors in the world and the meanings underlying these interactions. Education serves as the means by which insights into human behavior are gained. Self-knowledge causes reflection on attitudes, values, and tendencies toward specific behaviors. As the world continues to be more diverse, the ability to learn and grow is closely connected to a willingness to be introspective and to investigate the origins of cultural beliefs.

Diversity is process. Diversity engages the many different perspectives or ways of knowing within individuals. Whether truths are embedded in cultural learning, environmental impacts, ethnic background, perceptual filters, or practical experience, the vast diversity in knowing is a process unique to each individual. Awareness of these different ways of knowing, sharing, and collaborating with others increases learners' repertoires and makes the ability to learn more flexible and fluid.

Processes

The development of a curriculum based on nurturing, caring, and respecting individuals requires the viewing of the curriculum from a systemic perspective. Each component contributes to the development of the self in relationship to personal and interpersonal understandings. The curriculum incorporates a systems dynamic that takes into account the complex interactions among mutually supporting and interwoven elements. Educators look to create webs of inclusion in which the sharing of information and resources is key. Greater flow and mastery of information result from the increased number of connection points. The blending of Eastern and Western philosophies, the sharing of different ethnic backgrounds, and the merging of the mosaic of cultures present in today's schools offer curriculum developers a unique opportunity to prepare learners for the shrinking world in which they will become active participants.

In recent years, the curriculum has been described as a "rainbow," that is, the blending of separate colors or components so that the uniqueness, beauty, and worth of each part is represented. Thus, the whole is truly greater than the sum of its parts. In unity lie not only strength but also the opportunity to learn and understand ourselves through interacting in a culturally diverse world.

Some of the processes required to achieve the treasuring and acceptance of diversity are described below.

Acceptance and Trust. Assimilation and integration of diversity into learning organizations require that the environment focus on two primary conditions—acceptance and trust. Hateley and Schnidt (1995) state, "It is acceptance and trust that make it possible for each bird to sing its own song—confident that it will be heard—even by those who sing with a different voice" (p. 89).

Because singing with a different voice has not been highly valued in schools, individuals who are "different" or who deviate from the "norm" with respect to values, attitudes, beliefs, behaviors, race, religion, sexual orientation, mental acuity, and so on may face criticism and ultimate rejection (Nachmanovitch, 1990). Schools as instruments of social change must value the uniqueness and personal worth of each member. In so doing, schools as learning communities have tremendous potential to become arenas for developing acceptance and trust.

In the early 1970s, a New York Broadway play titled *The Me Nobody Knows* opened. The major theme of this play addressed the issue of trust and acceptance. Now, more than 20 years later, schools continue to be challenged with the need to create curricular opportunities that promote and value diversity. The intent is to foster an environment in which learners need not fear revealing their true identities. Schools must continue to strive to become interactive learning communities in which trust, acceptance, and openness are the cornerstones of curriculum, rich in its diversity and representative of the cultural pluralism of our society.

As the instrument for social change in society, a school and its curriculum possess the potential to challenge cultural stereotypes. Thus, the school does not have to be a microcosm of society. New learning communities, rich in diversity and committed to the development of human potential, are therefore free to develop.

Introspection. Introspective learning requires a willingness to nurture the development of an inner voice, as well as to provide the knowledge customarily equated with content learning and rational thinking. Introspection involves a "turning inward" on the self while listening to and trusting the inner guiding voice. To draw from this internal source, it is imperative that learners trust and accept their worth and value. Lacking this confidence in self-potential seriously limits the extent to which introspective knowledge may be gained.

The current curriculum is guided by the perspectives, visions, theories, and values held by the founding forefathers. It is unlikely that personalized and imaginative types of thinking were promoted in the reductionist curriculum that primarily valued rationalism and objectivity. Overtly valuing certain types of thinking more than others inadvertently excludes a segment of the population. Turkle and Papert (1990) have stated, "Equal access to computation requires an epistemological pluralism—an acceptance of multiple ways of knowing and thinking" (p. 1). To create learning environments that live the belief "All students do learn" and that answer the most fundamental question for educators—"How do they learn?"—we must begin to open the doors to their inner voices. These insights will act as guides to help students develop the processes needed to be lifelong learners.

Dialogue. The word *dialogue* comes from two Greek roots, *dia* (meaning "through" or "with each other") and *logos* (meaning "the word"). It has been suggested that this word carries a sense of "meaning flowing through." When people practice dialogue, they pay attention to the spaces between the words; the timing of action, not only the result; and the timbre and tone of voice, not only what is said. They listen for the meaning of the field of inquiry, not only its discrete elements. In short, dialogue creates conditions in which people experience the primacy of the whole (Senge, Roberts, Ross, Smith, & Kleiner, 1994).

Physicist David Bohm (1985) suggested that this new form of conversation should focus on bringing to the surface and altering the *tacit infrastructure* of thought. As Bohm conceived it, dialogue would kindle a new mode of paying attention, to perceive the assumptions taken for granted, the polarization of opinions, the rules for acceptable and unacceptable conversation, and the methods for managing differences. In essence, dialogue's purpose would be to create a setting whereby conscious collective mindfulness could be maintained. Some of the techniques used in effective dialogue are authentic listening, paraphrasing, questioning, summarizing, probing, and extending (Baker, Costa, Shallit in *The Process-Centered School: Sustaining a Renaissance Community*).

Innovation. Innovation is defined as the ability to introduce or bring in something new. Its creative force lies in the originality of thought and execution. Much has been written about left- (logical/linear) and right-(imaginative/creative) brained people. Successful managers and entrepreneurs have learned naturally how and when to use both sides of their brains, combining detail and logic with a sense of overview and invention. Frequently, in Western culture, the strengths of the right brain are associated with femaleness—intuitive, spontaneous, holistic, emotional, playful, nonverbal, diffuse, visual, symbolic, artistic, and physical. The left brain is associated with maleness and the following traits—positive, analytical, linear, explicit, sequential, verbal, concrete, rational, active, and goal-oriented. The importance of innovation rests in its ability to shift vertical thinkers toward the development of whole-brain thinking and androgynous voices—two skills necessary for the effective communication with people from different races, cultures, religions, and ethnic backgrounds. As Nachmanovitch (1990) writes,

> The mind that is tied up in investment and attachment is a mind that has fifty candles burning and will not notice the fifty-first when lit. When we surrender, we relax into a more subtle, sensitive mind that has few candles burning, or even none. Then when the creative surprise flares up, it can be seen clearly and distinctly, and most important, it can be acted upon. (p. 155)

Curriculum designers might afford students the following process opportunities to identify their dominant thinking: biofeedback experiences, internal and external brainstorming activities, reflective time, playful wondering and imagining, and classifiers/word cues.

Visualization. Visualization is the process of forming a mental image or seeing with the mind's eye. Native Americans call this the ability to use one's third eye. Visualizing or cinematics (Wonder & Donovan, 1984) is a powerful strategy for freeing oneself from left-brain thinking into daydreaming or right-brained work. This technique allows persons to preview problem situations, savor their fondest hopes, and test a plan of action.

Visualization is necessary for health, happiness, and creativity. It provides opportunities to defuse stress and to rehearse the emotions of a scenario. In situations in which diverse groups are engaging, visualization can be used to move members to empathically relate to others by seeing themselves as "walking in the other person's moccasins."

This type of directed visualization causes students to focus consciously on other individuals, noting specific details such as appearance, body language—all the nonverbal cues. To be successful, students must also engage left-brain skills for analysis of verbal and nonverbal cues. Eventually, the students will begin to produce a clearer image and understanding of the others. It is important during this process that students also note the feelings they experience as they visualize being another human. It is through this recognition that much learning will take place.

Curriculum developers and teachers might use role playing activities correlated to particular areas of study to enhance and develop these skills, such as envisioning life in the early 1800s. Teachers could ask what students smell, see, feel, and so on. In addition, questions that probe for alternative perspectives, dialogue, brainstorming, testing and hypothesizing assumptions, and journals are other avenues to enhance visualization skills.

Empathy. Empathy is the intellectual or imaginative apprehension of another's condition or state of mind accompanied by the reception of the feelings of the other into oneself. It is complete engagement with another person that allows for authentic listening to occur. Empathy means letting go of one's own mental tapes, images, and predispositions to see through another person's eyes.

In diverse classrooms, this position is often difficult to develop. Students frequently approach other students like this:

> I already know what sort of person I am, and I know what sort of person you are and what sort of people are in my class, and I know about this subject, this teacher, this school—now, what is it you have to say?

This is not authentic listening but what we define as *automatic listening.* Raising students' consciousness to this unconscious behavior is necessary so that it no longer controls them. They gain power over their selective hearing by being aware of it and trying to actively catch themselves engaging in automatic listening.

Fittipaldi (1993) states,

> The first step in generating a new future or creating a transformed organization is gaining the freedom to think in new ways. . . . The result will be enormous freedom to hear what is actually being said, to listen

> in a new way, to recognize and identify the current culture or paradigm that is limiting us. This will give us the power to see, generate, and fulfill new possibilities, which will result in new futures. (p. 236)

Empathic students have the capacity to share others' experiences to understand their lives. This begins with an interest in the facts of people's lives, but it gradually shifts to others' ways of thinking. Empathic learners get out from behind their own lenses and look through the lenses of other persons. Their purpose is not to judge but to understand. Empathic learning requires trust and patience. Its authority rests in the commonality of experience. Personality is seen as adding to perception, and so the personality of each member of the group enriches the group's understanding. Each individual must stretch her or his own vision to share another's vision. Through mutual sharing, the group achieves an understanding richer than any individual could achieve alone.

Relationship Building. The value of creating open relationships in learning situations rests on the flourishing of intuition and positive change. There are two important aspects to relationships: relationships between members of the community and relationships between content. The importance of developing both is based on the assumption that if anyone or any piece loses, no one and/or no piece really wins. Learners can bounce ideas and thoughts off the teacher or among themselves. There is no judgment of whether an idea is good, bad, or indifferent. Every student should know they can run something by a few other people in the classroom and then come away with an even deeper level of understanding.

Further, the educational system has a deeper responsibility to society then the mere delivery of content. Hawley (1993) cited a cover story in *Time* magazine that dealt with the "malformations cropping up in the American character resulting from an era of self-absorbed individualism" (p. 2). If school created communities in which the self and connectedness to others were valued, the United States could begin living by the motto of the Hard Rock Cafe, "Love All, Serve All." In beginning to relate to others and acknowledging their wondrous gifts, the self-absorbed individual may disappear from sight and the "malformations in American character" may vanish.

As Miller (1976) wrote,

> Growth requires engagement with difference and with people embodying that difference. If differences were more openly acknowledged, we could allow for, and even encourage, an increasingly strong expression by each party of her or his experience. This would lead to greater clarity for self, greater ability to fulfill one's own needs, and more facility to respond to others. (p. 42)

In addition, students in classrooms can benefit from relational learning as opposed to episodic learning, separate versus connected knowing. "The primacy of the whole suggests that relationships are in a genuine sense more fundamental than things and that wholes are primordial parts. We do not have to create interrelatedness. The world is already interrelated" (P. Senge, personal communication). Senge believes that individuals are born as natural systems thinkers but lose this skill in the course of formal academic training. Once students leave the traditional school setting, they are expected to relearn the skill—to see the bigger picture.

Certainly to curriculum developers, the primacy of the whole becomes compelling in the consideration of living systems. A person may be said to be composed of a head, a torso, and limbs; or of bones, muscles, skin, and blood; or of the brain, lungs, heart, liver, and stomach; or of a digestive system, circulatory system, respiratory system, and nervous system; or of many, many cells. No matter what distinctions we choose, we cannot grasp what it means to be human by looking at the parts (Senge, 1994). So we return to the argument posited in the first book in this trilogy, *Envisioning Process As Content: Toward a Renaissance Curriculum*—the argument against the disciplines as we have come to know them.

Spiritual Development. Sathya Sai Baba (n.d.) states, "The only way to achieve Unity amidst all this diversity is through spirituality" (p. 173). The spiritual development referred to here is people's commitment to and allegiance to their inner psychological and intuitive journey toward wholeness. This inner transformation is what brings meaning to learning. It requires that learning organizations are based on compassion, nurturance, and relatedness alongside achievement and action. Students will require more opportunities to pursue self-knowledge, conscious awareness, and an opening up of the mind and heart to new thoughts and ideas. McMillan (1993) suggests the following cornerstones for the workplace and schools:

1. Flexibility: acknowledgment of "inner" needs and suspension of work pressures as needed
2. Support: people and systems that are available if requested by the student/teacher/administrator
3. Education: available resources of information about the spiritual emergence process
4. Solitude: support for "quiet time," privacy, and permission to slow down as needed
5. Safety and simplicity: understanding and acceptance by fellow learners, without criticism (p. 114)

The development of the human spirit has long been recognized as the goal of education. We emphasize that we are not addressing religion but are advocating increased time for self-reflection, self-modification, self-assessment, and self-referencing. These metacognitive activities are developed in classrooms in which trust, openness, and community flourish.

Authentic Communicating. Authentic communicating is the mindful process of speaking with others in a way that is invitational and open. This requires the elimination of messages that covertly or overtly value the hierarchy found in most organizations, that distance others by use of a privileged vocabulary, or that subtly convey that someone may not be a member of the group. Authentic communication will serve to enrich the learning environment and create a forum for open and honest dialogue.

In particular, it has been found that word choice is grounded in an individual's preferred learning style (Costa & Garmston, 1993). When an auditory learner is in a dialogue with a visual learner, for example, they tend to have difficulty in understanding each other. The conversation may sound something like this:

Auditory Learner	*Visual Learner*
I heard the teacher say . . .	So the picture he created was . . .
Well, it really sounded like . . .	So what you were visualizing was . . .
Not quite, as I listened carefully . . .	Then it was more like seeing . . .

Until these two learners can find a neutral ground in which they can share ideas that resonate in both, they will continue to have difficulty understanding each other. Both women and men need to become conscious of the words used by the individuals with whom they are speaking. The burden may be somewhat greater for men because, contrary to popular myth, some researchers have found that men tend to do most of the talking in our society, whereas women do most of the listening (Belenky, Clinchy, Goldberger, & Tarule, 1986).

Intuiting. Intuiting is the process of listening for and attending to quick and ready insights or convictions that lack rational thought or inference, of contemplating perceptions based on feelings or other sensory stimuli, and of knowing without knowing. It is that sense that the head and the heart have become aligned and that there is no doubt. Intuition when used correctly is grounded in integrity, intellect, and inspiration.

The value placed on intuition is one of the areas of division between Eastern and Western philosophers. In many non-Western and nontechnological societies, subjective knowledge and intuitive processes hold a more esteemed place in the culture. In Western philosophy, positivism replaced the classical intuitivism represented by the work of Spinoza and Bergson. Both these philosophers held that it is only intuition that leads to the apprehension of ultimate reality. In Eastern religions and mystic philosophy, inner contemplation and intuitive understanding are primary routes to basic knowledge. We invite readers to consider a continuum similar to the position taken by Spencer (1993):

> By balancing our rational and intuitive abilities and accessing our imagination, we are able to reclaim many of the gifts that we left behind in childhood. In so doing, we can experience a sense of wonder at our own power to create new realities through relationships and work. (p. 249)

For skeptics, intuitive development is part of the new Creativity in Business course taught at Stanford University's Graduate School of Business. Several other top schools, such as Harvard and California State Universities, offer similar courses. Raising students' awareness of their inner voices, accompanied sometimes by physical sensations, increases their intuition. To cultivate intuition, students write down or speak about the intuitive insight. It takes practice to cultivate this faint inner voice, but intuiting is a valuable and reliable aid that can enhance decision-making and problem-solving strategies. Nachmanovitch (1990) writes,

> Reasoned knowledge proceeds from information of which we're consciously aware—only a partial sampling of our total knowledge. Intuitive knowledge, on the other hand, proceeds from everything we know and everything we are. It converges on the moment from a rich plurality of directions and sources—hence the feeling of absolute certainty that is traditionally associated with intuitive knowledge. (p. 40)

Transformation. Transformation is defined as the act of taking on a different form or appearance. In this case, it is associated with the ability to change—the stretching of the mind. The following excerpt brings to light the difficulty of engaging in true change.

Fear of Transformation

> Sometimes I feel that my life is a series of trapeze swings. I'm either hanging on to a trapeze bar swinging along or for a few moments in my life, I'm hurtling across space in between trapeze bars. . . . [Each time I let go] I am filled with terror. It doesn't matter that in all my previous hurtles across the void of knowing, I have always made it. . . . I have noticed that, in our culture, this transition zone is looked upon as a "nothing," a no-place between places . . . what a waste! I have a sneaking suspicion that the transition zone is the only real thing, and the bars are illusions we dream up to avoid the void, where the real change, the real growth occurs for us. . . . Hurtling through the void, we just may learn how to fly.
>
> *Danaan Parry*

Parry reminds us of the many times fear of failure has proved to be unjustified. When learners choose to "learn to fly," to take risks, to reach out to others, true learning or transformation takes place. Learners require experiences that will enable them to develop strategies to assist them in negotiating the void. They need to develop the intrinsic knowledge that they have the abilities and competencies "to safely fly over to the next bar." Curriculum design must provide experiences that challenge the existing comfort level, forcing learners to stretch and grow by engaging in risk taking, working with others, opening up to multiple perspectives, and developing an appreciation for the learning that results from incorrect solutions.

Yearning. Yearning is a disposition in which the individual desires something earnestly. In curriculum development, it is the responsibility of the designer to create a yearning for continued growth and development. The curriculum designer is viewed as any person connected with the content of a lesson or unit of work. Therefore, students are curriculum designers, as are teachers, administrators, textbook authors, and public officials. A yearning stems from within the person and involves wonderment, curiosity, and intrigue. It can be created through dialogue with a colleague or engagement with a phenomenon. It is at the heart of lifelong learning—that which leads a person to continually search for truth.

It is the searching for, the fiddling around with, or playing with content that engages the whole of a person. The process of learning or seeking the truth is what creates the yearning—not the answer. As Winnicott (cited in Nachmanovitch, 1990) wrote, "It is in the playing and only in the playing that the individual child or adult is able to be creative and to use the whole personality, and it is only in the creative that the individual discovers the self" (p. 50).

Summary

When we practice the processes of accepting and honoring diversity, we inevitably begin to practice the ancient art of shape-shifting.

> Shape-shifting is the very essence of communication. When we are trying to understand another person's ideas or we try to get them to understand ours, we shape-shift with that individual; that is, we make the effort to match energies with them. It is through this process of matching energies that we become one with someone or something. If the energies do not match, there is poor communication and you feel uncomfortable; or you make someone else feel uncomfortable. The same is true with being in the presence of animals or even places. (Hughes-Calero, 1991, p. 61)

Those skilled in interpersonal relationships have learned that it is all too easy to overlook a person's potential because a quick assessment cannot pick up the full depth and range of the individual. Individuals are capable of continual growth and development, provided they are encouraged and given appropriate opportunities. All too frequently, educators have ineffectively measured learners' potential. Students who seem impressive in school can turn out to be less impressive in life. They are the gardener's equivalent of annuals—flowers that bloom but have no staying power. Other students, who at first appear unimpressive, can bloom and develop, growing in stature and substance through time. They stand tall and strong in their own right and support the growth of others.

> Some say knowledge is power but that is not true. Character is power.
>
> *Sathya Sai Baba*

References

Baba, S. S. (n.d.). *Indian culture and spirituality.* Prasanthi Nilayam, India: Sri Sathya Sai Books.

Barrantine, P. (1993). *When the canary stops singing: Women's perspective on transforming business.* San Francisco: Berrett-Koehler.

Belenky, M., Clinchy, B., Goldberger, N., & Tarule, J. (1986). *Women's ways of knowing: The development of self, voice, and mind.* New York: Basic Books.

Biklen, D., Ferguson, D., & Ford, A. (1989). *Schooling and disability: Eighty-eighth yearbook of the National Society for the Study of Education.* Chicago: University of Chicago Press.

Blanchard, K. (1995). Foreword. In B. Hateley & W. Schnidt (Eds.), *A peacock in the land of penguins.* San Francisco: Berrett-Koehler.

Bohm, D. (1985). *Unfolding meaning.* Loveland, CO: Foundation House.

Costa, A., & Garmston, R. (1993). *Cognitive coaching: A foundation for renaissance schools.* Norwood, MA: Christopher-Gordon.

Davern, L., & Schnorr, R. (1991). Public schools welcome children with disabilities as full members. *Children Today, 20*(2), 21-25.

DeMartino, A. (1995). *Secondary inclusion: A study of congruence of perceptions of students, parents and teachers in Morris County.* Unpublished doctoral dissertation, Seton Hall University, South Orange, NJ.

Fittipaldi, B. (1993). New listening: Key to organizational transformation. In P. Barrantine (Ed.), *When the canary stops singing: Women's perspective on transforming business.* San Francisco: Berrett-Koehler.

Galant, K., & Hanline, M. (1993). Parental attitudes toward mainstreaming young children with disabilities. *Childhood Education, 69*(5), 293-297.

Hateley, B., & Schnidt, W. (1995). *A peacock in the land of penguins.* San Francisco: Berrett-Koehler.

Hawley, J. (1993). *Reawakening the spirit in work: The power of dharmic management.* San Francisco: Berrett-Koehler.

Hughes-Calero, H. (1991). *The flight of winged wolf.* Sedona, AZ: Higher Consciousness Books.

McMillan, K. (1993). The workplace as a spiritual haven. In P. Barrantine (Ed.), *When the canary stops singing: Women's perspective on transforming business.* San Francisco: Berrett-Koehler.

Miller, J. B. (1976). *Toward a new psychology of women.* Boston: Beacon.

Nachmanovitch, S. (1990). *Free play: The power of improvisation in life and the arts.* New York: G. P. Putnam.

Secretary's Commission on Achieving Necessary Skills (SCANS). (1991). *What work requires of schools: A SCANS report for America 2000.* Washington, DC: U.S. Department of Education.

Senge, P. (1994). Moving forward. In P. Senge, C. Roberts, R. Ross, B. Smith, & A. Kleiner (Eds.), *The fifth discipline fieldbook: Strategies and tools for building a learning organization.* New York: Doubleday/Currency.

Senge, P., Roberts, C., Ross, R., Smith, B., & Kleiner, A. (Eds.). (1994). *The fifth discipline fieldbook: Strategies and tools for building a learning organization.* New York: Doubleday/Currency.

Shepherd, L. (1993). *Lifting the veil: The feminine face of science.* Boston: Shambhala.

Shipka, B. (1993). Corporate poverty: Lessons from refugee camps. In P. Barrantine (Ed.), *When the canary stops singing: Women's perspective on transforming business.* San Francisco: Berrett-Koehler.

Spencer, S. (1993). Seven keys to conscious leadership. In P. Barrantine (Ed.), *When the canary stops singing: Women's perspective on transforming business.* San Francisco: Berrett-Koehler.

Turkle, S., & Papert, S. (1990, Autumn). Epistemological pluralism. *Signs, 16,* 1.

Waldrop, M. M. (1992). *Complexity: The emerging science at the edge of order and chaos.* New York: Touchstone.

Wonder, J., & Donovan, P. (1984). *Whole-brain thinking: Working from both sides of the brain to achieve peak job performance.* New York: Quill.

12

Inviting the Feminine Voice

Rosemarie M. Liebmann
Barbara D. Wright

The benefits of assimilating the kaleidoscopic worldview held by persons different from each other have been discussed in Chapter 11, "Processes for Diverse Voices." While formulating that chapter, we realized that prejudice against the feminine voice has prevailed far longer than other injustices embedded in the hierarchical ordering within cultural diversity. To stress the importance of looking at gender issues in schools against the backdrop of the wider picture and to emphasize the importance of the implications for teaching, we have treated this aspect as a separate although still connected topic.

The intent of this chapter is to reveal a hidden curriculum that sends females the message that they are subordinate to males and that their feminine viewpoint, often different from a masculine viewpoint, is not as highly valued. We begin by tracing the history of our patriarchal society, reflecting the messages delivered to women through theology, philosophy, psychology, social stereotypes, and education—the underpinnings of our culture. Of necessity, this will not be an exhaustive journey but an overview to provide evidence for concern.

We then present a set of processes that we believe will lead to a new voice that diminishes the male/female dichotomy embedded in our current society and replaces it with a more authentic balance—an androgynous voice. The benefits to our global society include increased learning resulting from a wider source of perspectives, more creative solutions to problems, and the involvement of all human beings. In essence, the total vision of society could be enlarged and transformed as the old is challenged and a new dynamic is achieved.

Prior to beginning this journey, we wish to emphasize that we are discussing the feminine archetypal processes of intuition and relatedness, in contrast to the masculine archetypal processes of objective rationalism and independence. The feminine processes that have been undervalued in Western culture are those that attract, connect, and hold people together. By honoring the feminine, we are not denigrating the masculine. Instead, we are emphasizing a worldview that honors the whole of who humans are. The reader is invited to envision a world that values the creative potential inherent in an androgynous voice.

Theology

In virtually every world culture before the advent of the three major monotheistic religions—Judaism, Islam, and Christianity—deity was female. She was a goddess worshiped under an infinite number of names and forms and in countless languages, societies, and places. Her artifacts are 30,000 years old or older (Johnson, 1988; Shepherd, 1993). She stood for peace, healing, communal living, and reverence for the earth. The goddess cultures initially developed the concept of civilization and the beginnings of religion, art, writing (alphabets), and timekeeping (Stone, 1976). "Evidence suggests," according to French (1992), "that for three and a half million years, humans lived in small cooperative [goddess-centered] communities in which the sexes were equal" (p. 9). In the banishing of goddess-centered cultures, however, the status of women was diminished. Stein (1990) writes,

> As near as archeology can now determine, the changes began in approximately 15,000-12,000 B.C.E and continued to completion by 2400 B.C.E. At this time in succeeding migration waves, northern hunting tribes moved south, conquering the Goddess matriarchies and destroying them. They brought the order that we know today—patriarchal world culture with its misogynist male god and biases against women. (p. 2)

The message of the Buddhist rule that only men can achieve nirvana, the Jewish law (until recently) that only men may study Torah, and the Christian law that only men could be deacons consistently implies that men are closer to God and therefore should have authority over women.

Philosophy and Feminism

Paralleling the teachings of the major religions, after 2400 B.C.E., philosophers of the ancient world also placed women in a subordinate role to men.

Gatens (1991) argues that there is a prevailing belief that metaphysics, theories of human nature, and epistemology are sex neutral when actually they are the theoretical underpinnings for the biases that become visible at a sociopolitical level. Gatens (1991) states, "Dichotomies have dominated modern philosophy: mind/body, reason/passion, and nature/culture. . . . These dichotomies interact with the male/female dichotomy in extremely complex and prejudicial ways" (p. 4). The historical associations between women, nature, passion, and the body are surprisingly influential in contemporary thought (Shepherd, 1993).

In modern philosophy, the male subject is revealed to us as self-contained and the owner of his own person and capacities. He is able to relate to other men as free competitors with whom he shares certain social-political-economic rights. The female subject is framed as prone to disorder and passion, leaving her economically and politically dependent on men. These views are justified by continual reference to the notion that a biological destiny is implanted in the female body and in women's nature. Women are often described not by their strengths but by what they lack as compared with men.

Historically, men were considered superior as a result of their role as warriors. Simone de Beauvoir (cited in Gatens, 1991) commented, "It is not in giving life but in risking life that man is raised above animal: that is why superiority has been accorded in humanity not to the sex that brings forth life but to that which kills" (p. 46).

As we look to our current curriculum in social studies, we notice de Beauvoir's comment to be the primary model set before students. Hours, weeks, and months are spent on the study of various wars, the conquering of nations, and the hostile takeover of governments. Social studies is taught from a historically masculine perspective of what is significant and important. Yet few students are encouraged to inquire into these findings and look at them through the values of an androgynous mind.

Psychology and Women

Two recognized works in women's psychology—Miller's *Toward a New Psychology of Women* (1976) and Gilligan's *In a Different Voice: Psychological Theory and Women's Development* (1982)—have revealed a new area of research strongly stating that female thought processes differ from, but are no less productive or valuable than, male thought processes. Although times have changed since Miller's publication, French (1992), along with Rothblatt (1995), Steinem (1994), and many other recent social commentators, indicates that efforts by women to enrich their lives are still readily misinterpreted as attempts to diminish or imitate men. Women who challenge the existing status quo risk being seen as creators of conflict and are expected to bear the psychological burden of not portraying the image of "true" women. As women become empowered socially, politically, and economically, their challenge is to maintain and continue these hard-won gains without becoming pseudo-men in the process. The challenge facing educators and curriculum designers is to develop the processes young women will need to be successful in a new and emerging world while at the same time meeting the needs of young men.

Integrated into Western society is the notion that profound psychological differences exist between men and women. Some of the characteristics that Western society ascribes to the image of "true women" in contrast to the image of "true men" are these:

- Females tend to believe in and value a sense of connectedness, whereas males tend to emphasize separation and autonomy.
- Males are unrealistically expected to discard or deny feeling weak, sensitive, or vulnerable, whereas females are encouraged to display a need for male protection.
- Most females have a greater sense of the emotional components of human activity than do most males.
- Males do the "important" work in society, whereas females tend to the lesser task of helping other human beings develop.
- Females tend to recognize the cooperative and creative nature of all human existence, whereas males value competition and the maintenance of the status quo.
- The need to serve others is not central to males' self-image. Once males have become "men," they may choose to serve others without fear of ridicule or a need to dominate. Females are expected to serve others.

The development of an androgynous voice—a voice in which self-enhancement and affiliation are both valued, a human voice that reflects the attributes of both masculinity and femininity—is becoming increasingly necessary as the world becomes more complex. As Miller (1976) noted,

> Practically everyone now bemoans Western man's sense of alienation, lack of community, and inability to find ways of organizing society for human ends. . . . It now seems clear we have arrived at a point from which we must return to a basis of faith in affiliation—and not only faith but recognition that it is a requirement for the existence of human beings. (p. 147)

The educational system needs to become an open, dynamic system that rewards divergent thinking, listening, and processing.

Social Stereotypes

> For many women, attention to their own inner experience often feels incompatible with attention to other; an ethic of caring for others carries the connotation of self-sacrificing or putting oneself last.
>
> *Judith Jordan*

The second wave of the feminist movement in 1960s has had its impact on the world. Yet at the end of the U.N. Decade for Women in 1985, a report on the state of the world's women concluded that women had made some gains in education, health, employment, and politics during the decade but that men still had most of the power (Sciolino, 1985).

In May 1995, an ABC television news documentary reported that two of every three persons living in poverty in the United States were females. Economic analysts project that women will be hired mostly in low-paid jobs (Noble, 1985).

Feminism has been associated with the decreasing birth rate, which has been linked to a desire of more women to attain higher degrees to achieve higher incomes. Although the number of women earning doctorates has been decreasing, women are better educated than ever before. Yet according to 1992-1993 surveys, they still receive lower pay than their male counterparts (Steinem, 1994). Women who work earn 15% less than men performing the same job, and men whose wives work earn 20% less than men whose wives do not work ("Work Versus Family," 1995). This disparity is frequently found in the educational arena, in which female professors and administrators are paid less than male professors and administrators. In addition, until recently, educators were paid poorly for services in general. The cause rests in the belief that the responsibility of helping other individuals grow is not "important work."

According to a television documentary on the International Conference on Women, women in the United States still have less voice in their government than do women in nonindustrial countries (e.g., 11% of federal positions in the United States are held by women; 13% of national government positions in Poland are held by women). In addition, research shows that females are treated differently from males in many other facets of society. Specifically, French (1992) points to the educational system when she writes, "Studies show that teachers of coed classes give two-thirds of their attention to boys, yet their students have the perception that girls and boys are being treated alike" (p. 126).

Discrimination against females has been documented in education through numerous studies. Steinem (1994) cites a multiracial study (released in 1987) that tracked a group of high school valedictorians through college. The study found that

> the intellectual self-esteem was about equal among females and males when they entered, but after four years, the number of young men who considered themselves "far above average" had grown, while the number of women who did so had dropped to zero. This was not related to grades, in which the women were equal to or better, but apparently to the frequent invisibility of women in what they were studying, the rarity of women in authority in classroom or campus, more "masculine" competition than "feminine" cooperation in the academic atmosphere. (pp. 184-185)

And even more recently, Kramer (1991), in a study on girls who were gifted, found that the need for status, fitting in, and being socially popular results in girls' willingness to hide their abilities and accomplishments. Kramer found that "girls distinguished between ability and effort, believing that gifted boys had ability and were smart, whereas . . . gifted girls . . . put forth effort and had only potential" (p. 358). This may in part result from teachers' passively reinforcing the sex role stereotypical behaviors (Brophy, 1985; Eccles & Blumfield, 1985).

Because young girls tend to focus on outside reinforcement, they may lose the independence necessary for finding their own direction, the willingness to stand up for and argue their own ideas, and the desire to follow those paths that are intrinsically rewarding (Boggiano & Barrett, 1992). This is why the primacy of grades over learning and a desire to please teachers and/or peers are evident in adolescent/teenage girls. Young girls' decision-making skills are based on an ethic of caring, rather than on being right or wrong (Belenky, Clinchy, Goldberger, & Tarule, 1986; Callahan, Cunningham, & Plucker, 1994). The result may be that girls learn how to play the "academic game" and get good grades with a minimum of effort.

The tragedy lies in that many young women are not using the cognitive skills available to them in productive ways. The desire to conform and the feelings of self-doubt sometimes result in manipulative behaviors that reinforce the social stereotype of femininity and lowered academic achievement. The goal, as expressed in the words of Ruether (1985), is to make "women as subjects at the center rather than the margin. Women are empowered to define themselves rather than be defined by others. Women's speech and presence are normative rather than aberrant" (p. 23).

It is frequently said that in general, women score better than men on tests of verbal ability and that men score better than women on most tests of mathematical skill. Similarly, average tests scores have been used to infer women as more intuitive and men as more logical. There are, however, always men who test in the women's range and women who test in the men's range. The overlap is always much greater than the range in which only women or only men score. When the test scores are studied in depth, men and women are found able to think more alike than unalike. In essence, the tests do not validate the popular stereotypes reinforced by many in society. Although the processes in which women engage may be different from those of men, women have shown that they are as intelligent as men.

The need for a new type of relationship between men and women is resulting in the formation of mixed-gender groups who discuss pertinent issues of sex differences and similarities. Together, they are striving for a blending of voices. Remaining now is to identify and nurture those processes that will change the future because we cannot rewrite the past.

An Acceptance of Complexity

There are distinct differences between men and women. The causes for these differences are debated on many levels and in many fields of study. For example, biological differences exist between the sexes. Gorman (1995) points out that women seem to have stronger connections between the two halves of their brain then do men, and recent research indicates that sex hormones are also involved in and influence the brain. Gorman continues, however, "The variation between the sexes pales in comparison with individual differences—and shows how marvelously versatile a 3-LB. mass of nerve cells can be" (p. 51).

Einstein's brain was found to have more glial cells than the brains of 11 other normal human male brains. Glial cells are "helper cells" that feed the neurons and clean up afterwards. They are 10 times more numerous in the brain than neurons and have been found to participate in the communication between the brain and the body. In Einstein's brain, significant differences were found in the number of these nurturing cells in those areas of the brain that are associated with the conceptual powers of imagery and complex thinking. Shepherd (1993) suggests that these nurturing cells are in some way connected with the feminine-masculine, androgynous thinking in which Einstein was able to engage.

A strong bond between the valuing of the left side of the brain and the domination of men over women has continued and has been reinforced by our scientific-technological Western culture. It sneaks into and is reinforced daily by men and women alike both overtly and covertly. But the beauty of our universe rests not only in our sameness but in our difference. Accepting with openness the complexity of humanity enriches our experiences and leads us to see the beauty of our cosmos with deeper understanding.

A Kaleidoscopic Society

From ancient Greece to the present, females have been defined by what they lack. What appears to be a sex-neutral philosophy is defined by the male experience. If there is to be a genuinely polymorphous sociopolitical body, it is clear that it needs to be capable of discriminating and respecting differences. As a result, it is crucial to begin thinking of ways in which those excluded from current political representation may be represented now and in the future. Such representation must avoid privileging historically valued human powers and capacities at the expense of powers and capacities that have been repressed or distorted. The dichotomies of thought that have dominated philosophical reflections from ancient Greece to modern times need to be reconceptualized and lived in an intertwined way. "A victory of continuism [is required] over duality" (Rothblatt, 1995, p. 22). From this chaos will grow the complexity of a kaleidoscopic society in which all humans are valued.

Processes That Honor the Feminine Voice

It is time for the mother's voice to be heard in education.

Nel Noddings (1984)

We have gone to some lengths to establish a rationale for looking at the hidden curriculum and the cultural subtleties that have marginalized and/or devalued feminine cognition for thousands of years. Language, with its many differing forms (intonation, word choice, body movements, syntax, presuppositions, and facial expressions), plays an important role in this communication, as do behavior and symbols. Language can cause persons to feel included or excluded, accepted or rejected, valued or denied.

And what impact do these latent, as well as manifest, messages have on female students? Why should educators be concerned? Recent studies in psychotherapy and self-hypnosis have revealed that people's thoughts control our beliefs, and our beliefs control our actions (Borysenko, 1988; Chopra, 1993; Gawain, 1978; Hay, 1987; Murphy, 1963). As human beings, our thoughts and our use of language communicate messages, intentional or unintentional, that reveal our innermost beliefs and values. As a result, some researchers are encouraging us to be conscious of monitoring our language, choosing to drop from our vocabulary words of negativity, criticism, fear, sarcasm, and bias toward ourselves and others. The idea is that "negative moods flourish through the use of words, that we 'language' ourselves into darkness" (Hawley, 1993, p. 88)—or, as in the case of so many young women, into intellectual weakness.

Educators need to create schools that demystify the avenues of communication from both within and without the organization. Public schools need to become complex adaptive systems that welcome change and search for commonalties as well as differences. There needs to be an openness in the way we communicate that allows for each person's voice to be heard. We need to look at the underside of our current curriculum to find ways to include the feminine voice. We need to encourage students to read between the lines, to look for what is implied but not said, and to search actively for ways to identify the value of all humanity.

Recognizing Presuppositions

Integrated into language are presuppositions that teach the hidden curriculum. Stories such as Sleeping Beauty, Snow White, and Cinderella remind young girls of Western man's perception that to be feminine requires one to be covertly strong, compassionate, and sensitive. Various media have delivered yet another message to young girls—they are to be "overtly sexy," and their appearance is more important than their intellects.

Unfortunately, for both males and females, the hero, in existing U.S. culture, is frequently the white, masculine "Lone Ranger" who as the gallant warrior comes to the rescue of the weaker female or the male who is seen in a lower position on the cultural hierarchical scale. They are the "High Noon Rambos" who are able to overcome superior forces without help. These early lessons are at the root of the mantra so many females—and males of different ethnic backgrounds—unconsciously repeat—"I am the weaker." Little girls are often reminded they are to be "sugar, and spice, and everything nice."

Monitoring Internal Dialogue

As Strickland and Coulson discuss in their chapter on creativity in the first book of this trilogy, *Envisioning Process As Content,* educators must teach learners the process of monitoring inner communication or self-talk. As the feminine in each person becomes more fully developed, this inner voice provides resources for knowing and understanding concepts at a deeper level. Individuals begin to tap into an inner strength that previously was not available. The transition manifested is increased self-concept and self-esteem. Young learners must hear and be conscious of the restrictions they place on themselves when they accept the patriarchal definitions of femininity and actively seek to free themselves from these social limitations. They must learn to trust the feminine sound of their inner voice.

One of the rules Hawley (1993) suggests and then applies to learning organizations is to create expectations of success and monitor exclusive and negative language that diminishes learning and creativity and therefore holds educators and students back. In essence, we need to carefully monitor our inner and intercommunication because the stories we tell and are told mold our perceptions of reality.

Communicating Authentically

Part of the reason for the superior/subordinate dichotomy rests in that women and men communicate differently (Gilligan, 1982; Gray, 1992; Tannen, 1990). It is not our intent to create the impression that all men communicate identically and that all women communicate in the same manner—there is a natural continuum. Men and women who are androgynous thinkers are able to leave the sex stereotyping behind and truly talk to one another with openness. What has been found, however, is that women tend to explore an idea from several different angles before making a determination. Men, on the other hand, tend to reach a decision without the need to look at alternatives (Gray, 1992). This creates a tension between the two groups because one sees the other as indecisive.

Communication gaps between men and women also surface when they are asked to listen to each other. Michelle Hunt (1994), a vice president of Herman Miller, describes how this phenomenon occurred during executive meetings she attended: "It was as if my mouth was moving but no one heard me. Five minutes later when a man voiced the same idea, everyone would say 'Great idea!' " (p. 419).

Carol Cohn (cited in French, 1992), who spent a summer studying with male experts in nuclear strategy, related, "To understand them—and speak so they could understand me—I had to learn their language, one made up of largely invented words, acronyms impenetrable to most of us" (p. 157). Cohn learned that the language of the nuclear scientist reflected the images of religion, birth, and male initiation rituals.

Rosemarie recently had an experience that brought this knowledge to a personal level. Her son, Gary, is a U.S. Marine. After his leave from boot camp, Rosemarie and her husband brought Gary to Camp Lejeune, North Carolina, for additional training. As they were leaving the base, one of the drill instructors engaged them in a conversation. Howard, Gary's father, and the drill instructor clearly understood each other. On the other hand, Rosemarie had no understanding of the acronyms that were freely used. In fact, frequently she had to ask her husband to explain certain language (BWT, i.e., Basic War Training) that Gary wrote about in his letters home. The language of letters was ingrained in these Marines and foreign to the outsider.

Analogies and metaphors used by men and women tend to differ. Frequently, analogies structured by men, in academia and health, are associated with power issues such as war, politics, and sports. Women tend to use softer metaphors that are allied with nature, family, and play. This basic difference continues to enhance the communication gap.

Communication barriers may also be connected with context. Waldrop (1992) reveals the difficulties involved in trying to get a group of economists and physical scientists to converse with one another. Each group held dearly to coveted theories and jargon. Each looked at the other with suspicion and unconscious superiority. Each group was committing a basic error in thinking—holding the answer before the problem was clearly defined. The tension continued until both groups realized that they were concerned with the same issue—complexity in economics and complexity in the physical sciences. The ability to recognize a common concept in their research bridged the communication gap by defining a shared interest and/or problem.

Reading Between the Lines

How might learners automatically recognize what is not being said? Griffin (1978) provides an excellent example of reading between the lines. While she was tracing the history of inheritance, she recorded her feminine voice into the existing knowledge:

> We shall tell you who gained and who lost *In this way* for there were those *the fathers* who held *knew that their names* and those who did not *would live on* those who were known *and that the great estates* and those *testifying to their glory and fame* who were unknown *would live on* those whose lives were vanished *and that power which spread from those holdings of land* those whose labor *would continue, generation after generation* like the labor of the fields, of the soil, *to be great in the minds of the living* would pass like the passing of breath from the living. (p. 52)

When the dual dialogue is separated, the familiar, male perspective is this:

> In this way the fathers knew that their names would live on and that the great estates testifying to their glory and fame would live on and that power which spread from those holdings of land would continue, generation after generation to be great in the minds of the living.

The unfamiliar, feminine voice raises consciousness to a different perspective:

> We shall tell you who gained and who lost for there were those who held and those who did not, those who were known and those who were unknown, those whose lives were vanished those whose labor like the labor of the fields, of the soil, would pass like the passing of breath from the living.

The ability to see what is not being said, to raise questions never asked before, is nurtured by preserving curious minds and the development of learners as inquirers and elaborators of thoughts, feelings, and assumptions. It requires learners to be conscious not only of their own thinking but of that of others. It takes authentic communication between critical friends and active listening. It requires androgynous communication skills and a willingness to challenge the existing methodolatry. Daly (1973) states, "The tyranny of methodolatry hinders new discoveries. It prevents us from raising questions never asked before and from being illumined by ideas that do not fit the preestablished boxes and forms" (p. 38). The methodolatry Daly is referring to is the scientific method so deeply embedded in our society and therefore in our schools.

Thinking Androgynously

Many women, as well as men, spend a lifetime trying to develop their true selves, with all the complexities this entails. The current educational system, however, tends to label individuals on the basis of assessments that provide only a part of the total picture. The categorization causes an expectation that individuals will behave in a manner consistent with a certain group—feminine/masculine, gifted/exceptional, athletic/artistic. The result is frustration and a stifling of unique talents and human spirits. Educators need to provide learning environments that permit students to bring their real selves to the classroom—not just the labeled self.

Instead of trying to separate, classify, and categorize individuals, educators and society at large might benefit from trying to understand the connections that bind people. As Wheatley (1992) states, "The world of relationships is rich and complex . . . the pattern that connects. . . . None of us are independent of our relationships with others" (p. 34). Wheatley argues that when we stop teaching facts and focus instead on relationships, we will begin to see ourselves as capable of extraordinary potential. In essence, when women are included as viable, thoughtful contributors to our culture, humanity's potential for greatness will be enhanced, nurtured, and created.

Awareness of the feminine need for relationships and connected learning suggests that we might also enlarge our perspective of processes to include the "all" of who we are. Griffin (1978) looks at thought processes through the construction of the word *think* in Chinese calligraphy, which uses both the *brain* and the *heart.* The intertwining of the brain and heart is, in Griffin's words, the highest form of maturity humans can achieve. This is consistent with our view of intuition, which we see as the "ah, ha!" experience—the peace and simultaneous excitement that comes from the alignment of one's head with one's heart.

Engaging in Dialogue

Educators need to raise questions that allow for responses that give voice to the learner's heart as well as brain. The intent of these questions should be to evoke dialogue, the central element of organizational transformation (Schein, 1994). Dialogue facilitates and creates new avenues of learning that result from the sharing of mental models. Dialogue is the avenue through which trusting relationships are built and through which individuals can freely speak their feminine-masculine minds. It is at the root of honest interchange in which individuals realize that they are valued and that their voices will be heard and integrated into each other's mental models.

Why are we advocating dialogue over debate? First, in a debate, someone wins and someone loses; in a dialogue, information is freely shared without winners or losers—only learners. Second, in a dialogue, a person listens non-judgmentally to the other person and attempts to understand the underlying assumptions on which thoughts, ideas, and perceptions are based. This art of listening—of being open and allowing something to enter without immediately intercepting it with thoughts and interpretations—requires a temporary suspension of judgment. Dialogue focuses on the thinking process and how past experiences have influenced current perceptions. The goal of dialogue is to help all members, male and female, reach higher levels of consciousness and creativity. Ideas begin to surface that may never have been voiced in a win/lose, right/wrong, separatists'/reductionists' curriculum—ideas that create new realities and possibilities. (See also Baker, Costa, & Shalit, "Norms of Collaboration," and Lipton & Melameade, "Organizational Learning: The Essential Journey," in the third book of this trilogy, *The Process-Centered School: Sustaining a Renaissance Community*.)

Developing Metacognition

Metacognition helps humans see, hear, and feel the chains that bind us to our current reality. It increases our awareness of premature cognitive commitments that could otherwise remain unquestioned. These premature cognitive commitments may have been transmitted to us as a result of covert messages from our family of origin, the society in which we live, or even the media. Left unquestioned and without recognition, they limit what we can know of the world around us. Through self-awareness, self-analysis, and metacognition, learners, female and male, attempt to understand their assumptions while they relate to the new thoughts and ideas expressed by others. It is during self-analysis that learners listen to their inner dialogue and can modify or adjust it in accord with new insights. Therefore, teaching the disposition of metacognition needs to become one of the overarching goals of curriculum.

Nurturing Connected Thinking

We know there are psychological differences between men and women: females tend to be connected learners (field dependent/relational) and males tend to be separate learners (field independent/reductional). The current design, compartmentalized and separated, of the traditional curriculum was and is appropriate for most young men. We are beginning to witness, however, a restructuring into thematic, cross-disciplinary learning. A significant impact has been made by the findings in the new sciences. New information is propelling us to reorganize our thinking, to accept that "no-thing" can be fully understood in isolation and that information is not static but "in-formation." As Steinem (1994) notes,

> We have for so long looked at most subjects through male eyes that remedial vision [through the eyes of women] . . . brings a new perspective. It may not completely change what has always been before us, but

> it adds depth, and a sense of the periphery which, as in a cell or a sprout, is where growth takes place. (p. 270)

One of the greatest benefits is the increased opportunity for learning as educators let go of the methods that worked in the past, that is, the industrial model school with its reductionist curriculum, and venture into new areas of connectedness, discovery, and creativity.

Developing Inclusive and Courteous Language

Communication skills take many different forms between males and females. We advocate the use of inclusive language that constructs itself in such a way to communicate "I see, hear, and respect you; I feel you have a lot to offer, and I sense I can learn from you," or perhaps, "I care about you." Inclusive language is positive and invites another into the community in an authentic way. It creates an organizational climate and personal attitude indicating that a person's ideas are valued and will be treated with respect. We all need to be aware of language that ridicules, mocks, or is discourteous to the learner—language used by teachers and students. We as authors, both in our respective fields and as mothers, have witnessed the pain inflicted on others by the use of careless, thoughtless language.

Language use within the school community should shift from vocabulary that is grounded in battles, struggles, and opposition to courteous vocabulary that is affectionate, friendly, and empathic. With a mind-set of love and respect, learning can become a dialogue with students rather than an exchange of facts.

Such a shift toward use of the feminine is evident in the language of chaos theory. In contrast to the stark language of mathematics, concepts in chaos science are described as *dust, webs, cups, foam,* and *fudgeflakes.* As chaos theory shifts the way we see our world, the voice of the feminine is also shifting the thinking processes. We are beginning to use new metaphors to describe the world in which we live.

Providing Guided Reflection Time

Women, particularly in higher academia, have voiced a need for processing time to connect newly acquired knowledge with previously existing knowledge (Belenky et al., 1986). This can be achieved if teachers provide a time in which questions on the relevance or context of the new learning are individually or collectively considered. This dialogue will serve to enhance the learning of both the teachers and the students. The questions need to shift from "What have the students failed to see?" to "What are they adding to the repertoire of knowledge?" If students publicly share private insights to stretch their own thinking and the thinking of others, construction of new truths result from sensing and feeling together and by reaching a consensus after erasing boundaries.

Self-reflection requires that we slow our busy lives down to provide time for openness, patience, alertness, and responsiveness. During quiet time, knowledge is produced. Insights occur during those moments when we no longer control our conscious voice and listen to our inner voice. The thoughts and ideas bubble up from our intuition.

Awakening Intuition

Four phases are involved in the intuitive process: (a) preparation—a question is directed to the unconscious and information is provided; (b) incubation—accumulated information simmers in the unconscious; (c) illumination—a solution is produced in a mysterious flash of insight; and (d) verification—fantasies are discerned from true inspiration.

The ability to be consciously aware of intuition and to bring it to the learning environment is foreign to many learners. As teachers, we need to help students understand that concepts need not be accepted at face value. Placing a concept on the board and asking students, "How does that make you feel?" causes students to be actively engaged. Students driven by unexamined emotional responses are prone to error because they are not using the whole of themselves. Physicist Eberhard Riedel (cited in Shepherd, 1993) states, "I consult my body about the correctness of an equation" (p. 59). His intent is to determine if the equation agrees with his sense of the process. This process, identifying and being aware of feelings, assists learners in making judgments. We advocate identification and awareness of the intuitive responses from all parts of the body, not just the head, as we gather information.

Zen masters have taught that when the student is ready, the teacher will come. The Zen master waits for the student to ask the right question as an indicator that the student is ready to integrate the answer. Intuitive knowledge, when nurtured, can help formulate these important questions. Further, intuition, guided by feelings and cognition, which are value laden, helps weed things out by telling us what we can or cannot accept. Feelings bring to learning a sense of love, a passion for the work, an excitement connected with discovery, and a zest for truth.

Attending to intuitive responses and creating a warm environment enable students to be more creative. The intuitive process requires a relaxed, receptive, playful state of mind. As educators, we should actively encourage the four stages of the intuitive process: preparation, incubation, illumination, and verification. It is necessary to question, interact with, and present objections to the revelations from intuition so that students will develop the ability to recognize truth from wishful thinking.

Developing a Tolerance for Ambiguity

One of the qualities attributed to the feminine aspect that needs to be developed in all of us is a willingness to live with ambiguity. In this rapidly changing world, the ability to value tentativeness and to tolerate uncertainty is becoming increasingly important. Ambiguity fosters the freedom to open new possibilities and options. This ability permits us to respond to each situation uniquely and requires flexibility in thinking as we begin to explore and navigate unknown territories. Instead of limiting ourselves to anticipated expectations, the tolerance for ambiguity permits individuals to engage in wonder and curiosity. Questions are raised such as, "What if this were true? What does it mean to the way we see the world?" The tolerance for ambiguity requires resourcefulness, cleverness, motivation, intuition, persistence, enthusiasm, creativity, and skill to contemplate the open-ended questions that will be generated. We will be answering and developing questions that require a broader perception—a movement away from a dichotomous world to a holonomous world—a world in which we use both masculine and feminine processes.

Enhancing Empathy

We advocate for the development of empathy, the ability to walk in another's shoes. This requires a deliberative, imaginative extension of individual thinking and an ability to be receptive and nonjudgmental. Empathy, as defined by Noddings (1984), "does not involve projection but reception. I do not project. I receive the other into myself, and I see and feel the other" (p. 30). This differs from the traditional definition of empathy (projecting oneself inside the other's mental models) and requires an opening of the self to experience the other—a shape shifting. It further requires the integration of reason, intuition, and the expertise of others—the ability to let the inner knowledge out and the outer knowledge in.

In Summary

It has been our intent to raise consciousness to the concerns of feminists and others who are aware of the hidden curriculum in which the feminine voice is marginalized or diminished. We believe that the processes offered for classroom teaching will benefit both students and teachers and create an atmosphere for learning in which creative thought will flourish. Today's classrooms need to be places in which students can understand that neighbors may see the world through a different lens, that interests should focus not on what people think but on how they go about forming their ideas, feelings, and opinions. We believe this can be accomplished through honoring the feminine voice, whether it be found inside a woman or a man. As we journey into increased opportunity for learning, venturing into new areas of connectedness, discovery and creativity, we expand our worldview.

References

Belenky, M. F., Clinchy, B., Goldberger, N. R., & Tarule, J. M. (1986). *Women's ways of knowing*. New York: HarperCollins/Basic Books.

Boggiano, A. K., & Barrett, M. (1992). Gender differences in depression in children as a function of motivational orientation. *Sex Roles, 26,* 11-17.

Borysenko, J. (1988). *Minding the body, mending the mind*. Reading, MA: Addison-Wesley.

Brophy, J. (1985). Interactions of male and female students with male and female teachers. In L. C. Wilkinson & C. B. Marret (Eds.), *Gender influences in classroom interaction* (pp. 115-142). Orlando, FL: Academic Press.

Callahan, C., Cunningham, C., & Plucker, J. (1994). Foundations for the future: The socio-emotional development of gifted adolescent women. *Roeper Review: A Journal on Gifted Education, 17*(2), 99-105.
Chopra, D. (1993). *Ageless body, timeless mind.* New York: Crown.
Daly, M. (1973). *Beyond God the father.* Boston: Beacon.
Eccles, J. S., & Blumfield, P. (1985). Classroom experiences and student gender: Are there differences and do they matter? In L. C. Wilkinson & C. B. Marret (Eds.), *Gender influences in classroom interaction* (pp. 79-114). Orlando, FL: Academic Press.
French, M. (1992). *The war against women.* New York: Ballantine.
Gatens, M. (1991). *Feminism and philosophy.* Indianapolis: Indiana University Press.
Gawain, S. (1978). *Creative visualization.* San Rafael, CA: New World Library.
Gilligan, C. (1982). *In a different voice: Psychological theory and women's development.* Cambridge, MA: Harvard University Press.
Gorman, C. (1995, July 17). How gender may bend your thinking. *Time, 146*(3), 51.
Griffin, S. (1978). *Woman and nature: The roaring inside her.* New York: Harper & Row.
Gray, J. (1992). *Men are from Mars, women are from Venus.* New York: HarperCollins.
Hawley, J. (1993). *Reawakening the spirit in work: The power of dharmic management.* San Francisco: Berrett-Koehler.
Hay, L. L. (1987). *You can heal your life.* Carson, CA: Hay House.
Hunt, M. (1994). Building an organization that recognizes everyone's uniqueness. In P. Senge, C. Roberts, R. Ross, B. Smith, & A. Kleiner (Eds.), *The fifth discipline fieldbook: Strategies and tools for building a learning organization.* New York: Doubleday.
Johnson, B. (1988). *Lady of the beasts: Ancient images of the goddess and her sacred animals.* San Francisco: Harper & Row.
Kramer, L. R. (1991). The social construction of ability perception: An ethnographic study of gifted adolescent girls. *Journal of Early Adolescence, 11,* 340-362.
Miller, J. B. (1976). *Toward a new psychology of women.* Boston: Beacon.
Murphy, J. (1963). *The power of your subconscious mind.* Englewood Cliffs, NJ: Prentice Hall.
Noble, K. (1985, December 12). Low-paying jobs foreseen for most working women. *New York Times.*
Noddings, N. (1984). *Caring.* Berkeley: University of California Press.
Rothblatt, M. (1995). *The apartheid of sex.* New York: Crown.
Ruether, R. R. (1985). *Womanguides: Readings toward a feminist theology.* Boston: Beacon.
Schein, E. (1994). On dialogue, culture, and organizational learning. In *The learning organization in action.* New York: American Management Association.
Sciolino, E. (1985, June 23). UN finds widespread inequality for women. *New York Times.*
Senge, P. (1990). *The fifth discipline: The art and practice of the learning organization.* New York: Doubleday/Currency.
Shepherd, L. (1993). *Lifting the veil: The feminine face of science.* Boston: Shambhala.
Stein, D. (1990). *Casting the circle: A women's book of ritual.* Freedom, CA: Crossing Press.
Steinem, G. (1994). *Moving beyond words: Age, rage, sex, power, money, muscles: Breaking boundaries of gender.* New York: Simon & Schuster.
Stone, M. (1976). *When god was a woman.* New York: Harcourt, Brace, Jovanovich.
Tannen, D. (1990). *You just don't understand me.* New York: Ballantine.
Waldrop, M. M. (1992). *Complexity: The emerging science at the edge of order and chaos.* New York: Touchstone.
Wheatley, M. (1992). *Leadership and the new science.* San Francisco: Berrett-Koehler.
Work versus family. (1995, July). *Training & Development, 49*(7), 71. (Available from the American Association for Training and Development, Alexandria, VA)

13

Measuring From in the Middle of Learning

Bena Kallick

The relationship is clear—a strong and thoughtful process leads to a better product. When there is a problem with the product, we must map our way backward from the product to the process to understand how to improve. Yet in many classrooms, educators take the time only to judge the product. And that judgment carries a finality that does not invite learners to consider how to refine and improve their work.

Imagine what it might be like to teach dance. Suppose that students were given considerable instruction without continuing critique and feedback and then were suddenly on stage for a performance. In the absence of good, critical feedback, the possibility of learners making the necessary corrections that would improve their performance is unlikely. They would be blind to audience or "other" in their work. As a result, they would find out how their work was received only under the pressure of a high-stakes performance. If that were the case, it would be difficult to keep the dancers motivated!

On the other hand, imagine performers who receive continuous feedback and critique about their work as they prepare for a high-stakes performance. They are able to self-correct, learn from the audience, and raise their performance to an even higher standard. The results of the instructional critique would be quite visible; either they made the moves the teacher suggested or they didn't—not like teaching math, or science, or social studies—or is it?

Visible in the classroom of dance is the movement that learners make as a result of their thinking, internalizing the instruction, and changing their movements to improve their performance. The difference between dance and social studies is more in what is visible, what is observed, than it is in the process of thinking, internalizing, and changing to improve performance.

Suppose educators focused on making observable the thinking and internalizing process through systems that provided assessment information? This chapter will explore assessment strategies that facilitate learning as we make a journey from process to product. The stops along the road will be the places where we are organizing ourselves, becoming self-observing about our disposition toward learning, how we access information, how we process and interpret information, how we communicate what we have learned, and, finally, how we intentionally plan for and build opportunities for continuous growth through feedback spirals.

Process Goals

When teachers, as well as learners, have clear statements about process goals, they have better access to appropriate instructional interventions. For example, in one classroom, students were asked to talk on tape about their writing process as they were writing. If students were to talk about the way they were organizing their pieces, they might describe the webbing of ideas that they saw. They might say that they were ordering the web of ideas so that they were in sequential order regarding the main ideas of their essays. After judging the essays, the teacher would then be able to return to the recorded organizational strategies and ask the question, "Did the strategies used lead to well-organized essays?" In other words, the teacher would be able to make visible the thought processes and strategies that the students were using and then make appropriate instructional interventions. The teacher might learn a considerable amount about students' thinking and then make use of a "just right" accommodation. It would also allow the students to reveal their thinking—what worked and what did not. It would convince the teacher that there is not a "one best" strategy; rather, students need to (a) make their strategies visible to themselves and others and (b) abandon strategies that do not produce the desired outcomes.

The above strategy is one, among many, that teachers are using to help students see the relationship between strategies, thinking tools, and structures that facilitate higher-quality performances. The first step in being able to choose the right strategy or tool for a particular performance begins with knowledge about (a) the qualities that characterize a good performance, (b) how high-quality performers think about their work, and (c) what the students know about themselves as learners.

Qualities of Good Performance

Teachers are often awestruck by exceptional work. Our immediate, holistic response is "This work is exceptional! Great! Wow!" Students need more information than "great," however, to be able to learn how to produce exceptional work. Students need to be surrounded by and learn how to analyze exceptional work. We all learn from exemplars of excellent performance.

A first step is being able to *describe* fine performance. The following is a procedure for describing work:

1. *Describe what you see in the work.* Do not describe what is not there—for example, do not say, "I do not see the proper use of punctuation." If it is not there, it cannot be described. This helps you and the students focus on what the work has to say. What is its voice? Its authorship? What is the author trying to do in the work? It requires a great deal of concentration and observation of detail. This process helps students see work before judging work.
2. *Make interpretations about the work.* Allow yourself to imagine what the author might be trying to do with the piece. At this point, you have moved from description to trying to understand, on the basis of information within the work, what the author's meaning might be.
3. *Analyze the work and establish the criteria to judge this work.* Evaluate on the basis of what has been established and noted in describing and interpreting the work.

The purpose of this exercise is to help students, as well as teachers, become better critics of work.

How Do Quality Performers Think About Their Work?

When we develop process goals, as many districts are presently doing, then we must find ways to assess growth in that area. To assess, we will need to describe the behaviors for which we are looking. One way to achieve those descriptions is by asking the question, "What do the behaviors of a scientist (historian, mathematician, etc.) look like?" For example, Judy Kelly at Croton-Harmon High School in New York describes the behaviors she expects from her ninth-grade earth science students as these:

- Applying knowledge to problems
- Performing direct observation
- Finding patterns
- Asking questions and developing hypotheses
- Gathering information and developing data
- Interpreting data
- Testing knowledge from the research of others
- Drawing conclusions
- Communicating results

If these are the processes and behaviors that are expected from ninth-grade students in science, how might they map back to seventh-grade students? fourth-grade students? first-grade students? We can see the genesis of a spiraling set of processes and behaviors that might be expected from students regardless of the content they are studying. So, in a fourth-grade science class, the teacher may be focusing on the content of plants and animals, and the expected behaviors and processes might include asking questions, setting up experiments, learning from direct observation, gathering and interpreting data, and communicating results. The focus on process suggests that students are expected to develop these behaviors as they move toward increasing independence in their work.

Self-Knowledge

In addition to content and process knowledge, students need to know how they learn best. They need to be able to answer questions such as these: What is the best environment for your learning? Where do you choose to study? Where do you choose to work creatively? How do you work with others? What is your preferred learning mode (visual, kinesthetic, etc.)? What do you consider your talents or strengths (arts, oral presentations, persuasive arguments, etc.)? Many teachers ask students to reflect on these questions regularly. This process of self-assessment provides students with data that may be useful as learners. In addition, it might provide useful information for teachers as they facilitate learning.

Self-knowledge builds from internal and external reflection and observation. Feedback from teachers serves as a rich data source. Teachers give evaluative feedback regarding thinking by focusing on (a) the students' dispositions or attitudes toward learning, (b) how students think about accessing information and what students consider important, (c) how students use a reasoning process to think about the information they are gathering, (d) how students use strategies to problem solve, (e) how students communicate the results of their learning, and (f) what is evidenced in their performance as they apply their learning to new situations.

Measuring Dispositions

Costa (1991) describes 12 attributes of intelligent behavior that might be the dispositions individuals need to have to be considered "smart." Many classroom teachers have searched for a way to make those attributes visible to students and to observers. As a result, the grids shown in Figure 13.1a and Figure 13.1b have become useful.

The grids are developed through conversations in the classroom. Students are asked, "What would it look like if a person were a good listener?" "What would it sound like if a person were a good listener?" Students generate a list of positively constructed observable behaviors. For example, in the "looks like" category, there might be responses such as "good eye contact" or "nods head when agreeing." The "sounds like" category might have responses such as "builds on the other person's ideas" or "clarifies when does not understand." Finally, the students and teacher agree to observe for these behaviors.

DIMENSION: Listens with Understanding and Empathy	Often	Some-times	Not Yet
Verbal Restates/paraphrases a person's idea before offering personal opinion			
Clarifies a person's ideas, concepts or terminology			
Expresses empathy for other's feelings/emotions			
Poses questions intended to engage thinking and reflection			
Expresses personal regard and interest			
Non-verbal Faces the person who is speaking			
Establishes eye contact if appropriate			
Nods head			
Uses facial expressions congruent with speakers			
Mirrors gestures			
Mirrors posture			

Figure 13.1a. How Am I Doing? Checklist

To begin, the teacher may ask the students to self-assess: How did I do with the behavior that is representative of an openness to learning? Once students feel comfortable assessing themselves, a second instruction might be for students to rate themselves as well as the others in their group. Students would then compare ratings and see how accurately they perceive themselves. Finally, the teacher may also rate the students and give specific examples of how students are evidencing the positive behaviors of good listening.

As the students begin to collect data about their behavior through time, they may create a graphic representation of their progress (or lack of it!). They will find it helpful to receive feedback from their peers, their teacher, and their own assessment of how they are doing. Examples of scoring rubrics are shown in Figures 13.1.a,b,c, and d.

DIMENSION: Openness to Diverse Perspectives	Often	Some-times	Not Yet
Restates/paraphrases a person's idea before offering personal opinion.			
Clarifies a person's ideas, concepts or terminology			
Expresses empathy for other's feelings/emotions			
Takes an allocentric point of view e.g.: "If I were in your position"			
Changes mind with addition of new information			

Figure 13.1b. How Are We Doing? Checklist

Accessing Information

Although many teachers have been using rubrics for scoring student work, they do not always break apart the components necessary for significantly processing content. One critical component is the ability to choose what is important from a vast amount of information that is available. If a teacher were to consider the process of accessing information important, here are some possible considerations to include in a scoring rubric:

- Selects information from at least three sources, each representing a different perspective
- Chooses credible sources
- Seeks multimedia sources, each evaluated for its source
- Bibliography represents thoughtful consideration of sources in relation to main topic; evidence of consideration is included in the text of the report
- List of sources is developed and justification for why the particular ones were chosen is cited by the source

Table 13.1 Scoring Rubrics

Intelligent Behavior Rubrics	
Metacognition	
Expert	Describes in detail the steps of thinking when solving a problem or doing other mental tasks. Explains in detail how thinking about thinking helps improve work and how it helps to be a better learner. Describes a plan before starting to solve a problem; monitors steps in the plan or strategy; reflects on the efficiency of the problem-solving strategy.
Practitioner	Describes his or her thinking while solving a problem or doing other mental tasks. Explains how thinking about thinking helps learning and helps improve work.
Apprentice	Includes only sparse or incomplete information when describing how he or she is thinking while solving a problem or doing other mental tasks. Sees only small benefits gained from thinking about thinking and learning.
Novice	Is confused about the relationship between thinking and problem solving. Sees no relationship between thinking and learning. Is unable to describe thinking when problem solving.
Persistence	
Expert	Does not give up no matter how difficult it is to find the answers to solutions. Evaluates the use of a variety of strategies to stay on task.
Practitioner	Does not give up when trying to find the answers or solutions. Stays on task.
Apprentice	Tries to complete tasks when the answers or solutions are not readily available but gives up when task is too difficult. Gets off task easily.
Novice	Gives up easily and quickly on difficult tasks.
Restraint of Impulsivity (I)	
Expert	Sets clear goals and describes each step to be taken to achieve goals. Schedules each step and monitors progress.
Practitioner	Sets clear goals and describes some of the steps to be taken to achieve the goals and sequences some of the steps.
Apprentice	Begins to work with unclear goals. Describes only a few of the steps to be taken to achieve the goals. Becomes distracted from schedule.
Novice	Begins to work in random fashion. Is unclear about or unable to state goals or outcomes or steps in achieving goals.
Restraint of Impulsivity (II)	
Expert	Evaluates a situation carefully and seeks advice from other sources to decide whether more information is needed before action. Looks for sources of information that might help and studies them to find important information.
Practitioner	Evaluates a situation to decide if more information is needed before acting. Information is searched for if needed.
Apprentice	Evaluates a situation quickly to decide if more information is needed before acting. Searches for only the most obvious information
Novice	Does not evaluate the situation to decide if more information is needed.

(continued)

Table 13.1 Continued

Intelligent Behavior Rubrics	
Flexibility (I)	
Expert	Uses time and resources creatively to find as many ways as possible to look at a situation. Evaluates these many ways to see how useful they might be. Expresses appreciation for others' points of view. Changes mind and incorporates others' points of view in own thinking.
Practitioner	Finds a variety of ways of looking at a situation and evaluates how useful they are. Describes some ways others' points of view are found to be new and different from own.
Apprentice	Describes different ways of looking at a situation from own perspective.
Novice	Looks at a situation in only one way and that way is often his or her own. Looks no further even when it is clear that it would be helpful to do so.
Flexibility (II)	
Expert	Consistently explores as many alternatives as time and resources will allow and analyzes how the identified alternatives will affect outcomes. The alternatives illustrate extremely diverse but highly useful ways of looking at situations.
Practitioner	Consistently generates alternative ways of approaching tasks and analyzes how the alternatives will affect those tasks. Some alternatives show originality in the approach.
Apprentice	Sporadically generates alternative ways of approaching tasks and analyzes how the alternatives will affect those tasks. Some alternatives show originality in the approach to the tasks.
Novice	Rarely generates alternative ways of approaching tasks. The few alternatives lack originality.

Group Cooperation	
A Scoring Rubric	
4	Demonstrates interdependence. All members contribute. Shows indicators of cooperation and working together, compromising, and staying on task. Disagreements are welcomed as learning opportunities. Completes task with accuracy and within time limits. Members listen to others' points of view. Paraphrasing, clarifying, and empathizing are evident.
3	Members disagree but reach agreements through arguing and debate. Some paraphrasing and clarifying is evident. Group sometimes strays from task. Some members remain silent or refrain from participating.
2	Some members are off task. Group rushes to complete task in the most expedient way because of the pressure of time. Evidence of arguing or encouraging others to get it over with.
1	Few on task. Evidence of arguing and disinterest. Some members occupied with other work.
0	Chaos. Task not completed. Many put-downs. Some members leave before task is complete. Complaints about having to participate in task.

This treatment of judgment helps the teacher understand what was going on in the students' minds as they developed their research reports. Of course, any of these descriptors can be tailored to the course of study and the developmental age of the students. What is important is the communication that the teacher signifies by valuing well-chosen and varied access to information.

Processing Information

Processing can be broken into two areas: reasoning process and strategies for thinking and problem solving. Reasoning implies what takes place as students try to think through a situation. Strategies imply tools to improve the reasoning process. Once again, teachers can signal their interest in students' developing these processes by stating clearly that students will be scored on the basis of evidence of their reasoning and use of strategies.

Writing might be a good example of how this is played out. Students would need to submit their revisions as well as their final drafts. Teachers might be specific about how they will review the revisions in light of the final drafts. For example, did the students make revisions based on reader response? Did they minimally revise as if in an act of obedience, or did they seriously revise on the basis of their own considerations of others' responses? Perhaps student journals might also be submitted so that the teachers can see how the students think about the conferences concerning writing.

Many teachers keep process folios—the artifacts representative of the process students went through to arrive at a particular exhibition or paper. Once again, the artifacts give teachers access to the thought process. How did the students organize their thinking? How did they make notes? Were there specific strategies that were useful to the final product? How well were the students able to metacogitate? How well do the artifacts of the process folios substantiate the final products?

In some classrooms, teachers provide students with a specific structure for reporting regarding process. In the example shown in Figure 13.2 a,b,c,and d, the teachers ask the students to create their own time management plan. In addition, they score each part of the plan as it emerges. They avoid being too prescriptive but do insist that students be aware of the need to organize, plan, and lead their study to higher levels of thinking. This simple structure provides an opportunity for the teachers to coach for quality performance. Rather than waiting until the end, when the project is complete, the teachers have found a way to offer continuing assessment feedback throughout the project.

Communication of Results

This is where teachers begin to make judgments about the degree of success the students have achieved in their final products. Two particular aspects are of interest at this point: (a) Is the medium appropriate and well defined? (b) In what way has the attention to process resulted in a quality product?

To avoid falling into the "the medium is the message" trap, teachers must beware of glitz! Sometimes students capably package their material in a manner

World History Class

Doug Young - Social Studies
Chris Louth - English

Croton-Harmon High School
Croton-on-Hudson, NY

CHINA EXHIBITIONS

For our next unit, we are going to depart from the usual chronological approach to our area study and start with exhibitions which deal with China's past, present, and future. Your job, should you choose to accept this mission, is to research and present your topic while being very aware that your audience has limited knowledge of your subject. You will become an authority on your topic as well as a resource for our future work with this fascinating country.

As before, the exhibitions should take a minimum of 3-5 minutes per student. Your presentation will be a combination of content, interest, creativity, preparation. and polish. Maps will be a "must" for this presentation, so think about ways to incorporate them. Your checklist and criteria sheet will be given out within the next day or so.

Also, as in previous exhibitions, you may choose to work on your own or with a group of students (hopefully some of you have learned a valuable lesson about cooperative exhibitions).
The list below suggests possible methods of presentation and topics. Also feel free to develop your own ideas. In order to avoid duplication, there will only be one topic per class (i.e. Mao Tse-Tung, Opium Wars, etc...)

TOPICS

Changing Role Of Women
The Future of Hong Kong
The New Open Door Policy
Tiananamen Square Revolution
Confucianism
Future of Taiwan
Peasants and the Communist Revolution
Dr. Sun Yat-sen (Father of Modern China)
Two China Policy
Urban and Rural Life Compared
China's Aging Leadership
Chinese Style Communism
History of Rebellion in China
One Child Families
History of Chinese Style Communism
The Long March
Four Modernizations
Chiang Kai-shek vs. Mao Tse-Tung

MEDIUMS

1. Write a poem, rap, or song which will be handed out, explained and performed.
2. Write and present to the class a short story on one of the topics listed.
3. Write and perform a skit or debate on a contemporary problem.
4. Create a debate between two people (Mao Tse-Tung & Chiang Kai-shek) on the issue of the future of Hong Kong or Taiwan.
5. Visual aids: for any of the above you must use a collage, poster, painting, drawing, cartoon, or props to add meaning to your presentation.
6. Come up with an idea of your own, or combine some of the above ideas. You don't have to be limited by these suggestions but all projects must get approval.

Figure 13.2a. Example of Structure for Reporting Process
SOURCE: Developed by Doug Young and Chris Louth. Used with permission.

NAME ______________________________

Exhibitions China 1991: All parts must be completed for full credit.

I. Objective/Goal of Performance as Selected and Developed by Student: (10 points)

Was the goal met in the presentation? Explain your reasoning.

	Exceptional	Proficient	Satisfactory	Limited	Needs Improvement
Self-Evaluation	______	______	______	______	______
Teacher Evaluation	______	______	______	______	______
	10	9	8	7	6

	Self	Teacher
II. **Research** (5 points) Multiple Library Sources (3 required) Proper bibliographic format	______	______
III. **Development of Issue** (10 points) Insightful, relevant, and thoughtful development of topic as selected by student Explanation:	______	______
IV. **Presentation** (10 points) Preparation and Polish Organization: Introduction, body, conclusion Demonstration of creativity Explanation:	______	______
V. **Speaking Qualities** (10 points) Voice usage to emphasize ideas Eye contact Gestures Poise/Polish Explanation:	______	______
VI. **Mastery of Exhibition** (5 points) Response to audience questions Clarified/explained research Gave additional information when asked Demonstrated real....not memorized....knowledge about topic Explanation or example: Rebuttal:	______	______
TOTAL POINTS	______	______

Figure 13.2b. Example of Structure for Reporting Process
SOURCE: Developed by Doug Young and Chris Louth. Used with permission.

CHECKLIST FOR EXHIBITION

All of the following must be answered prior to presenting your exhibition. For each, a date and explanation on a separate piece of paper is required. Each student in the group is to turn in their copy of the checklist. This preparation counts as a test. (100 points)

DATES

_________ 1. Pick a focus. What do you hope to find out through your investigation to help the class see and understand because of your presentation. (5)

_________ 2. What kind of research do you need and explain your reasoning. (5)

_________ 3. Which medium(s) will you use for your exhibition and explain why you are choosing that mode. What props are you going to use? (10)

_________ 4. Draw up a schedule/time line for completing the project with meeting times inside and outside of class established and adequate time at the end to practice. Be sure to explain what each partner's role and objective is. (5)

_________ 5. Analyze and summarize the data you research from the library. Give a summary of each source you used. (20)

_________ 6. What new conclusions can you now make based on your work. (10)

_________ 7. How has your focus changed as a result of the data gathered and conclusions drawn. In other words, now state the specific objective of your exhibition. (5)

_________ 8. Write a rough draft/outline/script/etc. of the exhibition which must contain the following: (20)

_________ Introduction - Make it snappy

_________ Body - Use at least three sources

_________ Conclusion - Is there a wrap up

_________ Bibliography - Be sure it is correct

_________ 9. To help you decide whether or not your exhibition is as fully developed as it should be, create four questions with answers about your exhibition. These are to be chosen by using a key word from each of the 4 levels (one from application, analysis, synthesis, and evaluation) on the Cognitive Domain sheet. After you answer your own questions, ask yourself the following: "Will the audience be able to answer these questions from my exhibition? If not, what needs to be changed or developed." (20)

Please be sure to organize all materials you might need prior to class. (Props, maps, graphs, posters, picture drawings, and AV equipment.) Aside from class time, you may want to practice and do a self-evaluation. If I can help, please stop in. Don't wait until the day before you are scheduled to present.

Figure 13.2c. Example of Structure for Reporting Process
SOURCE: Developed by Doug Young and Chris Louth. Used with permission.

PRESENTER(S); TOPIC: SUMMARY:	PRESENTER(S): TOPIC: SUMMARY:
PRESENTER(S): TOPIC: SUMMARY:	PRESENTER(S): TOPIC: SUMMARY:
PRESENTER(S): TOPIC: SUMMARY:	PRESENTER(S): TOPIC: SUMMARY:

Figure 13.2d. Example of Structure for Reporting Process
SOURCE: Developed by Doug Young and Chris Louth. Used with permission.

that is so creative and attractive that we lose sight of the end goal. The medium should be appropriate for expression of the message. As Frank Lloyd Wright suggested, there is a clear relationship between form and function. We need to pay attention to the relationship between process and product so they come together.

For example, a high school biology teacher suggested that the students might present their learning in a variety of forms. One such form suggested was a poster. The teacher decided to ask the art teacher how to judge the posters. The art teacher studied the work to be presented by poster and replied, "It would be impossible to present the amount of material you are looking for in a single poster. Students will be forced to do either a superficial job or an inadequate job. You need to require a series of posters." The form would be inadequate for the content in a single poster.

With the trend toward multimedia presentations, educators will be constantly facing this question. On the one hand, students may have learned a great deal from the process of storyboarding, scanning multiple sources for appropriate visual images, making decisions about music that signifies the mood of the work itself, and finding useful metaphors. On the other hand, the final presentation may be lacking power for the audience. As we move toward more possible ways for students to demonstrate their knowledge and understanding, we will have to separate our assessments into at least two parts: (a) the process of planning, thinking, and designing and (b) the final product or performance.

Feedback Spirals

Process assessment suggests that learning needs to be viewed as dynamic: Learners are in a state of continuously working to improve, grow, and learn. The present evaluation system focuses more on summative judgments—scores, grades, and numbers that reflect a reductive summary about students' performance. Formative assessments serve as measuring tools for giving students specific and descriptive feedback throughout the learning process.

Feedback spirals (Costa & Kallick, 1995) provide a sometimes simple but more often complex recursive pathway and strategy for gaining information about the effects of actions in the system. People, whether in organizations or as individuals, employ feedback spirals by gathering evidence through scanning their environment for clues about the results of their actions. For example,

Some feedback spirals are internal: The artist mixes colors on a palate. When the color is still not to the artist's liking, he or she thinks, "I'll mix a little more blue."

Some are external: The artist displays his or her works and then interviews and listens to patrons about their reactions.

Some feedback spirals are intricately entwined: A teacher poses a higher-level question and then searches students' verbal and nonverbal responses for evidence of mental engagement. Students give responses and search their teacher's face, verbal response, and body language for clues that may signal acknowledgment.

Some feedback spirals are grand in design: A school system implements a whole language program and designs a system for gathering evidence of its achievements.

Others are enhanced with technology: A spaceship's sensors monitoring the blast-off detect a liquid oxygen leak, and the launch is scrubbed.

Some feedback spirals are immediate: A thermostat monitors the room's heat and turns on or off the air conditioner immediately on reaching a preset temperature.

Others take years: Sociologists follow sets of identical twins from birth through age 40, searching for clues about the nature and influence of heredity and environment on human life.

And others are as yet incomplete: Geologists, using highly sensitive equipment, monitor the earth's slightest movements in search of patterns and stresses to enable prediction of earthquakes.

A school-related example of internal and external feedback spirals is when members of a school planning team dialogue to refine and shape an understanding about a particular outcome statement such as "self-directed learners" (internal). Team members realize, however, that their meaning may not be shared with others, and they interview and listen to other community members and faculty to gain their perceptions and meanings of "self-directed learners" (external).

Feedback spirals are not intended to define the bottom-line, summative, terminal conditions or behaviors. Rather, they are used as cyclical guides to learning and continued progress. Feedback spirals themselves are learning devices. This is because human thinking and learning are dynamic, changing processes. Students can employ feedback spirals by gathering evidence throughout their learning process. Following is a description of the feedback spiral shown in Figure 13.3.

Clarify goals and purposes: What is the purpose for what you are doing? What beliefs or values does it reflect? What outcomes would you expect as a result of your actions?

Planning: What actions would you take to achieve the desired outcomes? How would you set up an experiment to test your ideas? What evidence would you collect to help inform you about the results of your actions? What would you look for as indicators that your outcomes may or may not have been achieved? *And* how will you leave the door open for other discoveries and possibilities that were not built into the original design? What process will you put in place that will help you describe what actually happened?

Take action/experiment: Implementation of plan.

Assess/gather evidence: Implementation of assessment strategy.

Study, reflect, evaluate/derive meaning: How are these results congruent with your values? What meaning do you make of these data? Who might serve as critical friends with whom you might converse about your learning, to coach, to facilitate, and to mediate your learning from this experience? What have you learned from this action?

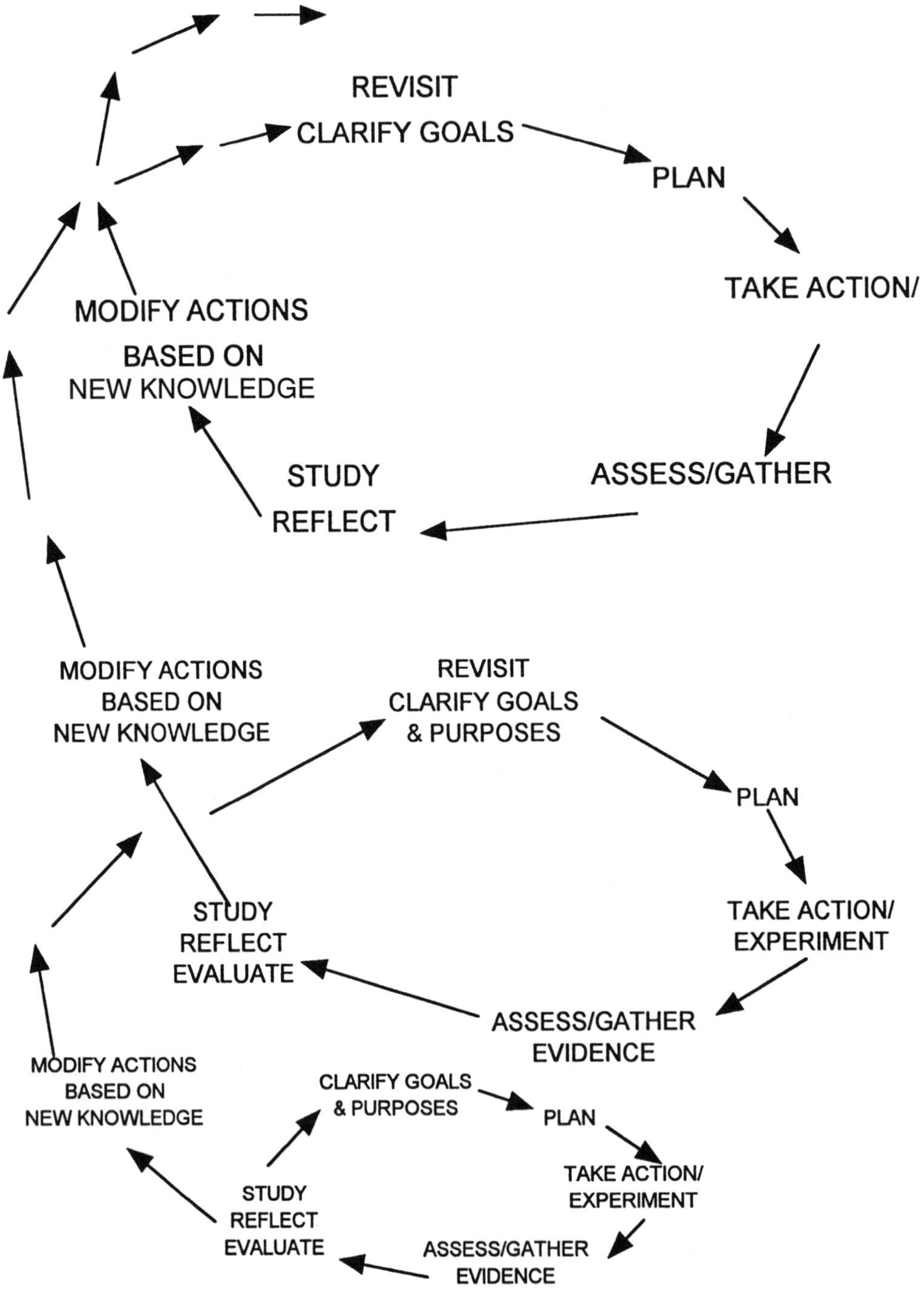

Figure 13.3. Continuous Growth Through Feedback Spirals

Modify actions on the basis of new knowledge: What would you do differently in the future as a result of your reflection and integration of new knowledge? Is this worthy of trying again?

Revisit/redefine: Do your goals still make sense? Are they still of value to you? Do you need to redefine, refocus, or refine them? Are you moving in the direction you intend? (This returns to the first step in the spiral of goal clarification.)

Application to a New Situation

The real test is finally achieved when students are able to transfer what they have learned to a new situation. At this point, the question is, what do the students do when they are not sure what to do? We as teachers need to be prepared to make close observations so that we can, like the dance teacher, see the students performing.

The focus on process or strategies as significant measures directly relate to the question of transfer. When students are able to use an explicit language for process and are able to be metacognitive (aware of their ways of knowing), they are more likely to be able to transfer those strategies and processes to new situations. So the final test of the success of teachers' work on process will be providing students with opportunities to face new problems and challenges that they have not yet faced and to see what they do when they are not instructed about what to do. Exhibitions, specially designed performance tasks, and other problem-centered options provide rich opportunities for students to demonstrate their independence and interdependence when they are not being continuously instructed. In this situation, the teachers serve as assessors in the classroom and are able to document the activity.

Summary

When process is a valued part of learning any given content, we change our focus. As with an optical illusion, when we focus on one aspect (the figure), the other aspect recedes (the ground). So it is with the relationship between process and product. When we make process the focus, the product recedes. Both process and product, however, are always inherent in the full picture of learning. If we do not use assessment strategies to provide feedback and criticism about the process of learners' work, we will be missing the rich opportunity to learn from learning. When we evaluate the finished products, it is too late for the learners to learn while doing. We must measure from in the middle of learning.

References

Costa, A. (1991). The search for intelligent life. In A. Costa (Ed.), *Developing minds: A resource book for teaching thinking.* Alexandria, VA: Association for Supervision and Curriculum Development.

Costa, A., & Kallick, B. (1995). *Assessment in the learning organization: Shifting the paradigm.* Alexandria, VA: Association for Supervision and Curriculum Development.

The Essence

Process as Content

Louis Rubin

The volumes in the *Process as Content* trilogy are rooted in the persuasive conviction that thought serves as the essence of the educational process. Because there are distinct modes of thinking for the accumulation, interpretation, and application of knowledge, each of these warrants due curricular emphasis. Moreover, because students can know without understanding—and understand without perceiving implication or use—good schooling must ensure that acquiring and exploring the powers of insight are significant by-products of learning. In short, learners must know things—know what they really mean—and know how they can be used.

Such arguments are of particular moment at a time of massive ferment and upheaval in the quest for effective reform. Federal initiatives such as Goals 2000: Educate America and the Elementary and Secondary Education Act, for example, aim at high expectations for all students—measured by what they know and can do—and structured, presumably, by sensible conceptions of consequential teaching and worthy subject matter. Much depends, however, on what knowledge and capabilities are deemed worthy and what learning experiences are harnessed to their attainment. It is hardly surprising, therefore, that in the wake of ideological insecurity, an ambiguous curriculum spawns confusion.

Margaret Mead (personal communication, 1965) once noted that "the task confronting today's schools is to teach the young how to solve yet unborn problems, through still unknown solutions." Her point was that students now in school will face an inevitable and immense array of social problems. Without knowing the precise nature of these difficulties, however, we cannot teach their solutions. Our only viable option, then, is to teach youth *how* to solve problems. It is in this spirit, perhaps, that the editors saw fit to organize the volumes around the premise that teaching that (a) generates knowledge and understanding, (b) poses related problems, (c) demonstrates potential steps to their solutions, and (d) integrates direct practice in problem solving not only can increase comprehension and retention but—of even greater consequence—can enhance intellectual capability as well as the capacity to use acquired knowledge constructively. Knowledge is most useful when it propagates intuition. The distinction between inert and active knowledge, in sum, lies in the degree of functionality.

Furthermore, a growing body of research-based theory suggests that connectivity is central to the construction of meaning and the sense of application. Too often, we tend to break down complex operations, assuming that learning is at its best when discrete conceptual components are taught separately. Psychologists contend, however, that only when the pieces are reconstructed into a workable entity are true meaning and significance grasped. In the absence of such reconstruction, a disjointing of perception occurs. There are instances, for example, when an idea is best comprehended by contemplating the whole rather than the sum of the parts. In piecing together an unassembled table, to wit, some find it easier to form a mental picture of the end product rather than to insert peg A in slot B. Similarly, the child tinkering with the family computer may fathom its intricacies as fast—or faster—than the adult laboring through a manual. Put succinctly, the fracturing of reality has its liabilities.

We are once again, ironically, in the periodic cycle of debate over the relative merits of segregated and integrated curriculum. There are those who maintain that much is gained when concepts from different subject areas are coalesced into a holistic perspective, as well as those who contend that the discipline's unique methods of inquiry and knowledge structure are lost in homogenization. Both views have their validity, and the error may lie in opting for one over the other—rather than exploiting the advantages of each. Generic and universal thinking modes clearly exist. For example, mathematical understanding, literary insight, and historical interpretation require distinct cognitive operations that can be taught in conjunction with knowledge acquisition and use. "Knowing" and "using" are discrete—but corollary—dimensions of learning. The interplay between perception and use, moreover, can also serve as a unifying mechanism for integrating classroom and real-world experience.

Because human minds function in an interlocking sequence of networks through which we meld multiple sources of comprehension, formulate meaning, and grasp significance, events and encounters are meshed, juxtaposed, and counterbalanced in a continuing web of cognitive activity that eventually enables us to make sense of things. For this reason, the aims of education are assumed to be encapsulated in both the subject matter and experiences of schooling. Students are shaped, thus, by the range and complexity of whatever occurs in the classrooms and the consequent interplay with perceptions gained elsewhere. Yet the curriculum does little in the way of orchestrating and consolidating the emotional and intellectual activity such occurrences encompass. Perkins and others repeatedly have reminded us that useful learning evolves when students assemble, analyze, and interpret diverse information and gradually create personal meaning that leads to conceptual applications. But our ways of choreographing learning and instruction typically assume that chunks of this and that can be added, subtracted, or combined willy-nilly.

It also is tempting to assume that if random efforts to raise standards, improve instruction, update content, and enhance curriculum organization are each managed competently, schools will benefit and students will be better served. It has now become plain, however, that such temptation is naive. Disjoined innovation, although advantageous in piecemeal ways, does not circumvent the need for connection and synergy. The degree to which such initiatives attend to linkage, congruence, and common cause is of consummate importance. Policymakers, nevertheless, often approach their task unilaterally; content specialists advocate revisions inspired by their subject matter; textbook manufacturers are guided by marketplace appeal; leadership is geared to one temporal fad of the moment or another; revisions are initiated in response to the clamoring assertions of vested interest groups; opportunists exploit the commercialization of learning; and intelligent cohesion in service of the strengthening of mind has become a lost cause.

Worse, because one aspect of restructuring frequently affects others, single-minded change invariably has a downside. Pedagogical innovations, as a case in point, are governed by the practitioner's adeptness in using them skillfully. Similarly, policy changes—placing greater emphasis on cultural diversity, for instance—necessitate coupling with compatible instructional methodology. Seemingly lacking, however, are viable ways to integrate reform in broad, closely aligned patterns.

In the same vein, much attention during the last decade has been devoted to thoughtful curriculum implementation: using rational theory in a context and manner that enhances organizational cohesion, combining efficient instruction with discerning evaluation, and so on. The aftereffects have not been encouraging. In subsequent efforts to unravel the problem, three significant conclusions emerged: First, good curriculum constructs, used unintelligently, produce little good and sometimes considerable harm; second, disordered attempts to reform and restructure have a short life as well as limited advantage; and, third, implementation difficulties make it plain that good constructs can be perceptibly weakened by artless management. And, in the absence of de facto centric planning, some provision for effective coalescence is essential. The trilogy fashioned by the volumes' editors sets forth the compelling logic that a process curriculum—anchored by modalities of intellection—can provide badly needed unity.

A variety of recent educational policies have sought to resolve current dilemmas by regulating minimum standards, toughening assessment procedures, and intensifying content criteria. Few of these, however, have achieved their intended effect. There is, thus, a growing suspicion that even good improvement policies are difficult to actualize with any degree of success—first, because they are isolated and lack connection with other independent organizational provisions; and, second, because they frequently fail to make due allowance for the pragmatic problems schools confront.

Even when implemented effectively, moreover, they may not accomplish their intent because the reformers often decipher problems inaccurately, neglect to anticipate the barriers in prevailing practice, and ignore the lessons of historical analogy and precedent. Additional hurdles lie in the gulf between curriculum and reform strategies. If process as content is to affect teaching practices, it must address the broad spate of attendant factors involved. Preparation, licensing criteria, performance assessment, instructional objectives, and student evaluation must be tied to the nurture of process capability. A realignment of purpose and focus will also need to cope with vagaries of organizational change, competing concerns, and theoretical divisiveness. And more impediments exist in the possible fallout between means and ends—the aims of process curriculum and the necessary course of action. The restructuring literature provides little in the way of guidance or workable blueprints for dealing with the stumbling blocks of disparate policy, divergent implementation tactics, and the combined overload of excessive school obligations. All this suggests that our greatest need is a shrewder fix on the matters of greatest importance. A major challenge thus arises: How can we best establish new goals within the system, mount a coordinated thrust toward process-based education, and create collaborative forces to energize the changeover?

What sort of networking, for example, would enable schools to take advantage of existing models? How might improvement programs evolve new teaching and learning procedures yielding symbiotic benefit? Can the necessary connective tissue be most effectively accomplished by the architects—or the users—of process-based innovations? Can concurrent attention be focused on a process curriculum *and* its corresponding need for pedagogical approaches?

The significance of these requirements is highlighted by problems stemming from recent reform endeavors. Emphasis has focused on three primary goals: (a) formulating better organizational approaches to professional development; (b) introducing intellectually more demanding content, wherein teachers guide students in constructing cumulative personal meaning as well as a sense of its use; and (c) eliminating restrictive controls that inhibit teachers and administrators from right-minded self-direction. Progress has been uneven. Some teachers, caught up in the promise of the intended reform, stay committed. Others, out of disinterest, disillusionment, or confusion, lose interest. Highly motivated at the outset, they gradually abandon a process approach and return to old patterns of pedestrian teaching and the lures of convenience. Hence, although newer texts reflect a conspicuous leaning toward cognitively oriented curricula, most instruction remains dominated by teacher-talk and didacticism.

What might constitute an optimum melding of subject matter and cognitive development? Skills developed through repetitive drill—such as rote memorization knowledge devoid of understanding—neither provoke thought nor enlarge the intellect. Conversely, skills developed through discerning practice, and comprehension evoked by inferring, interpreting, and organizing meaning that is applied in related problem solving, result in a richer, more functional, knowledge stockpile and a considerably expanded efficacy for productive thinking.

The critical challenge confronting curriculum practitioners, consequently, is to sequence optimally useful subject matter, incorporate process-centered learning activities, integrate a variety of instructional formats in diverse contexts, ensure that all of these experiences extend mental proficiency, and devise assessment measures that verify the accomplishment of process and content objectives. When teachers help students access information and ideas, cognitive processing can occur. But only when learners actually "get it"—relating new conceptual insight to previously acquired understanding—does knowledge become functional. It follows, therefore, that content and thinking are best taught and evaluated simultaneously.

New instructional materials and testing prototypes are beginning to embrace a conception of teaching and learning wherein functional knowledge is seen as a blend of knowing and using. The 1994 National Assessment of Educational Progress geography tests are illustrative. Subject mastery was construed not as naming world capitals and rivers but rather as the ability to interpret maps; describe significant physical and cultural features of regions; discuss political, social, and economic characteristics of world areas; and so on. The assessment, in turn, dealt not with simple recall but with the competence to analyze, compare, and generalize—to think.

In a sense, process education lends additional weight to Dewey's convictions regarding activity-centered curricula and what currently is referred to as constructivist learning theory. Reduced to its essence, the theory postulates that concepts within subject areas can be taught in a manner that encourages students to draw on their own social experience in constructing meaning. Such personally constructed understanding can also be used in classroom analysis of social phenomena to inject situated cognition—learning in actual contexts. Teaching that enables students to grasp meaning in their academic tasks, to correlate concepts from different subjects, and to fuse such learning with the outside world creates an impressive repertoire of useful skills.

Viewed in the large, then, the volumes' implications are of considerable consequence—particularly in pointing the way to replace our present leaden approach with boldly invigorated curriculum designs. New frameworks can structure disciplinary concepts and process-linked instruction into a cognate nexus embracing texts, methodology, and evaluation. Teachers, obviously, will need to redefine goals and procedures, as well as adopt a broader range of intentions, but the advantages would be substantial. Once empowered and unfettered, intellectual processes develop a life of their own, acquiring through repeated use cumulative strength, complexity, and applicability. Few reform efforts could make more of a difference.

Index

CORWIN
PRESS

The Corwin Press logo—a raven striding across an open book—represents the happy union of courage and learning. We are a professional-level publisher of books and journals for K-12 educators, and we are committed to creating and providing resources that embody these qualities. Corwin's motto is "Success for All Learners."